THE ELDER P

D1615542

⌐ ❁ ⌐ l ⌐

. . . . .

THE ELDER PITT

Marie Peters

LONGMAN
London and New York

Addison Wesley Longman Limited
Edinburgh Gate
Harlow Essex CM20 2JE
United Kingdom
and Associated Companies throughout the world.

Published in the United States of America by Addison Wesley Longman Inc.,
New York.

First published 1998

ISBN 0 582 25958 4 CSD
ISBN 0 582 25957 6 PPR

British Library Cataloguing in Publication Data

A catalogue entry for this title is available from the British Library

Library of Congress Cataloging-in-Publication Data

A catalog entry for this title is available from the Library of Congress

Set by 35 in 11/12pt Baskerville
Produced by Longman Singapore Publishers (Pte) Ltd.
Printed in Singapore

CONTENTS

LIST OF MAPS

PREFACE

I have welcomed the opportunity to write a study of the elder William Pitt in this series of Profiles in Power. For many years, I had a special interest in his political career and gathered material towards a biography. Then, some time ago, I came to the conclusion that a full account which would meet modern standards of scholarship and expectations of biographies was neither possible – largely because of the problems of sources considered in my introduction – nor useful, and that thematic studies were a more satisfactory way of assessing the significance of Pitt's career. I moved on to broader interests, leaving much of my material unexplored. Now, however, the concept and constraints of this series remove the need to be comprehensive about the life story while encouraging use of those unexplored resources in an assessment firmly rooted in the political context of the times.

Within the guidelines of this series, I have attempted to write a study which exploits all accessible sources, not simply those newly available, and incorporates the insights of the exciting recent work on the period. I have written primarily for the student with little prior knowledge, trying to cover the whole of Pitt's career – his periods of failure as well as success – in such a way as to illuminate the major characteristics and issues of mid-eighteenth-century British politics. No biography can entirely escape the tendency to exaggerate the importance of its subject; I hope students may be encouraged to investigate other actors and developments more thoroughly than has been possible here. I hope, too, that a fresh view, grounded in original research, of one political life will have something of interest for the specialist. My account is deliberately 'revisionist', in the sense that it scrutinizes sceptically the hagiography which still clings to Pitt's name and tends to set him outside the norms of politics. But no study would be satisfactory which did not attempt to explain the heroic stature accorded him by many (although never all) contemporaries, even while some recognized his flaws. It is perhaps significant that my account has been written as far away as one can get from Britain on this globe. In my childhood, people here in New Zealand still believed that – under Churchill, whose career has many parallels to Pitt's – the mantle of the British Empire extended round the world; my generation was trained and steeped in European culture; but, in the course of my career, a multitude of influences has led us to a sometimes painful reassessment, although not a rejection, of that culture as we have come to growing appreciation of our roots in these South Pacific islands.

In the course of my long preoccupation with Pitt at such a distance I have incurred more than the usual academic debts. My work stands on the shoulders of that of many scholars, whose contribution, unfortunately, it has not always been possible to acknowledge fully in a book of this nature. Many libraries, in Britain, North America and Australia, have responded to requests from our expert and efficient interlibrary loans service. Generous periods of leave and research grants from the University of Canterbury, one combined with a Visiting Fellowship at Corpus Christi College, Cambridge, have enabled me to enjoy at first hand the ambience and service of places as different as the Public Record Office, the British Library, the Bodleian, and the University Library, Cambridge, the Huntington in San Marino and the Clements Library in Ann Arbor, and many local record offices and private collections in Britain. I am grateful for permission to cite their resources, and particularly to Rosemary Dunhill, Hampshire County Archivist, for her help over the Malmesbury Collection. Transcripts held by the History of Parliament Trust have filled some otherwise glaring gaps in my cover of private papers. Colleagues on the other side of the world – most notably Paul Langford, Peter Marshall and Frank O'Gorman – have sustained me with encouragement. To Frank I owe particularly the incentive to undertake this brief life of Pitt, while both he and Paul patiently commented on the first draft. Colleagues at home, particularly David McIntyre, John Cookson and, in the past, Glenn Burgess, and several generations of students have kept me stimulated, while colleagues on leave, former students and friends – notably Margaret Escott – have chased up loose ends of research for me. My family have borne with my preoccupation, while, above all, my husband, who is also a colleague, has sustained me with encouragement and has patiently read my text with his acutely critical eye. To all I offer my heartfelt thanks, and my apologies for the shortcomings which remain.

LIST OF ABBREVIATIONS

Add. MSS	British Library, Additional Manuscripts
Chatham Correspondence	William Stanhope Taylor and John Henry Pringle (eds), *Correspondence of William Pitt, Earl of Chatham* 4 vols (London, 1838–40)
Correspondence	W.S. Lewis (ed.), *The Yale Edition of Horace Walpole's Correspondence* 47 vols (New Haven, CT, 1937–83)
HL	Henry E. Huntington Library, San Marino, CA
HMC	Royal Commission on Historical Manuscripts
HP	History of Parliament Trust, London, transcripts
Memoirs George II	Horace Walpole, *Memoirs of King George II*, ed. John Brooke, 3 vols (New Haven, CT, 1983)
Memoirs George III	Horace Walpole, *Memoirs of the Reign of King George the Third; first published by Sir Denis Le Marchant Bart.*, ed. G.F. Russell-Barker, 4 vols (1894)
Parl. Hist.	*The Parliamentary History of England from the Earliest Period to the Year 1803*, [ed. William Cobbett], 36 vols (1806–20)
PRO	Public Record Office, London
PRO 30/8	Chatham Papers, Public Record Office*

Simmons and Thomas   R.C. Simmons and P.D.G. Thomas, *Proceedings and Debates of the British Parliaments respecting North America, 1754–1776* 6 vols (New York, 1982–7)

* The foliation of this collection is sometimes confused; where I have been aware of a conflict, I have followed the usage of the recently revised Calendar, but much of my work was done before it was available.

Spelling and punctuation have been lightly modernized in transcriptions from manuscripts, but not in those from modern printed editions. References are given to readily available printed sources where these are reasonably reliable, even when the manuscript source was consulted. Unless otherwise stated, the place of publication of works cited is London.

INTRODUCTION

. . .

CONTEXTS: WAR AND POLITICS

War and the threat of war dominated the lifetime of the elder William Pitt. He was born in 1708, in the midst of Britain's first great modern war, the War of the Spanish Succession. The Duke of Marlborough's allied army had just added Oudenarde to the string of victories against the French which was securing for the newly United Kingdom a leading role in European affairs for the first time in the modern period. The most widely accepted justification for this expensive involvement was the protection of the Revolution Settlement of 1689 against Louis XIV's recognition of James II's son as James III. Over recent decades, many had begun to see a balance of power against French hegemony in Europe as a necessary protection of Britain's interests, commercial as well as dynastic. But many also looked beyond Europe for a share in commerce and colonies at the expense of Spain and France.

Pitt grew up as the succession of the German Hanoverians to the British throne in 1714 was secured. With the Hanoverians came commitment to European affairs but also an ongoing debate about how the commitment could best be managed: in what areas, by what alliances, with what resources, whether ships, subsidies or troops. When Pitt came into politics in 1735, there had been more than twenty years of relative peace. But, as the young man's political views began to be shaped, that peace gave way to renewed war. He, too, was excited with others in the opposition he joined, as British appetites for gains from the Spanish empire in

1

Central America were again whetted. He, too, quickly forgot those dreams as, from 1740, fears were renewed about the extension of French power in Europe – an extension, this time, at the expense of Britain's allies, the Austrian Habsburgs, in the War of the Austrian Succession. Like everyone else in the kaleidoscopic European situation of the mid-century, in which debate continued about where Britain's interests lay, Pitt became a learner in foreign policy.

Wars were to shape the rest of Pitt's career, as he made his name in foreign policy. He saw Britain successfully maintain a great-power role in Europe while he helped to entrench antagonism to Bourbon France (and Spain when the Bourbon family was united) as a hallmark of British policy. As the contest with France intensified beyond Europe and became much more important than the lure of the Spanish empire, Pitt presided, at the brilliant zenith of his career in 1756–61, over the war which marked Britain's emergence as the leading imperial power, not only in the Americas but also to the east, in India. After that, real power eluded him. Having done little, as Earl of Chatham, in his few months of effective office in 1766–67, to aid the solution of the problems of imperial organization that Britain's new status brought, he spent his remaining eleven years, when not debilitated by illness, in fruitless opposition. In 1778, in the midst of another war, he collapsed into his final illness while speaking against the independence of the American colonies. He died a month later, as once more Britain faced the Bourbons and came in the next five years to bitter defeat. Chatham's life ended, it seemed, in nemesis. However, this grave imperial crisis, bringing not only the loss of the American colonies but also the threat of disintegration of the small but growing British presence in India, was in the longer run only a temporary setback in the growth of empire.

This success abroad, as great power and metropolis of a growing empire, encompassed Pitt's life and is often identified with him. There were, in fact, much more significant explanations than the purely personal. Success was made possible, in the first instance, by the stabilizing of English constitutional arrangements. These came to make England the envy of Europe rather than the byword for insecurity she had been in the previous century, while allowing the development of financial systems which efficiently tapped national wealth. The generally unruffled subordination of other parts of the British Isles, less by constitutional arrangements than by an informal union of elites, was also an essential prerequisite.

Crucial to constitutional stability was the taming of volatile party politics which, in Anne's reign, when Pitt was born of a Tory father and Whig grandfather, wracked the parliamentary classes, regularly spilled out into the constituencies and society, and complicated the management of Scotland and Ireland. Party politics had their roots in longstanding ideological divisions over the nature of monarchy and the Church of England and toleration for religious dissent, exacerbated by the Revolution of 1688–89 and extended by debates over involvement in Europe. After 1714, securing their own dominance with that of the new dynasty, the main body of the Whigs continued their transition, begun at the Revolution, from 'country' opposition to support of the court. The Tories, tainted, often unjustly, as Jacobites (supporters of the exiled Stuarts), could no longer easily tap the natural majority for Church and monarchy they had long enjoyed and were thrust on to the back benches or out into the counties. There and in growing urban areas, especially London, their populist edge, rooted in long-remembered dislike of busybody Puritans, was sharpened by new alienations from Whig rule. Stability culminated, from 1721, in the twenty years of power of Robert Walpole, whose political skills, from 1721, did most to evolve a workable political system – a parliamentary monarchy – out of the volatility of the past generation, while moderating something of the bitterness of party divisions.

Pitt cast his lot with the Whigs, though not with Walpole, but throughout his career sat light to party ties – which, in any case, while often ideologically compelling and pervasive, never had the tightly organized or mass base of modern parties. In the course of his career, he was to contribute to and benefit from developments which fundamentally altered the nature and role of parties: the reshaping of a forceful alternative 'patriot' opposition ideology in his earlier career and the fracturing and partial reforming of party identities in the much changed 1760s and 1770s.

Britain's success abroad in Pitt's lifetime was powered above all, however, by the growth of commercial wealth,

3

particularly the thrusting dynamism of Britain's trade beyond Europe, aided by a maturing of the American colonies which few would have foreseen at the beginning of the century. This diversifying economy raised a varied and prosperous middle class below the landed elite, which had emerged also prosperous and increasingly assured from the travails of the previous century, and the gentry, whose confidence grew as this century proceeded.

In Pitt's lifetime, tensions between landed and middle classes were usually far outweighed by the cohesive strength of a relationship of recognition from above and emulation from below and the fusion (in Paul Langford's interpretation) of one broad, propertied 'ruling class'. The mid-century world which saw the zenith of Pitt's career and into which Pitt's children were born was – at least for most of the middle and landed classes – stable, wealthy, comfortable and cultivated in ways hardly imagined in 1708. But it was still anxious and prone to crisis. Commerce sought opportunities in war but was vulnerable to its vagaries; the equilibrium of a parliamentary monarchy was always liable to upset, whether real or imagined, and from the 1760s was increasingly susceptible to pressure from those not fully incorporated into its politics which was slowly to bring fundamental change.

In fact, the formal political system of court, cabinet and parliament, though undoubtedly oligarchical and in some ways increasingly so, was never closed to sporadic pressure from outside, especially when the elites were divided. In the course of the eighteenth century, a more continuous political interest on the part of those on the edges was fostered, not only by economic and social change, but also by the development of a vigorous press after the lapsing of pre-publication censorship in 1695. By 1702, London had a daily paper; by the 1730s, a range of forms – dailies, tri-weeklies and weeklies – was established; the number of publications and their circulation continued to grow over the mid-century, while weekly provincial papers also flourished. In addition, there was a variety of other periodical publications, as well as pamphlets, while prints, broadsides and ballads extended the message beyond the readily literate. These works may not have reached much beyond the middle classes of the towns or the gentry in the countryside to touch the bulk of the population; their purposes were seldom solely political.

But they certainly enriched a vital political culture which could influence parliamentary elections, especially in larger constituencies – few in number but high-profile and, in petitions, addresses and instructions to MPs, with well-established means of expression capable of further sophistication. In the course of Pitt's career, this culture was to break increasingly frequently and effectively – though seldom autonomously or as the sole determinant of events – into the heart of national politics.

Pitt, coming as something of an outsider on to the political stage, needed to play on these vulnerabilities, uncertainties and novelties. In doing so, and by seeming so instrumental in imperial expansion, he came to be identified by many of his time and later with the new: he was seen as a patriot above party, peculiarly sensitive to the interests of 'the people' and particularly to those of the expanding world of commerce and commercial people. This view of him is largely mistaken; his undoubted stature rested more surely on other foundations.

. . .

THE POWER OF ORATORY AND REPUTATION

Pitt's career is in some ways a strange subject for a series of Profiles in Power. He may have been driven by the urge to wield and extend Britain's power in the world; he may have been seen as bringing that power to unprecedented heights. But he himself effectively held political office of the first rank for little more than five of the 40 years or so of his active career. With dazzling heights of brief success that career combined long periods of bitter frustration and the depths of abject failure. Yet few contemporaries would have denied his power. He held sway in their minds, not by virtue of office, but by the power of the spoken word. Coming to politics with few inherited advantages, Pitt derived his chief political strength from the way he learnt to sway the forum at the heart of the formal play of politics, the House of Commons. When he rose, his tall, spare frame – 'with the eye of a hawk, a little head, thin face, long aquiline nose, and perfectly erect'[1] – and, above all, the emotive power of his words commanded the attention of the House and cowed opponents as few others could do. His rhetorical power gave credence to his claims to the status of 'patriot'. Those who tried to prick his bubble with the sarcastic title 'great commoner'[2] found that it was taken over as a generally recognized title of honour, one which conveyed the immense authority of his physical presence and undoubted intellectual power. In Pitt's middle and later career, the element of drama in his oratory was sometimes heightened by his appearance as an invalid on his crutch, supported by friends or servants, his limbs swathed in bandages, occasionally accompanied by shouts of acclamation from the crowds outside. Even in the House of Lords, a very different forum which he never controlled to the same extent, he did not lose his power to command attention.

As this power over minds was confirmed by brilliant success in war at the zenith of his career, it was amplified by word of mouth, correspondence and the printed press to the growing audience of the political nation. Pitt was unique among leading politicians in his time in the extraordinary interest he evoked outside parliament, at least from the late 1750s, and in the way he shaped people's image of themselves as Britain staked its place on the international stage. Yet the very source of Pitt's power – this reputation, largely constructed by the spoken word yet necessarily operating in the world of political compromise – made him peculiarly vulnerable to criticism. In his time, Pitt was accused of empty bombast in his oratory, of unprincipled inconsistency and unscrupulous ambition in his conduct. The way he played the political game, how he brought his considerable abilities and, in due course, his formidable reputation to bear on the components of power – crown, court, parliament, patronage and party, press and political nation – was never typical of his time and often deeply flawed. Nevertheless, the fluctuations of his career – which to a considerable extent reflect the uncertainties of his age – can throw much light on the nature of politics in those decades of profound change.

Historians have traditionally attributed enormous power to Pitt.[3] Taking up contemporary celebration of him as the chief architect of victories won in 'every quarter of the globe',[4] early biographers began to shape this view by suggesting the means by which his dominance was secured. William Godwin, generally by no means uncritical of Pitt, attributed to him in wartime 'comprehensive genius, ...

indefatigable industry'. John Almon's gossipy accounts of a subservient Admiralty, browbeaten colleagues and administrative zeal added apparent substantiation, while, rather later, Francis Thackeray's adulatory study, influenced by a new emphasis on military analysis prompted by the Napoleonic wars, contributed an over-arching strategy and comprehensive planning to Pitt's supposed achievements.[5]

Macaulay reacted to Thackeray by returning the picture of Pitt as war minister more to the proportions given by his contemporaries, allowing him spirit but not comprehensive views, while later finding much to criticize in his behaviour in the 1760s.[6] The predominantly Whig historians of the early Victorian period, however, generally accepted the established view of Pitt as great patriot and war leader, while discovering other virtues to admire. While they criticized George III and largely adopted Horace Walpole's dismissive account of the Duke of Newcastle, Pitt's partner in the wartime coalition, they praised Pitt as parliamentary orator, incorruptible defender of liberty and spokesman of the people.

This rising tide of admiration dried to a trickle in the high-Victorian period of free trade, *laissez-faire* imperialism and concern for economy, which found more to praise in the younger Pitt. In the early twentieth century, however, when a newly self-conscious imperialism, uneasy about foreign challenges and domestic criticism, coincided aptly with celebration of the bicentenary of Pitt's birth and the development of professional history, the heroic picture of Pitt was fully constructed. He was transmuted into a great imperial statesman with a clear vision of Britain's destiny beyond Europe which reached towards the ideal of an 'empire based on liberty'.[7] At the same time, a growing interest in naval strategy attributed to Pitt the kind of systematic thinking about strategy which had lessons for the very different age of the steamship and cable telegraph.[8] The first substantial biographies of Pitt which appeared at this time, by Basil Williams and the Prussian, Albert von Ruville, although too scholarly to capitulate entirely to this heroic view, were shaped by it.[9] It was entrenched and magnified in all subsequent biographies until very recently; it remains largely intact even in Stanley Ayling's consciously post-imperial view of 1976,[10] while analyses of British strategy over the centuries still appeal to it.[11]

In its fully constructed form, this historians' myth about Pitt represents him as from his youth marked out for an outstanding political career. Soon, it is suggested, he became the far-sighted statesman who, having watched impotently while the Duke of Newcastle 'blundered' in the 1740s and 1750s, turned attention in the Seven Years War to Britain's 'true' interests outside Europe, kept it there despite the opinions of his colleagues, and co-ordinated a 'world-wide' strategy which allowed the navy to fulfil its role in European waters while supporting 'combined operations' there and in theatres beyond Europe. According to this view, Pitt exercised effective oversight over nearly every branch of government and, particularly, ensured the success of American operations by his sympathetic understanding of conditions there and his detailed oversight and support. This heroic view is often combined with an emphasis on those virtues the Whig historians saw in Pitt, so that, in his later career, he is presented as the standard-bearer of Whig liberalism in the domestic and imperial disputes of the 1760s and 1770s, one whose influence, if only he had been heeded, might have saved the American colonies.

This view of Pitt standing head and shoulders above his contemporaries and powerfully dominating his world, prescient even when powerless, still in varying degrees continues to influence much scholarly writing on his period.[12] However, the more rigorous study of eighteenth-century politics in the 60 years and more since the first publications of the great historian of that century, Sir Lewis Namier, has raised quite different questions about Pitt the politician, questions often strongly reminiscent of the more sceptical view taken by some of his contemporaries and sustained by Macaulay and others.[13] Behind the mask of patriot and imperial statesman lurks the intensely ambitious politician. Because he came from outside the elite predestined for power, he harboured a fierce determination to protect his independence; he often used ideas and policies instrumentally to his ambition, rather than constructively. Disruptive and often arrogant, he was a complex character playing a deep political game in a fluid and changing world.

The time is ripe for a thorough reappraisal of Pitt's political life in his times as they are now understood, a reappraisal which can penetrate the veneer of mythology and hold these various views in balance. Jeremy Black's recent biography has begun this process of contextualization.[14] This book attempts to advance it further, especially for Pitt's later career, and to unfold his life as he lived it and contemporaries saw it, not allowing it to be coloured prematurely by the glow of his later reputation but taking due account of that reputation when it is won.

. . .

THE MAN AND 'MADNESS'

There will always be major difficulties in the way of a satisfactory biography of Pitt, even one attempting to deal only with his political career. We will never have that knowledge of the man that a biographer of a person of his stature in more recent times would expect as a matter of course, the knowledge which would allow recovery of his complexity as a full historical personality. Unlike most of his contemporaries, except to his wife and then usually on private matters, Pitt did not often commit his thoughts to paper. There are few letters to trusted colleagues and little other comment. So, despite the magnificent recent chronological calendaring of the Chatham papers in the Public Record Office which has made work on them much easier, there is still, except for brief periods, great difficulty in knowing what Pitt's real views and intentions were. Even more important for one whose power rested so much on the spoken word is the fact that the records of parliamentary debates are very imperfect. This is particularly the case for the Seven Years War period; and the ongoing discovery of revealing fragments in letters and diaries of others hardly fills the gap. We may have known for some time that Dr Johnson, writing up the debates of 1741 for the *Gentleman's Magazine*, composed for Pitt his supposed sarcastic confession to 'the atrocious crime of being a young man' in answer to rebuke from the venerable Horatio Walpole.[15] We do not know exactly what Pitt said, or even all the occasions on which he spoke.[16] At times, especially in his later career, increasing competition among magazines and newspapers produced fuller and possibly more reliable accounts. But still there is reason to suspect they were manipulated by publicists anxious to claim his support,[17] while Pitt himself never countenanced the publication of his speeches.

Even a reassessment limited to Pitt's political career must go beyond the public man, however imperfectly known, and make some attempt to understand the formation of the personality that helped to shape ideas and behaviour. For this purpose, this study makes cautious use of the available fragments of evidence, both long-known – from which sometimes too much has been wrung – and new. Much of this evidence concerns Pitt's chronic ill health.[18] It is probably insufficient to allow firm conclusions about the nature and interconnectedness of Pitt's many complaints, even by a medically qualified biographer. This work certainly does not attempt such conclusions. However, it can be said that, from school and university days, Pitt suffered frequently from a variety of ailments in various parts of the body – limbs, stomach, bowels, head – generally loosely referred to as 'gout'. A 'veteran invalid', he called himself quite early,[19] and his crutch, his limbs bandaged in red flannel or black velvet, his sedan chair with a fixture for his gouty legs, became public hallmarks. But there was more than physical illness; perhaps from his thirties, Pitt was also prone to nervous or psychological disorders which he and his doctor came to refer to as 'lowness'[20] and we might call clinical depression. Brian Tunstall diagnosed Pitt's condition as manic-depressive insanity.[21] Certainly, at two periods in his life, 1767–68 and 1775–77,[22] he was totally overwhelmed and mentally incapacitated to a degree which contemporaries thought 'approaching to insane melancholy'. His condition deeply moved those few who were permitted to see 'the lowest dejection and debility that mind or body can be in' and misery 'beyond conception'.[23]

Pitt's constant struggle against such manifold complaints was probably the most formative influence on his personality and the gravest handicap to his career. It deeply affected his relations with other people, helping to turn him from a sociable young man into an impatient, irritable recluse who increasingly hardened the shell he put between himself and others beyond his family. Frustration at the limits ill health put on his undoubted abilities enhanced the natural tendency to arrogance and autocracy which made him such a difficult colleague. Other characteristics – rapid swings of

NOTES

mood from deep despair to exultation, histrionic pronouncements, the reckless political extremism which sometimes led
observers to call him 'mad' when he was not depressed –
were also shaped by his condition. More importantly, his
performance in parliament and office was often critically
affected, or he was inaccessible at crucial times. Certainly,
his ill health fashioned the curious rhythm of his political
life, in which periods of intense activity often alternated
with disillusioned withdrawal.

The interaction between his illness and political behaviour perplexed Pitt's contemporaries. Sometimes, unsympathetic observers suspected him of 'political gout', of using his
ill health to avoid difficult situations. Often these accusations are without foundation; his complaints were persistent
enough not to require feigning. But just how stress and
intractable political problems affected his health is not
clear. There were circumstances – those of war, for example
– in which he was able to work regardless of illness, inter-
viewing officials and diplomats while bedridden, but many
occasions – when he was first Secretary of State in the minority Devonshire–Pitt administration of 1756–57, or in the
opposition of 1770 – when, while ill, he seemed more ready
and able to bestir himself on some issues than others. Interaction between illness, personality and political performance
there undoubtedly was; its precise nature is unfathomable,
part of the complexity of the man.

. . .

NOTES

1. Lord Edmond Fitzmaurice, *Life of William, Earl of Shelburne,
    afterwards First Marquess of Lansdowne* 3 vols (1875–76), I,
    p. 77.
2. *Test,* 1 Jan., 9 April 1757; cf. Basil Williams, *The Life of William
    Pitt Earl of Chatham* 2 vols (1913), I, p. 292n.
3. What follows owes some debt to Richard Middleton, *The Bells
    of Victory. The Pitt–Newcastle Ministry and the Conduct of the
    Seven Years' War* (Cambridge, 1985), pp. 219–32; for one
    major theme of Pitt's historical reputation, cf. Marie Peters,
    'The myth of William Pitt, Earl of Chatham, great imperial-
    ist: Part I', *Journal of Imperial and Commonwealth History* 21
    (1993), pp. 31–4.

4. John Entick *et al., The General History of the Late War* 5 vols (1763–64), I, dedication.

5. [W. Godwin], *The History of the Life of William Pitt, Earl of Chatham* (1783), p. 80; [John Almon], *Anecdotes of the Life of the Right Honourable William Pitt, Earl of Chatham* 3rd edn, 3 vols (1793), I, pp. 307, 310, 321, 333–4; Francis Thackeray, *A History of the Right Honourable William Pitt, Earl of Chatham* 2 vols (1827), I, pp. 597–9.

6. Thomas Babington Macaulay, 'William Pitt, Earl of Chatham' (1834), 'The Earl of Chatham' (1844), both first published in the *Edinburgh Review*.

7. W.L. Grant, 'Canada versus Guadeloupe, an episode of the Seven Years' War', *American Historical Review* 17 (1912), p. 738.

8. Julian S. Corbett, *England in the Seven Years' War: a study in combined strategy* 2 vols (1907).

9. Williams, *The Life of William Pitt* (still the most satisfactory biography, but note e.g. II, pp. 123–5); Albert von Ruville, *William Pitt, Earl of Chatham* 3 vols (1907).

10. Stanley Ayling, *The Elder Pitt Earl of Chatham* (1976).

11. E.g. Michael Howard, *The British Way in Warfare. A Reappraisal* (1975), pp. 7, 10–12, 14; Paul Kennedy, *The Rise and Fall of British Naval Mastery* (1976), pp. 101–4.

12. Cf. Peters, 'Myth', p. 34 and n. 39; it is not entirely absent from Geoffrey Holmes's account in Geoffrey Holmes and Daniel Szechi, *The Age of Oligarchy. Pre-industrial Britain 1722–1783* (1993), e.g. pp. 260–4.

13. Peters, 'Myth', p. 34 and nn.

14. Jeremy Black, *Pitt the Elder* (Cambridge, 1992).

15. Mary Ransome, 'The reliability of contemporary reporting of the House of Commons, 1727–1741', *Bulletin of the Institute of Historical Research* 19 (1943), p. 75.

16. Williams's list, in *The Life of William Pitt*, II, pp. 338–51, is an invaluable and remarkably complete starting point; cf. pp. 335–7 on reliability.

17. On the problem of parliamentary reporting see Simmons and Thomas I, pp. viii–ix, xii, and introductions to later volumes.

18. The letters of Dr Anthony Addington, the Chatham family's doctor from 1767, are in the Chatham Papers in the Public Record Office, PRO 30/8/15 and 16.

19. Pitt to Ann Pitt, Dropmore Papers, Series II, Add. MSS 69289, no. 44, n.d. [1750s].

20. A common eighteenth-century complaint; see Roy Porter, *Mind-Forg'd Manacles. A History of Madness in England from the Restoration to the Regency* (1987), pp. 241–6, 232–4.

21. Brian Tunstall, *William Pitt Earl of Chatham* (1938), pp. 6, 12, 391.
22. Ibid., pp. 69–70, 104–8 detects two earlier periods of 'insanity', 1744 and 1751–3. At both times, certainly, Pitt was seriously ill.
23. James Harris, memoranda, 12 July 1767 (reporting a conversation with Lord Lyttelton), Hampshire Record Office, Malmesbury Collection, 9M73/G748, cf. 'Report says that he is mad', Sackville to Irwin, 7 April 1767, HMC, *Stopford-Sackville* I, p. 121; Whately to Lyttelton, 30 July 1767, Hagley Hall, Lyttelton Papers, vol. 6, f. 260; Nuthall to Camden, [5 Aug 1767], Camden Papers, HP; cf. below, p. 182.

Chapter 1

THE YOUNG DEMOSTHENES, 1735–46

. . .

YOUTH, 1708–35

The family into which William Pitt was born on 15 November 1708 had until recently been small landholders in the county of Dorset, aspiring to little more than local office. Although a senior branch, established in Hampshire in the early seventeenth century, had prospered and put its elder sons into parliament, not until the generation of Pitt's grandfather did wider prospects open for the junior branch. They came from the newly dynamic world of commerce. That grandfather, Thomas, made a fortune out of both interloping and legitimate trade to India in the unsettled late seventeenth-century years of the East India Company and was Governor of the Company's factory in Madras from 1698 to 1709. Transferring much of his fortune home in the form of the large diamond which gave him one of his nicknames, he used his wealth to acquire estates with which came considerable influence in parliamentary boroughs and to marry his five surviving children into titled families. William was the second son of Thomas Pitt's eldest son, Robert, a man of much lesser stature than his father, and his wife, Harriet Villiers, of an old, aristocratic family and granddaughter of the fourth Viscount Grandison.[1]

The time-honoured application of wealth derived from commerce to land and aristocratic marriage alliances had transformed the family's lesser gentry status. But the evidence does not allow much speculation about the influence on William of this diverse background. As a young boy he had some contact with his paternal uncle, James, Earl

Stanhope, an experienced soldier and leading Whig, and in his schooldays his formidable paternal grandfather saw enough of him to recognize him as 'a hopeful lad'.[2] The letters of his young manhood suggest more familiarity with his mother's side of the family.[3] His paternal inheritance was perhaps the source more of tension than of inspiration. With his grandfather's wealth came 'the Governor's' feuding family relations and something of his tempestuous character – evident even in the young man's correspondence, in occasional heated outbursts.

Conventionally enough for a family of the status to which the Pitts could now aspire, from 1719 to 1726 William was sent to school at Eton, where, in contrast to his brother, Thomas, he applied himself and did well, being commended to his father by his tutor as 'of so good abilities, and . . . so good a disposition' as to 'answer all your hopes'.[4] However, Eton's harsh regime may have begun the warping of an affectionate disposition. Certainly, much later in his life, Pitt was to comment that 'he scarce observed a boy who was not cowed for life at Eton',[5] and his own sons were to be educated at home.

Then followed eight unsettled years during which the impecunious younger son's search for a suitable career was disrupted by family upheaval. In 1726 Governor Pitt's death brought William a small annual income. Any thought on his father's part that Pitt might become a clergyman – a natural career opening in a landed family that had church livings in its gift – was given up by the time he left Eton. Nevertheless, as a career in the church would have required, Pitt went up to Trinity College, Oxford, in 1727, despite his father's grumblings about expense. But after only a year, and possibly because of his father's sudden death in its course, he moved on to further study in Utrecht, renowned as an international centre of Protestant learning, more forward-looking than Oxford if now rapidly declining. For this study, Pitt had some support from his brother, who, as elder son, had inherited the family property. By the beginning of 1730, however, William was back in England, kicking his heels on various family country estates. Then early in 1731 another career, with a small immediate income but promise of much more, was opened for him with the help of a friend from Eton days, George Lyttelton, whose sister his brother married about this time. Lyttelton introduced William to his wealthy and influential soldier uncle, Richard, Viscount Cobham, in whose regiment of horse William was granted a cornet's commission. He spent parts of the next two years in camp but in 1733–34 he was off to the continent once more, probably again with his brother's help, for the grand tour which was a normal part of the education of a young man of social standing. Pitt's was a mini-version of such a tour, as befitted his limited means; it took him for seven months to France and Switzerland, but not to Italy, the prized goal of wealthy grand tourists. The correspondence of these unsettled years shows a young man both sociable with friends and warmly affectionate towards his family, especially his sister Ann. Yet there were evident tensions with the brother on whom he was so obviously dependent for material support and, in ill health, for example, other clear signs of strain.

The general election of 1734, the first since Pitt came of age, opened yet another avenue to explore. The electoral influence built up by his grandfather gave Thomas Pitt substantial control in three constituencies, and returning his brother for one of them would have been a natural move. However, not until Thomas had secured his own and his sister's husband's return, and had decided to reject an offer to buy out William's claim on a seat at Old Sarum, was William returned to represent the electors of that pocket borough – all five of them – in February 1735.[6]

Under the unreformed electoral system, in which constituencies varied widely in the size of their electorates, there was nothing at all unusual in a politician sitting for a pocket borough. For only seven months in more than 30 years in the Commons did Pitt represent more than 100 voters. On the other hand, the young man who now entered parliament was not necessarily yet committed to making his way in politics. Under the unreformed system, many stood for parliament for a variety of non-political motives.[7] Pitt's letters at this time reflect less the promise seen in him by his tutor and his grandfather and the broadening of his traditional classical education by continental experience than the normal pastimes of a not particularly serious-minded young man – amorous encounters both flirtatious and more serious, and even 'a course of drunken conversation'.[8] And, while he was undoubtedly indignant at the proposal to buy out his electoral interest, he apparently had no settled political views in late 1734.[9] Indeed, he may well have intended to advance his military career by recommending himself, through his parliamentary behaviour, to a powerful patron. Within two months, however, he had set a political course. And over the next seven years his political ambition developed as he realized his abilities.

. . .

WALPOLE'S WORLD

The political world into which Pitt came in 1735 was dominated by the commanding figure of Sir Robert Walpole. For fourteen years, Walpole had held office in the leading position of First Lord of the Treasury, astounding contemporaries by a grip on power unprecedented in recent times. Coarse and ostentatious yet warm and humane, still able to play the bluff country squire to admiring backbenchers while flaunting his new status and wealth, Walpole was a calculating political manager, combining shrewd judgement of individuals with a penetrating appreciation of underlying trends. The exercise of his superb political skills at court and in parliament demonstrated an effective new kind of premiership, one which took account both of the continuing importance of personal monarchy and of the changing role of parliament, especially that of the House of Commons in financing the state. His political skills, together with judicious policies, had moderated the bitter party strife which had so threatened stability in the three decades before 1721, even softening the alienation felt by Tories at their exclusion from office since the Hanoverians came to the throne in 1714. As justly self-proclaimed defender of the Revolution Settlement and the Hanoverian succession, Walpole had impeccable claims, both ideological and pragmatic, to Whig credentials.

However, by the early 1730s, Walpole's ascendancy was being challenged. In the later 1720s, the able opponents Walpole had excluded from his amalgam of court and Whig supporters, known as the Old Corps of the Whigs – notably the brilliant debaters in the Commons and Lords, William Pulteney and John, Baron Carteret – mounted an increasingly sophisticated parliamentary opposition with a small core of committed supporters. From 1730 they achieved some

17

tenuous co-operation with the still substantial body of Tories in parliament and their able former leader, Henry St John, Viscount Bolingbroke, who had returned from exile in 1725 but was still excluded from his seat in the Lords for his earlier Jacobite dabblings. More important to this opposition than the disappointed ambition of brilliant leaders was the programme developed to encourage the co-operation of dissident Whigs and Tories and expounded in a vigorous press campaign led by the newspaper, the *Craftsman*, with major contributions from Bolingbroke. This 'country' or 'patriot' programme revived and adapted a stream of criticism of the exercise of power influential from at least the 1690s. It mounted a vigorous critique of Walpole's supposed neglect of British interests abroad and accumulation of power at home by means which were held to corrupt the foundations of the mixed constitution and endanger liberty. The programme – elaborated by some of the most able pens of the day, among them Jonathan Swift, Alexander Pope, John Gay and, for a time, Henry Fielding – was capable of a variety of emphases attractive both to old-fashioned Whigs, alarmed at their party's compromises in office, and to popular Toryism. It was in many ways backward-looking and unrealistic. But, especially in major political scandals in the early 1730s, there was enough in Walpole's 'Robinocracy' – the derogatory term was coined from the diminutive of Robert – to give the critique credibility. Later, the critique was to prove adaptable to more radical ends, both in Britain and America. Thus the opposition to Walpole was of the greatest importance in ensuring the continuity of this influential eighteenth-century political discourse. In modes of opposition as much as of rule, Walpole's period of dominance provided the bridge from the seventeenth to the eighteenth century.[10]

The potency of the opposition programme was demonstrated most strikingly in the excise crisis of 1733.[11] By a campaign which set a pattern of propaganda and action for later opposition 'storms', Walpole was forced into a humiliating withdrawal of a major and constructive proposal which would have permanently reduced the land tax by extending excise duties to wine and tobacco in place of much less efficient customs duties. A chorus of protest across the country, skilfully orchestrated by the merchants and corporation of the City of London and the opposition press, operated on both Walpole's majority in both houses of parliament and his support at court. Walpole was able to recover from this major miscalculation with the help of the firm if belated support of the king and his own skill in appealing to Whig loyalties in parliament. However, the election of 1734, one of the most acrimonious of the century, showed the extent of the damage to his standing. The force of government and private patronage in the much more numerous constituencies with small electorates enabled him to retain a workable majority. But that majority was substantially reduced by losses in those constituencies – most counties, and boroughs with large electorates – open to wider opinion.

The excise crisis laid bare the mechanics of power and opposition in the early Hanoverian world. Walpole's consummate political skills won the excise war and his opponents entered the new parliament daunted and divided. Yet there is no doubt that the opposition had won the propaganda battle – most notably in persuading country gentlemen to vote against their interest in a reduced land tax. Moreover, the injudiciously abrupt dismissals Walpole required of the king in order to restore his position at court and in the Lords brought prominent new recruits to the opposition – notably the experienced diplomat, the Earl of Chesterfield, relieved of his court office, Lord Cobham, now no longer colonel of Pitt's regiment, and a number of influential Scottish peers. An even more prestigious recruit in the person of Frederick, Prince of Wales, a friend of Chesterfield, looked increasingly probable, as Frederick's stormy relations with his parents followed the pattern already becoming typical of Hanoverian monarchs with their adult heirs – one Walpole had exploited in opposition in 1717–20, when George II was Prince of Wales. An open breach now would threaten the restored political calm. Vain, shallow and unpredictable as Frederick was, any rival court around him could still offer to opposition politicians protection against charges of dynastic disloyalty and some patronage, the more valuable as George II was already in his fifties.

This political world offered difficult choices to a young man entering parliament. Support for the great statesman who dominated it could offer the experience and fruits of office or prospects in any other career. Yet it was clear that the real intellectual excitement – and the quickest way to capture attention – lay in joining the glittering array of talent who criticized the Robinocracy. And to a young man Walpole may well have seemed past his prime.

. . .

STARTING OUT AT THE END OF AN ERA, 1735–42

Within two months of his election in 1735, Pitt signalled his attraction to politics and to opposition by a 'distinguished' maiden speech in support of a bill to remove royal office-holders (or 'placemen') from parliament – a favourite plank of the patriot programme.[12] Youthful enthusiasm and loyalty to his one patron must certainly have drawn Pitt towards opposition. But his brother had been a government supporter for some time, and very probably it was Walpole who, in 1731, had met the £1,000 cost of William's commission in order to secure his brother's electoral influence.[13] Pitt's surprise that the proposed accommodation at his expense over the seat for Old Sarum was to be with one 'declared in opposition' rather than someone 'more agreeable to Sir Robert' was therefore natural. This surprise suggests that he was not thinking of taking a similar course.[14] He seems not to have been aware of his brother's changing sympathies, a change suggested by the return of George Lyttelton, Thomas's wife's brother, for Okehampton in March 1735. Lyttelton, it appears, had drawn Thomas – as he had already drawn William – into the orbit of his uncle, Cobham. Thus the influence on William of both brother and patron came to coincide in a commitment to opposition which in retrospect seems inevitable.

By the summer of 1735, Pitt was enjoying the distinguished company at Cobham's magnificent country seat at Stowe.[15] Here, by his hospitality, rather than by speeches in the House of Lords, Cobham – bluff soldier more than politician and apparently never to make a speech in the Lords – was beginning to shape the implacable opposition to Walpole first mysteriously aroused by the excise bill, then confirmed by his unprecedented dismissal after a noteworthy military career. Cobham's young nephews, Richard Grenville (his heir) and George Lyttelton, were returned to parliament at the same time as Pitt. Affable, promising young men of assured status, with few signs yet of later foibles, they readily adopted Pitt as one of 'Cobham's Cubs' – the spearhead of Cobham's vicarious display of his new-found patriot principles.

It was not long before the Cubs won their first notoriety as, with their patron, they began to move into the orbit of the Prince of Wales. In April 1736, Pulteney provocatively moved an address to the king on the occasion of the prince's marriage, a marriage well known to be displeasing to the king. On this occasion, all three Cubs made 'very remarkable speeches', aptly summed up as insinuating, 'not in very covert terms', that the nation owed the match and the dynastic stability it promised much less to the king than 'to the Prince demanding it of his father, and the voice of the people calling for it too strongly not to be complied with'.[16] Later in the year, Pitt was said to be 'perpetually with the Prince, and at present in the first rank of his favour'. The next February, all three Cubs spoke again on the even more provocative Pulteney motion, only narrowly defeated, asking the king to grant the prince an establishment of £100,000 a year.[17] Meanwhile, in May 1736, Pitt's notoriety had been enhanced by his dismissal from his cornetcy. Compensating reward came after the tensions between the prince and his parents became an open breach in July 1737, when Lyttelton became Private Secretary and Pitt Groom of the Bedchamber to the prince, Pitt's position bringing him a welcome £400 a year.[18]

Pitt's career had thus taken a decisive political turn.[19] He had begun to discover the power to command attention by his oratory but, in his careless giving of offence to the king, displayed a recklessness in deploying it that was to become characteristic. However, for a time, he and his young friends played only a sporadic role in opposition. They supported the patriot cause in debates on moves in 1737 and 1738 to reduce the size of the army. On this issue, typical 'country' arguments, favouring a militia instead of a professional force which was seen as a threat to the constitution, were deployed alongside considerations of the foreign situation. Lyttelton and Pitt added gibes at the subordination of placemen.[20] But Pitt was silent on large issues like the religious questions of the 1736 session, which dangerously challenged Walpole's control of Church–Dissent hostilities, or Sir John Barnard's proposal of 1737 to reduce interest on the national debt.

Pitt was eventually more attracted to the attack on Walpole's peaceful foreign policy which became the focus of opposition in the late 1730s.[21] Merchants in the City of London took up again the longstanding issue of the so-called 'depredations' of Spanish *garda costas* in the Caribbean against what they considered to be illegal British trading practices there. Public opinion could easily be aroused over this issue and opposition leaders readily took it up. In March 1738, a flood of merchants' petitions to the Commons on the depredations gave Pulteney the opportunity to demand strong action – only to have his resolutions emasculated by Walpole.[22] A year later, on 8 March 1739, the opposition campaign came to a climax when the Convention of the Pardo, negotiated with Spain to settle the disputes, was presented to the House. In one of the great parliamentary occasions of the century, the opposition, supported by further petitions, opposed the Convention and were only very narrowly defeated.

In 1738, Pitt was noticed only once, propounding the uselessness of negotiation with Spain.[23] The next year, on the Convention, he attracted far greater attention. He was reported to have spoken 'very well, but very abusively' of the 'national ignominy' of yet another negotiated settlement 'odious throughout the kingdom', which, he claimed, sacrificed longstanding vital interests of trade and self-defence while offering the 'public infamy' of financial reparations. Spain, he suggested, had more reason than Britain to fear a war in America, and delay would only strengthen the Bourbon union with France.[24] Pitt's sentiments were little different from those of more prominent opposition speakers. However, his virulence brought Walpole supporters to their feet in reply. Walpole himself made notes on his speech, which won for Pitt the accolade of a public kiss from the Prince of Wales. Indeed, Pitt's much greater enthusiasm on this occasion was probably prompted less by his own opinions than by the prince's very recent commitment to open parliamentary opposition.[25]

However, Pitt's parliamentary contributions remained erratic even as the tempo of opposition to Walpole mounted. Despite the Convention, war came in October 1739. Bellicose opinion against Spain was further fuelled by the early success of Admiral Vernon in capturing Porto Bello, a base for the *garda costas*. A vigorous press campaign and a spate of instructions to members of parliament, beginning in 1739 and continuing through 1740–41, combined concerns about both the domestic and the foreign aspects of the Robino-cracy. The multi-faceted swell of complaint began to resemble that against the excise, but its range became far wider. In the 1739–40 session, the opposition pressed Walpole hard on a place bill and defeated him on a bill to register seamen, which was claimed to threaten civil liberties. By the 1740–41 session, the prospects in the West Indies looked far less promising and serious complications threatened as war broke out in Europe.[26] The growing confidence of the parliamentary opposition, buoyed by the tide of opinion outside, came to a further climax in the famous motion of 13 February 1741, for an address to the king to dismiss Walpole.

No speeches from Pitt are recorded for the 1739–40 session, although he seconded a motion demanding that no peace be made without recognition of the major issue of principle in the disputes with Spain, the right of British ships to navigate the high seas without being searched.[27] But from the beginning of the 1740–41 session, when he and Lyttelton were 'very warm' in the address-in-reply debate, he was much more active. In January, he confronted Walpole over a proposed enquiry into naval mishaps, claiming that 'we are now to examine whether it is probable that we shall preserve our commerce and our independence, or whether we are sinking into subjection to a foreign power'. And later in the session he opposed the revival of the scheme to register seamen defeated the year before.[28] Most notably, in the great debate of 13 February, which ranged widely over Walpole's domestic and foreign policy, Pitt 'in his emphatic language' supported the motion by citing precedents for the removal of ministers on political rather than legal grounds. He criticized 'the satiety of power' that had increased debts and multiplied taxes at home, but concentrated on what he called 'a subversion in the state of Europe which [had] cost a long war'. He saw the 'house of Austria lessened, but . . . a deference to the counsels of France', and gross mismanagement in war with Spain.[29]

This time, Pitt and his fellow Cubs distinguished themselves from the rest of the prince's followers, who left the House without voting.[30] Many of the Tories, who were discomfited by such a blatant personal attack on the king's minister, also left. Their qualms allowed Walpole a striking victory, which brutally showed up the divisions of his opponents and deflated their confidence. However, Walpole's relief was brief. In the election of the spring of 1741 his majority was further dented, this time by defeats in the close constituencies brought about by the loss to opposition of powerful patrons: the Prince of Wales, who controlled many Cornish seats, and the Duke of Argyll in Scotland, alienated by Walpole's clumsy handling of Scottish discontents.[31] It required a further series of debates and votes in the new parliament to demonstrate that Walpole was weakened beyond recovery.[32] Perhaps constrained by the prince, Pitt took part only in the last crucial policy debate, on an address for an enquiry into the conduct of the war.[33] When, in February 1742, Walpole was defeated on an election petition and saved from the enquiry by only three votes, he persuaded the stubbornly reluctant George II that he had to go. An era had ended.

. . .

WHITHER NOW?

In the instability that followed, Pitt was eventually to find opportunities to enforce his claims to advancement in the political career he had now so clearly chosen and to the office he needed for financial security. But his immediate prospects were slight, constrained not least by the fragility of the parliamentary opposition. It was deeply divided, as Pitt's sporadic public role in opposition, like that of more prominent figures, vividly illustrates. As a follower of Cobham and the Prince of Wales, Pitt associated much less with the dissident Whig leaders, Pulteney and Carteret, who were often widely suspected of readiness to reach terms with the administration, than with leading peers like Chesterfield, whose public voice in the new opposition paper, *Common Sense*, supported a 'broad-bottom' alliance of Whigs and Tories and looked for the renewal of 'declining morals, and liberties' under a virtuous prince.[34] These associates were unimpeachably Whig, but at Stowe Pitt rubbed shoulders with recently converted Jacobites like Lord Cornbury,[35] and in the House he supported Tory motions. Alliance with the Tories had the tactical advantage that it might force a major ministerial reconstruction in which the Whig peers and even lesser followers like Pitt could hope for office. However, they also knew from the voting and electoral behaviour of the Tories how fragile alliance with them was.

In fact, parliamentary opposition alone did not bring Walpole down; his fall was the result of accumulating political and personal strains, not least those of a war he did not welcome. And the fragility of the opposition was soon amply demonstrated in the outcome of that fall. Aided by Walpole's advice and the mistakes and divisions of the opposition, the remaining leaders of the Old Corps were able to persuade the king (if he was in any doubt) to reject more thoroughgoing options in favour of a limited reconstruction, bringing in Pulteney and Carteret and a few of their followers.[36] This outcome was a reminder that, while the House of Commons might in special circumstances be able to force the king to give up a minister, the initiative lay with him in reconstituting his administration. By following the pattern of the reconstruction which ended the 1717–20 opposition in which Walpole had been prominent, this outcome was one step on the way to confirming Walpole's pattern of dominance and was probably essential to maintaining the degree of stability his skills had ensured. However, it was dismissed as a 'job' by many of his opponents in and outside parliament. It left a deep and continuing sense of disillusionment at the failure to achieve a renewal of government on patriot lines which would have to be contained if stability was to endure.

It was hardly to be expected that Pitt would gain any office in this reconstruction, especially when many more prominent were left high and dry. Furthermore, he was deserted (although not deprived of office) by his more powerful patron when the vacillating Prince of Wales made peace with his father. Pitt's other patron, Cobham, despite the restoration of his regimental command, typically took an inflexible stand against any accommodation, even of the prince with his father.[37] Pitt's very subordinate role at this stage is emphasized by the fact that he played no recorded part in the opposition discussions accompanying the reconstruction, even the very large Fountain Tavern meeting of 12 February 1742.[38]

The manner of Walpole's going, almost as much as his long dominance, confirmed the House of Commons as a major theatre of political debate and contention for power. There, over seven years of sporadic confrontation with the redoubtable Walpole, Pitt had learned some parliamentary skills. He had attracted some attention, though often only as one of a group of 'young gentlemen, who took great personal libertys'. At the time of his dismissal from his cornetcy he was noted as 'a young man of no fortune, a very pretty speaker, one the Prince is particular to, and under the tuition of my Lord Cobham'.[39] Most notably in the debate on the Convention with Spain, he had tasted the thrill of mastering the House with 'the prettyiest words, and the worst language . . . ever heard', although few apart from a French observer as yet discerned an exceptionally able parliamentarian in the making.[40] Nor, except perhaps in expression, was there anything to distinguish his sentiments from those of others in opposition. Unlike his friend, George Lyttelton, Pitt had shown no interest in the extra-parliamentary aspect of opposition.[41] So far, he had played a young man's part, testing his options for advancement somewhat recklessly, evidently without much consistency of purpose.

By 1741, however, his correspondence suggests excited anticipation of a decisive thrust against Walpole[42] – and he and his friends had shown in the House that they were not the prince's puppets. In 1742, as the parliamentary opposition reformed to face Walpole's successors, it gave vent to the widespread disillusion at the outcome of his fall by setting up a parliamentary enquiry into his years in power which might provide legal grounds for punishment by impeachment – the clumsy device to secure accountability revived in the seventeenth century. Pitt's two speeches of vigorous support suggest that he genuinely shared the disillusion. Certainly he showed remarkable venom against Walpole as he answered objections to the enquiry and once again ranged widely over the complaints of alleged misuse of power in domestic affairs and gross mismanagement of affairs abroad that had allowed French power and ambitions to increase. Both speeches drew attention to the 'voice of the people' in complaint and claimed that it ought properly to be heard and expressed by the House of Commons.[43] His speeches reinforced his claims as a rising politician, winning him one of the last places on the secret committee of enquiry.

The committee's proceedings were soon stonewalled by essential witnesses, however, and, despite its lengthy reports, no action eventuated.[44] The failure of this attempt to add legal penalties to Walpole's defeat was a further step towards entrenching the more flexible political processes of accountability his practice had exemplified. But the sense of bitter disillusion was not allayed. Here Pitt, with his Cobham connections and his budding oratory, was to find his opportunity.

. . .

WAR AND THE PATH TO OFFICE, 1742–46

Despite the success of the Old Corps in avoiding major disruption following Walpole's fall, the political situation was far from settled. In the administration, the 'new Whig' recruits vied for supremacy with the remaining leaders of the Old Corps, Henry Pelham (Walpole's chosen heir), his brother, the Duke of Newcastle, and the Lord Chancellor, Lord Hardwicke. Like Walpole parvenus in national politics, Revolution Whigs by dint of service rather than family, the latter all had solid political and administrative experience behind them and a shrewd appreciation of the political system as shaped by Walpole. They soon out-manoeuvred Pulteney. He bore the brunt of the outcry against false patriots and when, in July, he was persuaded into accepting a peerage as Earl of Bath, his political career was effectively over. Pelham then seemed set to become the recognized leader in the Commons. A year later, when he was appointed First Lord of the Treasury, he had in his hands the makings of an ascendancy like Walpole's. But Carteret, Secretary of State, was a much more formidable rival. Although widely distrusted by his new and earlier colleagues, he was a gifted Europeanist with diplomatic and political experience and a fluent command of languages. His broad views, his German and his easy affability quickly won the favour of the king. Thus arose the distinct possibility that the sources of power Walpole had so skilfully combined would be separated and a more courtly 'prime minister' might emerge.[45]

This possibility, and the likelihood of further political instability – which opposition politicians might exploit – were gravely exacerbated by the complex new issues arising in Europe. There, the unexpected death of the Emperor,

Charles VI, in October 1740 brought into operation his carefully negotiated provisions – the Pragmatic Sanction, which Britain supported – to protect the Habsburg inheritance of his daughter, Maria Theresa, who could not be elected emperor. In December 1740, Prussia's new king, Frederick – whose skills as statesman and soldier were to make him Frederick the Great – defied it by invading Silesia, Austria's richest province. France soon widened the challenge with extensive victories in Germany in 1741.

The Austrian succession posed the biggest question to arise in Europe since Britain's emergence as a great power in the struggle over the division of the Spanish empire settled in 1713–14. The balance of power then established and later defended was now seriously threatened by the 'rape' of Silesia, which launched the recently cobbled-together state of Prussia, Europe's rising military power, into a longlasting competition with the hitherto mighty Habsburgs which was to change the face of Europe. More immediately, the successes of the leading European power, France, aroused anew the threat of French hegemony.

This Britain could not ignore – even though the opportunity distracted France from the possibility of joining Spain in the Caribbean war. The policy of the Walpole era of generally peaceful management of controversial issues in concert with other powers could not cope with the ambitions raised by the Austrian succession. So in 1741, Britain intervened to help Maria Theresa – whose desperate plight aroused popular sympathy in Britain – and early in 1742, without any parliamentary dissent, the new ministers continued subsidies for Austria and potential allies and dispatched British troops to the army being assembled in the Austrian Netherlands.[46] Very soon, however, the rapidly changing circumstances of war inflamed again the debate about how best to protect Britain's European interests which had gone on since the turn of the century. All attention was diverted from concerns outside Europe as, on this bitterly divisive issue, both Carteret's distrustful ministerial colleagues and those remaining in opposition, not least Pitt, found their opportunities.

Carteret, who, as Secretary of State dealing with northern Europe, had principal responsibility for British moves, favoured an active policy like that of William III. This deployed British money, troops and ships and aimed to build up alliances to support Maria Theresa in all spheres of Habsburg influence – the Netherlands, Germany, Italy. This policy was firmly backed by George II, who had an experience and knowledge of continental affairs much greater than most of his ministers and was deeply interested, as he always was, in foreign policy. Also in his mind were the concerns of his beloved German electorate, where, except in wartime, he spent as much time as possible every summer. Already, in face of the French victories of 1741, the king had negotiated a humiliating convention of neutrality for his Hanoverian dominions which directly conflicted with British policy. The convention was quickly repudiated, but at the cost of promises of British help in the defence of Hanover.

Carteret's policy had some success. The Austrian campaigns of 1742 brought a dramatic deterioration in French fortunes in Germany, while the Treaty of Breslau, guaranteed by Britain, was negotiated between Austria and Prussia. At the zenith of the policy in 1743, the allied army, under the personal command of George II, won its own victory over the French at Dettingen, on the Main, while the Treaty of Worms brought Maria Theresa a very useful new ally, Sardinia. But not all was well. Carteret failed to detach the new Emperor, Charles Albert of Bavaria, from the French, who also reactivated the Family Compact with Bourbon Spain. Other British ministers were far from happy with the scale of British activities, not least because the expense was difficult to defend in parliament. The opposition were able to suggest that British interests – as distinct from those of their allies – would be much better defended by strictly limited continental commitments, or even by concentration solely on war by sea.

The reversal of French successes in 1742 – which made help to Austria seem much less necessary – gave the opposition the first issue on which to focus this debate. In the summer of that year, the ministers had to agree to take 16,000 Hanoverian troops into British pay in order to avoid a reduction of the Hanoverian war effort. This move gave force to allegations in the press that British interests were being subordinated to those of its foreign monarch[47] – a charge which had been a standard 'country' accusation since the 1690s. The issue also tapped deep springs of popular distaste for the Hanoverian monarchs and their Whig politicians, which George II's frumpish court and personality, his well-known obsession with routine and his volatile temper, did nothing to allay. As Pulteney (by then Earl of Bath) warned Newcastle in September, the ministers were giving their opponents a potent new issue on which to focus public disillusion.[48]

Caught up in the power of this feeling, Pitt was given an issue on which he emerged as a speaker of first-rank importance. He took the lead in the Commons as the issue burst into view at the opening of parliament in November 1742. Then, according to Richard Grenville, 'Pitt spoke like 10,000 angels' against Britain's payment of Hanoverian troops.[49] A little later, the particular virulence he brought to the argument was shown when he argued that the hiring of troops was but another instance of the way in which 'this great, this powerful, this formidable kingdom is considered only as a province to a despicable electorate'. Such reckless personal venom could only compound his offence to the king and extend it to his heir – the Prince of Wales had already said that 'Pitt might as well have spit in his face as spoke as he did'.[50]

Pitt's part in these foreign policy debates early in 1743 won him a new kind of notice. To one back-bencher (who had been in the House since 1734), on this 'infamous job of the H[anove]r t[roo]ps' Pitt stood out as 'in the opinion of several as well as me . . . a greater man than any I have ever sat with', one who 'if he preserves his integrity will be transmitted to posterity in the most illustrious of characters'. To others, he was beginning to 'speak like a man of business', and as one 'who does not intend to be under any one'.[51] Most significant was the opinion given to Henry Pelham by Sir Robert Walpole (now Lord Orford), that Pitt might be included on Pelham's first Treasury Board. 'Pitt is thought able and formidable', he wrote; 'try him and show him.'[52]

The Hanoverian issue was vigorously taken up in the press from December 1742, in close collusion with opposition politicians like Chesterfield, who took the lead in the Lords, and the Earl of Marchmont (one of the Scottish peers dismissed after the excise crisis). Cobham maintained his behind-scenes role as 'the secret life and spirit of the party' in animus against Carteret. Carteret's successes in 1743 encouraged the accusation that the threat of France was being exaggerated in Hanoverian interests. The press campaign rose to a climax in October and November.[53] In October, Chesterfield concluded that, to exploit the strains becoming evident in the administration, '[a]ll we have to do . . . is to prepare for battle' in parliament and 'to blow the Hannover flame to the height'.[54]

Once again Pitt spearheaded the attack in parliament, probing these strains with a new sharpness of political purpose. He claimed that Hanoverian influence had hampered and distorted Britain's war effort, putting the king in danger of losing the affections of his people. At the same time, 'Lord Carteret was severely reflected upon, and styled . . . an execrable, a sole minister, who had renounced the British nation'.[55] At the battle of Dettingen, Pitt said, the king had been 'hemmed in by German officers, and one English minister without an English heart'. Pitt's strong language was widely noted.[56] His attack went on throughout the session. In January, Carteret was berated as 'a Hanover troop minister', while 'the amiable part of the Administration' was urged to give up policies 'which only tend to advance another's power in the closet'. Later still, Pitt charged Carteret with establishing 'a Prerogative Administration'.[57] Although Pitt's extremism sometimes antagonized potential supporters, the opposition attack achieved some high votes damaging to the administration.[58]

There was more to Pitt's attack than rhetoric. Behind the detailed criticisms of the campaigns, he was developing an alternative policy that would recognize Britain's interests in Europe but not strain the country's resources as the long war of Anne's reign had done: a limited commitment, to the defence of some but not all of Maria Theresa's territories and to an alliance against France only at the request of, and in concert with, other powers. Much of this was well-established argument; much was closely paralleled in discussions in the press.[59] However, as Pitt developed his case, the question of British troops in the army in Flanders divided the opposition.[60] In December 1742, when the opposition reversed their support for the troops, Pitt had rejected the charge of inconsistency on the grounds that what had been a request for money and auxiliary troops had become an 'aggressive' policy of committing British troops.[61] Now he and Lyttelton, with Chesterfield and Marchmont, refused to oppose the continuation of British troops in Flanders, while others, including Cobham and the Grenvilles, reverted to the traditional line of opposing any British commitment except possibly by subsidies. The issue was bitterly argued out in an opposition meeting at the Fountain Tavern on 10 January 1744. The next day, in the Commons, the divisions became clear when Pitt and Lyttelton stuck to their agreement to vote against continuing the British troops, but did not speak. A week later, in attacking the vote for the Hanoverians, Pitt carefully distinguished this question from the wider issue of intervention on the continent. Other opposition speakers did not.[62] The bitter chronicler of these differences, the poet and political intriguer Richard Glover, attributed Pitt's views to his hopes of office.[63] Pitt himself offered three not entirely consistent explanations: that 'the nation being involved in a war, the ministry ought not to be disarmed'; that the ministry was not now supporting a 'war of acquisition', but seeking peace; and that there was a need 'to keep up sufficient strength on the continent to oppose France'.[64] Only the last argument was fully consonant with his emerging policy of limited intervention.

Within weeks, another dramatic change in the fortunes of war gave force to this last justification as Marshal Saxe led a French army into the Netherlands. French preparations for an invasion of Britain with possible Jacobite collusion became obvious. In March, war between Britain and France was formally declared. As these threats emerged, Pitt persisted with his more moderate line. He firmly declared his loyalty, warmly supported an increase of the army and navy, and dissociated himself from Tory protests at various moves against Jacobites.[65] Nor did he always join other Cobhamites in opposition moves.[66] These new hints of moderation were far from universally recognized; to many Pitt was still the hot young firebrand – who appeared to support an enquiry into the state of the navy 'in the most indecent manner'.[67] Nevertheless, his sustained efforts in this session[68] reinforced his claim to be recognized as a leading parliamentary speaker with some independence of his aristocratic patrons.

Furthermore, these efforts made him a much more credible contender for office. More immediately, they apparently took their toll. Pitt spent most of the parliamentary recess at Bath, crippled by the first major attack of the complex 'gout', possibly associated with depression, which was to afflict him all his life.[69] Incapacitation struck at a crucial time. Over the summer, the course of the war heightened divisions in the ministry. The French invasion threat was foiled by the weather, but Saxe's advance in the Netherlands, although stalled, was not reversed, while the situation worsened in Germany and Italy. The previous year, as the ineffectiveness of Carteret's expensive schemes made them even less justifiable to parliament, the Pelhams had made intermittent overtures to opposition peers, especially Chesterfield and Cobham, in which Pitt played an occasional subordinate role in bringing the parties together.[70] Now the Pelhams saw their chance to break Carteret. In November, they demanded his dismissal. In three weeks of negotiations the opposition peers chose to support the Pelhams, not Carteret (who had recently become Earl Granville). The king was forced to submit. In place of a dozen or so of Granville's and Bath's 'new Whigs', enough of the opposition were brought in to create the appearance, at least, of the 'broad-bottom' administration they had long desired. The 'new allies' included a few Tories, Lyttelton, and the second Grenville brother, George – who had joined the Cubs in parliament with another brother, James, in 1742, and whose steady conscientiousness was already making him more active than Richard.[71]

The Pelhams had forced the king to recognize the need for ministers able and willing to defend policies in parliament. Yet the king won on one count. Pitt was the only leading Whig excluded. During the negotiations, Pitt made no difficulties. Indeed, unlike Cobham, who at first irascibly resisted any deal with Walpole's heirs, he had been one of the majority in an opposition committee which voted not to insist on policy stipulations.[72] But, with the king grudging about any changes, there was no hope that he would accept the most vitriolic of opposition speakers in the office Pitt chose to press for, that of Secretary at War. This was not only an important office of second rank, but also one which required much attendance on the king on matters in which he took a keen interest. Pitt had to go along with the opposition peers in their acceptance of the Pelhams' assurances that they would attempt to mollify the king in time.

In fact, for the moment, Pitt acquiesced readily.[73] There can be no doubt that he wanted office – while his choice of office suggests a high estimation of his bargaining power.[74] His complaisance was perhaps the result of continuing illness. The ensuing parliamentary session was to see the first of his many appearances 'with the mien and apparatus of an invalid', leaning on his crutch,[75] and he spoke very little. But that session also confirms a more probable reason for acquiescence – that he continued to see his future with the Pelhams rather than with the remnants of the old or with Granville's new opposition.

Certainly, in the new session, which was remarkably peaceful, Pitt amply demonstrated his potential usefulness as a government spokesman. His two recorded speeches helped to hold together the still fragile 'broad-bottom' alliance on difficult issues of foreign policy. On 23 January, he 'made a very strong and much admired speech' – indeed a striking overview of recent policy – defending the proposal of an increased number of troops for Flanders on the grounds (once again) that the administration's measures had substantially changed. No longer were they abetting Austria, he said, in 'romantic schemes' of acquisition, but were directed (in concert with the Dutch) to limited objectives and peace. Lambasting Granville and praising Pelham in equal measure, he declared his belief that 'a dawn of salvation to the country had broken forth'.[76] On 18 February, despite his former bitter hostility to the Hanoverian troops (who were no longer to be employed by Britain), he defended as 'a meritorious and popular measure' the ruse of granting increased aid to Maria Theresa so that she could pay for at least half of them. With 'all the art and temper imaginable', he smoothed some prickly Old Corps feelings raised by his speech.[77] Both measures passed with negligible opposition. And, unlike other members of the former opposition whether now in office or not, Pitt in this session took no advantage of several other opportunities to embarrass the administration. Particularly when, in March, he regularized his breach with the Prince of Wales by at last resigning his household post, Pitt's commitment to the Pelhams seemed clear.

They responded with warm gratitude for his 'fulminating eloquence'.[78] But their appreciation was not likely to bring Pitt to office while, all through 1745, the king remained manifestly hostile to them, continuing to favour a greater commitment to the war in Europe than they recommended and remaining open to the influence of Granville as informal 'minister behind the curtain'.[79] Meanwhile, the war situation deteriorated on all fronts, particularly in the Netherlands, relieved only temporarily by news in July of the fall to a colonial force of Louisburg, the French fortress controlling the mouth of the St Lawrence. That same month brought the worst news of all: of the landing of Charles Edward, the Young Pretender, James II's grandson, in Scotland. The long-held fear of a Jacobite rebellion rapidly became a threatening reality as he advanced unchecked through Scotland into England by November. The possibility of a further French invasion attempt to support him could not be discounted. The administration, badly served by its Scottish managers, was caught unprepared. Their standing with the king plummeted further, while the Duke of Cumberland, the king's younger and much more able son, who, at 23, had just assumed command of the allied army in Flanders, was recalled with his troops to meet the threat.

In these dire circumstances, parliament, recalled in October, earlier than usual, was likely to be unpredictable. The administration could rely on a certain degree of loyal response; on the other hand, there would be awkward issues for opponents to seize on.[80] Pitt, fully active again, had the chance to demonstrate his value to the Pelhams more forcefully. He sought judiciously to advertise his own loyalty and concern for proper measures; at the same time he attempted to embarrass the ministry and exploit its divisions without completely alienating the Pelhams. Thus he opposed as untimely an amendment to the address calling for the 'patriot' remedies of shorter parliaments and elections free from influence, but on 23 October he moved for the recall of the remaining British troops in Flanders to meet the threat of rebellion. This motion was clearly opportunistic: most of the troops were already under orders to return and it was obviously unwise to advertise this possibility to the French.[81] But the motion, seen by some as 'very respectful',[82] appealed to the House and was defeated by only eight votes. Five days later, Pitt attempted to exploit the shortcomings of the administration's Scottish officeholders, who were supporters of Granville, by seconding a motion, of which

Pelham was forewarned, for an enquiry into the causes of the rebellion. This time, a comfortable majority saw the motion as premature.[83] And Pitt also helped to agitate the deeply divisive issue of the rank to be given to officers serving in the controversial private regiments to be raised by noblemen.

This pressure, applied with the obvious sympathy of the Cobhamites in office, secured approaches from the Pelhams. For the first time Pitt negotiated on his own behalf, initially with Pelham on 25 October and then as part of a larger group of Pelhamite and 'new ally' peers on 16 November. He signalled a new independence by taking a tough stance, laying down three popular 'patriot' conditions at the initial meeting. The first two – 'constitutional bills', particularly a place bill to exclude lower-ranking army and navy officers from parliament (a strange comment on Pitt's own experience), and the removal of remaining Granville supporters – were acceptable enough to the Pelhams but would, if pressed, have only exacerbated their relations with the king. Negotiations broke down chiefly on the third, the very fully debated demand for a major redirection of war policy towards acting only as 'auxiliaries' on the continent, with strictly limited help to the Dutch, and concentrating 'as principals' on maritime conflict with the Bourbons.[84]

Pitt now stepped up his pressure in parliament. This new stage in his views on the war – 'his favourite notion of a maritime war', as Newcastle was soon calling it[85] – was brought into the open on 21 November. Then, without notice this time, he moved an address to the king to augment the navy. In a striking speech notable for its abuse of Pelham, he claimed '[w]e are designed by [nature] for a maritime power. Experience sufficiently confirms . . . when we endeavour to exert our strength by sea we become the dread of the world when by land the contempt of it.' He dwelt on the advantages to trade to east and west that the success of the last campaign by sea had brought, in contrast to that by land, drawing attention particularly to the fall of Louisburg.[86] In normal circumstances, such a rousing appeal to 'the natural way of exerting our strength' would have won much support. Now, however, the thin House readily accepted Pelham's argument that, as Horace Walpole put it, '[s]hips built a year hence' were little use 'to suppress an army of Highlanders, now marching through England'.[87] There were even larger majorities against Pitt when he pressed for the recall of cavalry from Flanders, and again when, following the announcement of the arrival in England of Hessian troops, he attempted to exploit the usual unpopularity of foreign mercenaries. With rebellion rampant in the north, not even the Tories would risk the taint of disloyalty.

It was obvious to all now that Pitt was 'ravenous for the place of secretary at war'; he was within reach of securing his ambitions in some form. But this unfathomable behaviour seemed deliberately to have flagged away his chances. With a mere 40 or so votes in the House, he had, it seemed, 'nothing left but his words, and his haughtiness, and his Lytteltons and his Grenvilles' against 'the whole royal family, all the Cabinet Council, and both Houses of Parliament in a matter that concerned all Europe'; he seemed to have made impossible the compromises necessary to gain office. 'I cannot decypher Pitt's behaviour', exclaimed Chesterfield, who wondered whether he intended 'setting himself at the head of a Party, however small, independent of us'.[88]

Pitt's demonstration of independence had indeed been carried too far. Pelham might not fully agree with the king that Pitt's defeats in the House made negotiation unnecessary,[89] but he made no further approaches. It was Pitt who had to change tack. Early in the new year, as the Young Pretender retreated to Scotland, a French invasion failed to materialize, and the situation abroad improved, Pitt renewed contact indirectly through the Duke of Bedford, a powerful young peer of patriot inclinations who had joined the administration in 1744 as First Lord of the Admiralty. Pitt expressed only 'an inclination to know our foreign scheme', handed over negotiations to Cobham and became co-operative again in the Commons. Newcastle approached Cobham, who accepted the 'foreign scheme', and agreement was reached on further places for Cobhamites. But once again the king absolutely refused to consider Pitt as Secretary at War. Pitt complaisantly withdrew his claims.[90]

Then, however, in mid-February, the issue of Pitt's preferment as part of a deal to secure the Cobhamites was swallowed up in the much larger problem of the king's intensifying hostility, as the crisis of 1745 passed, towards his ministers and their policy of seeking matching commitments from the Dutch to the war in the Netherlands. Now, with the worst of the crisis over, the Pelhams and their Old Corps supporters enforced their protest at the king's attitude with quite unprecedented mass resignations. When an attempt to form an alternative ministry around Bath and Granville (Pulteney and Carteret of old) failed within days, the Pelhams insisted, as one part of the extensive terms for their return, that the king should 'perfect the scheme' for giving 'honourable employment' to Pitt.[91] The employment he was offered, however, was not as Secretary at War, but, first, the sinecure office of Joint Vice-Treasurer for Ireland, and then, when the chance arose in May, that of Paymaster General – an office which required no attendance on the king.

. . .

ARRIVAL

The Pelhams' stand ended the political uncertainty that had followed Walpole's resignation with victory for his heirs and his 'system' for making parliamentary monarchy work. By successfully insisting that the king should be seen to give his confidence to the ministers who took responsibility for his measures and could secure parliamentary support for them, the stand elucidated an important corollary to that system. The obverse was total defeat for Granville – the courtly favourite who had claimed 'give any man the Crown on his side and he can defy everything'[92] – and apparent humiliation for the king. The victory went to those with superior judgement of political realities. However, while it confirmed practical limits that had long existed on the king's freedom of action, within those limits it did not alter his political influence – as Pitt's career was to continue to demonstrate.

From 1743, Pitt had attached his prospects to the Pelhamite Whigs, in the process muting his 'patriotism' and abandoning contact with Tories. He benefited from their final victory. He was not essential to it; but satisfying him could make the administration's task in parliament easier, and Henry Pelham's instincts were for inclusiveness, at least of Whigs. So, Pelham held in May, Pitt 'must be had, and kept', even at the risk of surprise to members of the now resurgent Old Corps that 'Mr Pitt should be thought on for so high and so lucrative an employment' as that of Paymaster.[93] Pitt thus became a politician in his own right. The breach with Cobham, which had been incipient since 1744 as Pitt tested his independence, was soon open; Cobham's irascible inflexibility had become a liability; the other Cubs were Pitt's loyal allies.[94]

Pitt had demonstrated his usefulness chiefly by his role in opposition. At first that role was largely shaped by his patrons; perhaps even in the early 1740s he was still influenced by Cobham's inveterate hostility to Carteret and Hanoverian troops. But, having discovered his abilities, his political ambition grew. The issues of war and political instability opened opportunities. Pitt did not create the skilfully orchestrated anti-Hanoverian outcry; he did not as yet appreciate the potency of its out-of-doors aspect; but by 1743 it had enabled him to emerge as the chief opposition spokesman in the Commons. Now he was clearly playing for office.

However, in exploiting the possibilities of opposition, Pitt's political judgement was marred by an extremism which often deterred likely allies[95] and was most obvious in his gratuitous and costly offensiveness to the king. Without the divisions at court, he could have continued to fulminate impotently in opposition. He was further weakened by that reluctance to build political alliances – with Chesterfield, for example, or the young Duke of Bedford – which was becoming apparent in these years. Bolingbroke found him 'supercilious', Cobham thought him 'narrow . . . and a little too dogmatical', Chesterfield perspicaciously commented that 'he has neither love nor hate in his disposition'.[96] And the final process of coming to office made apparent the limits that still constrained his independence: he had to give up his policy stipulations, hand over his case to peers, and endure the denial of his chosen office by the king. It was not easy to break unconnected into the narrow circle of aristocrats who controlled political power in mid-eighteenth-century Britain.

After youthful extravagances in support of the Prince of Wales, Pitt had made foreign policy his chief concern, showing only an intermittent interest in the domestic aspects of opposition campaigns. The issues of these years gave him a rapid education in the demands of Britain's recently acquired great-power status. He had shown himself, on a number of occasions, capable of surveys of foreign affairs of some power and insight which insisted on the paramountcy of British interests, particularly in reducing the 'exorbitant' power of France. He seems, however, not yet to have reached any consistent conclusions on how this end could be achieved. He had shared the quite unrealistic opposition expectations about war with Spain in the New World, but his reiterated complaints against Walpole were far more concerned with supposed mismanagement of European affairs. In the early 1740s he had certainly propounded a limited defensive role for Britain in Europe in opposition to Carteret's grand schemes. No doubt his vigorous stands won some reputation as a 'patriot' – in 1744, Sarah, dowager Duchess of Marlborough, had bequeathed him £10,000 'upon account of his merit in the noble defence he has made of the laws of England, and to prevent the ruin of his country'.[97] But Pitt vacillated over how Britain's role might be exercised, whether by mere auxiliary aid or the commitment of British troops; the call for greater concentration on maritime war – a 'blue-water' policy – came only late in 1745 after the fall of Louisburg. He was as perplexed as anyone, it seems, by the difficulties created for Britain – especially for the 'old system' of alliance with Austria and the Dutch which had served British interests since 1689 – by the rise of Prussia, the consequent shift in Austrian priorities to Germany and the decline of the United Provinces.

To some extent, these changes in emphasis could be defended as well-considered responses to the changing fortunes of the continental war – initially wildly fluctuating and then increasingly gloomy, as the Netherlands became the focus of British concern. But at least equally obvious is their adaptation to Pitt's political need to demonstrate his value as an ally. It is tempting to conclude that his aim was primarily a share of power, not a redirection of it. Now he had at last achieved this aim, at a similar age to Walpole and Pelham when they were given second-rank office. What prospects lay before him?

. . .

NOTES

1. The best account of the family's background, derived largely from family papers preserved at Dropmore and calendared

in vol. 1 of HMC, *Fortescue*, is in Basil Williams, *The Life of William Pitt Earl of Chatham* 2 vols (1913), I, ch. 1.

2. HMC, *Fortescue*, I, p. 76.

3. Unless otherwise indicated, the following account of Pitt's pre-1735 years is based either on the limited family correspondence in Dropmore Papers, Series II, Add. MSS 69288–9, or on Williams, *The Life of William Pitt.*

4. Add. MSS 69288, no. 2.

5. Lord Edmond Fitzmaurice, *Life of William, Earl of Shelburne, afterwards First Marquess of Lansdowne* 3 vols (1875–6), I, p. 72.

6. Romney Sedgwick, *The House of Commons 1715–1754* 2 vols (1971), II, p. 355, I, pp. 228, 350–1.

7. Lewis Namier, *The Structure of Politics at the Accession of George III* 2nd edn (1960), ch. 1.

8. Add. MSS 69289, no. 4.

9. William to Ann Pitt, 24 Oct., 7 Nov. 1734, Add. MSS 69289, nos 17, 18.

10. The simplest description of this opposition is H.T. Dickinson, *Walpole and the Whig Supremacy* (1973), ch. 8, the most influential, J.G.A. Pocock, *The Machiavellian Moment. Florentine Political Thought and the Atlantic Republican Tradition* (Princeton, NJ, 1975), ch. 14, esp. pp. 477–86. On radical adaptations, see Marie Peters, 'The *Monitor* on the Constitution, 1755–1765: new light on the ideological origins of English radicalism', *English Historical Review* 86 (1971), pp. 706–27; Linda Colley, 'Eighteenth-century English radicalism before Wilkes', *Transactions of the Royal Historical Society*, fifth series 31 (1981), pp. 1–19.

11. The best account is Paul Langford, *The Excise Crisis. Society and Politics in the Age of Walpole* (Oxford, 1975).

12. HMC, *Egmont*, II, p. 171.

13. Sedgwick, *The House of Commons*, II, pp. 353, 355.

14. See n. 9 above.

15. Described briefly but vividly in Tony Aldous, 'A bestowal for Stowe', *History Today* 41 (Jan. 1991), p. 6.

16. John, Lord Hervey, *Some Materials Towards Memoirs of the Reign of King George II*, ed. Romney Sedgwick, 3 vols (continuous pagination) (1931), p. 553.

17. Ibid., pp. 613, 667; HMC, *Egmont*, II, p. 355.

18. Lady Anne Irwin to Lord Carlisle, 20 May [1736], commenting on the 'alarm' the dismissal raised in the army, HMC, *Carlisle*, p. 172; cf. *Gentleman's Magazine* 6 (1736), p. 278, and [John Almon], *Anecdotes of the Life of the Right Honourable William Pitt, Earl of Chatham* 3rd edn, 3 vols (1793), I, pp. 32–5; Hoare-Pitt Papers, Public Record Office, PRO 30/70/1/3, 1 Feb. 173[8], ALB/2.

19. As verses addressed to him by his friends at Stowe make clear: PRO 30/8/27, f. 178; Almon, *Anecdotes*, I, p. 29.

20. Jeremy Black, *Pitt the Elder* (Cambridge, 1992), p. 38, cf. HMC, *Egmont*, II, pp. 350–1 (18 Feb. 1737); *Parl. Hist.*, X, cols 464–7 (3 Feb 1738).

21. Paul Langford, *The Eighteenth Century 1688–1815* (1976), pp. 110–15.

22. William Coxe, *Memoirs of the Life and Administration of Sir Robert Walpole* 3 vols (1798), I, pp. 573–83.

23. By a French reporter; see Leo Francis Stock (ed.), *Proceedings and Debates of the British Parliaments respecting North America* 5 vols (Washington, DC, 1924–41), IV, p. 507 and n.; cf. PRO 30/8/74, f. 376. It seems reasonably certain that it was William, not his Tory cousin, John Pitt, who spoke.

24. John Selwyn to Thomas Townshend, 10 March 1739, in Coxe, *Walpole*, III, p. 519; Stock, *Proceedings and Debates*, IV, pp. 773–5; cf. PRO 30/8/74, f. 11, the corrected text of part of Pitt's speech.

25. Coxe, *Walpole*, I, p. 594n., III, p. 607 (John Selwyn to Stephen Poyntz, 17 March 1739, wrongly dated 1739–40); Sedgwick, *The House of Commons*, I, p. 44.

26. See below, p. 28.

27. *Memoirs George II*, I, p. 5, n. 19, cf. *Commons Journal* 23, pp. 386–7 (21 Nov. 1739), and PRO 30/8/74, f. 96 (draft).

28. Coxe, *Walpole*, III, p. 557 (18 Nov. 1740); *Parl. Hist.*, XI, col. 1009 (26 Jan. 1741), XII, cols 103–5, 115–17 (March 1741).

29. Coxe, *Walpole*, I, p. 653; I.G. Doolittle, 'A first-hand account of the Commons debate on the removal of Sir Robert Walpole, 13 February 1741', *Bulletin of the Institute of Historical Research* 53 (1980), pp. 134–5; *Parl. Hist.*, XI, cols 1359–64. Pitt's notes are at PRO 30/8/74, ff. 1–8.

30. Doolittle, 'A first-hand account', p. 134, n. 121.

31. Most notably, the Porteous riots, over a smuggling incident, and the consequent punishment of the city of Edinburgh.

32. John B. Owen, *The Rise of the Pelhams* (1957), ch. 1; Sedgwick, *The House of Commons*, I, pp. 46–50.

33. Walpole to Mann, 22 Jan. 1742, *Correspondence*, XVII, p. 297; cf. PRO 30/8/74, f. 11.

34. Lyttelton to Pitt, 23 May [1741], PRO 30/8/48, f. 244; Paul Langford, *A Polite and Commercial People. England 1727–1783* (Oxford, 1989), p. 48.

35. PRO 30/8/27, ff. 177–80.

36. Owen, *The Rise of the Pelhams*, pp. 87–103.

37. Philip Lawson, *George Grenville. A Political Life* (Oxford, 1984), p. 10; Lewis M. Wiggin, *The Faction of Cousins. A Political*

Account of the Grenvilles, 1733–1763 (New Haven, CT, 1958), p. 97.

38. Almon, *Anecdotes*, I, pp. 78–9; Sedgwick, *The House of Commons*, I, pp. 51–2.

39. Coxe, *Walpole*, III, p. 516 (10 March 1739); Lady Irwin to Carlisle, 20 May [1736], HMC, *Carlisle*, p. 172.

40. Coxe, *Walpole*, III, p. 609 (17 March 1739); Black, *Pitt the Elder*, p. 36.

41. George Lyttelton, *Considerations on the present state of our affairs, at home and abroad* and *Farther considerations on the present state of our affairs, at home and abroad, as affected by the late convention* (1739).

42. See e.g. letters from Lyttelton and to Gower and Chesterfield, PRO 30/8/48, ff. 243–4, 259, vol. 33, ff. 65–71, vol. 6, ff. 28–33, *Chatham Correspondence*, I, pp. 1–4.

43. *Parl. Hist.*, XII, cols 482–96 (9 March), 553–63, 567–72 (23 March 1742). The first speech was on a motion for an enquiry into the last twenty years, which was lost by two votes; a second motion, for an enquiry over ten years, was narrowly passed.

44. Owen, *The Rise of the Pelhams*, pp. 101–9. A motion early the next session, supported by Pitt, to revive the enquiry, was easily defeated: *Commons Journal* 24, p. 38.

45. Cf. Owen, *The Rise of the Pelhams*, pp. 121–5, esp. Hervey's comments quoted on p. 125.

46. Ibid., pp. 132–3; Robert Harris, *A Patriot Press. National Politics and the London Press in the 1740s* (Oxford, 1993), p. 110.

47. Harris, *A Patriot Press*, pp. 119–20.

48. Ibid., p. 120.

49. Richard to George Grenville, 22 Nov. 1742, in William James Smith (ed.), *The Grenville Papers* 4 vols (1852–3), I, p. 19.

50. *Parl. Hist.*, XII, cols 1033–6 (10 Dec. 1742); Henry Fox to Lord Ilchester, 18 Nov. 1742, in Earl of Ilchester (ed.), *Letters to Henry Fox, Lord Holland* (1915), p. 93.

51. Edward to Elizabeth Montagu, 21 Dec. 1742, HL, Montagu Papers, MO1717; James Oswald, quoted in Williams, *The Life of William Pitt*, I, pp. 104–5; John Campbell, quoted in Black, *Pitt the Elder*, p. 47.

52. William Coxe, *Memoirs of the Administration of the Right Honourable Henry Pelham* 2 vols (1829), I, p. 93.

53. Harris, *A Patriot Press*, pp. 40–4, ch. 5, which explains (esp. pp. 147–9) why the subordination to Hanover argument was so potent; Sedgwick, *The House of Commons*, I, p. 53; [Richard Glover], *Memoirs by a Celebrated Literary and Political Character* new edn (1814), p. 9 (quotation).

54. Chesterfield to Gower, 2 Oct. 1743, Granville Papers, PRO 30/29/1/11, f. 286.
55. *Parl. Hist.*, XIII, col. 136n., cf. 152–70 (1 Dec. 1743). The term 'sole' (or 'prime') minister suggests unconstitutional aggregation of power.
56. *Parl. Hist.*, XIII, cols 141–3nn. (6 Dec. 1743), cf. Mure's notes, 7 Jan. [1744], in W. Mure (ed.), *Selections From The Family Papers Preserved At Caldwell* 2 parts (3 vols) (Glasgow, 1854), part 2, I, pp. 57–8; Black, *Pitt the Elder*, pp. 51–2.
57. *Parl. Hist.*, XIII, cols 465, 471nn. (18–19 Jan.), 678n. (19 March 1744), cf. 470n., 473n., 692–3nn., 700n.
58. Esp. in Jan. 1744; Owen, *The Rise of the Pelhams*, pp. 207–11.
59. *Parl. Hist.*, XIII, cols 152–70 (1 Dec 1743), 385–6n. (15 Dec. 1743); cf. Harris, *A Patriot Press*, esp. pp. 141–4.
60. The arguments resembled those of 1741–42, over the degree of support to be given to Maria Theresa; Harris, *A Patriot Press*, pp. 110–12.
61. Williams, *The Life of William Pitt*, I, p. 104; Walpole to Mann, 9 Dec. 1742, *Correspondence*, XVIII, p. 123.
62. Glover, *Memoirs*, pp. 28–30; *Parl. Hist.*, XIII, col. 469n.; cf. Black, *Pitt the Elder*, pp. 54–5 (John Tucker's account), 56.
63. Glover, *Memoirs*, pp. 18–30.
64. Ibid., p. 29; Newdigate notes, quoted in Black, *Pitt the Elder*, p. 56; *Parl. Hist.*, XIII, col. 469n.
65. *Parl. Hist.*, XIII, cols 647–8, 666–7, 670nn.
66. Ibid., cols 678, 700nn.; Lawson, *George Grenville*, pp. 23–5.
67. Walpole to Mann, 16 Feb. 1744, *Correspondence*, XVIII, p. 399; Black, *Pitt the Elder*, p. 57.
68. They included some trade measures: *Parl. Hist.*, XIII, cols 898, 654nn.
69. See above, p. 10.
70. Owen, *The Rise of the Pelhams*, pp. 193–6; Chesterfield to Gower, 2 Oct. 1743, PRO 30/29/1/11, ff. 285–6, gives some hint of Pitt's role, and cf. Owen, *The Rise of the Pelhams*, p. 196.
71. Owen, *The Rise of the Pelhams*, pp. 223–50.
72. Glover, *Memoirs*, pp. 30–5.
73. Owen, *The Rise of the Pelhams*, p. 248.
74. Walpole's suggestion (to Mann, 26 Nov. 1744, *Correspondence*, XVIII, pp. 551–2) that Pitt deliberately chose an office he knew the king would refuse in order not to compromise his influence in the Commons is belied by Pitt's earlier and later behaviour.
75. *Parl. Hist.*, XIII, col. 1054n.
76. Ibid., cols 1054–6nn.; Walpole to Mann, 1 Feb. 1745, *Correspondence*, XIX, pp. 4–5; cf. Black, *Pitt the Elder*, p. 59.

77. *Parl. Hist.*, XIII, cols 1176–8nn.
78. Ibid., col. 1056n. (quotation); Newcastle to Chesterfield, 8 Feb., 26 March 1745, in Richard Lodge (ed.), *The Private Correspondence of Chesterfield and Newcastle, 1744–46* (1930), pp. 9, 41.
79. Owen, *The Rise of the Pelhams*, pp. 267–83.
80. Ibid., pp. 283–97, covers the session.
81. Cf. Chesterfield to Gower, 11 Nov. 1745, PRO 30/29/1/11, ff. 294–5.
82. Shaftesbury to James Harris, 24 Oct. 1745, in Earl of Malmesbury (ed.), *A Series of Letters from the First Earl of Malmesbury* 2 vols (1870), I, p. 7.
83. Owen, *The Rise of the Pelhams*, p. 286; Black, *Pitt the Elder*, pp. 63–4.
84. Newcastle to Chesterfield, 20 Nov. 1745, in Lodge (ed.), *Private Correspondence*, pp. 78–86.
85. Newcastle to Devonshire, 21 Nov. 1745, quoted in Black, *Pitt the Elder*, p. 65.
86. British Library, Stowe MSS, 354, ff. 248–9.
87. Walpole to Mann, 22 Nov. 1745, *Correspondence*, XIX, p. 168. Horace, the third son of Sir Robert, was a connoisseur of the arts and letters, whose extensive correspondence and sometimes acerbic memoirs are invaluable, if hardly dispassionate sources of informed observation. Their reliability is assessed by Sir Lewis Namier and John Brooke, *The House of Commons 1754–1790* 3 vols (1964), III, pp. 596–7.
88. *Correspondence*, XIX, pp. 168–9; Fox to Hartington, 28 Nov. 1745, quoted in Owen, *The Rise of the Pelhams*, p. 290, cf. Fox to Ilchester, 21 Dec., in Earl of Ilchester, *Henry Fox, First Lord Holland, His Family and Relations* 2 vols (1920), I, pp. 121–2; Chesterfield to Gower, 30 Dec. 1745, PRO 30/29/1/11, ff. 297–8, cf. 11 Nov., ff. 294–5.
89. Owen, *The Rise of the Pelhams*, p. 286.
90. Newcastle to Chesterfield, 18 Feb. 1746, in Lodge (ed.), *Private Correspondence*, p. 108; Owen, *The Rise of the Pelhams*, pp. 292–4; Black, *Pitt the Elder*, pp. 67–8.
91. Newcastle to Chesterfield, 18 Feb. 1746, in Lodge (ed.), *Private Correspondence*, p. 108; Owen, *The Rise of the Pelhams*, pp. 293–301 (quotations p. 299).
92. Quoted in John B. Owen, *The Eighteenth Century 1714–1815* (1974), p. 54.
93. Pelham to Lord Ilchester, 1 May 1746, in Ilchester, *Letters to Henry Fox*, p. 12; cf. Legge to Bedford, 3 May 1746, in Lord John Russell (ed.), *Correspondence of John, fourth Duke of Bedford* 3 vols (1842–6), I, p. 89.
94. Wiggin, *The Faction of Cousins*, pp. 113–14; *Correspondence*, XVIII, p. 551n. (Dec 1744); *Parl. Hist.*, XIII, col. 393n.;

Newcastle to Chesterfield, 5 March 1746, in Lodge (ed.), *Private Correspondence*, p. 119; Robert J. Phillimore (ed.), *Memoirs and Correspondence of George, Lord Lyttelton, from 1734 to 1773* 2 vols (1845), I, p. 251, citing Marchmont, 11 Feb. 1746; Alexander Hume Campbell to Marchmont, 6 Jan. 1747, HMC, *Polwarth*, V, p. 192.

95. Cf. Owen, *Rise of the Pelhams*, pp. 200–1, 205, 212, 213; Lawson, *George Grenville*, pp. 17–18.

96. [G.H. Rose (ed.)], *A Selection from the Papers of the Earls of Marchmont* 3 vols (1831), I, pp. 74, 80; Chesterfield to Newcastle, 11 Jan. 174[6], in Lodge (ed.), *Private Correspondence*, p. 100.

97. Williams, *The Life of William Pitt*, I, p. 125.

Chapter 2

DORMANT VOLCANO? PITT AND THE PELHAMS, 1746–57

. . .

PELHAMITE POLITICS

The securing of the Pelham administration in February 1746 brought with it a period of unusual ministerial and parliamentary stability. With the essential, albeit initially reluctant, support of the king assured, Henry Pelham had at last effectively reconstructed the bases of power which Walpole had enjoyed, while reuniting with the Old Corps most of the dissident Whigs. But the seeming calm was all too brief, lasting only until Pelham's premature death in March 1754.

Pitt's career, too, entered a more settled phase. He was now more firmly committed than ever to the Pelhams. The cost – further muting of the patriot stances which had so potently tapped public disillusionment with post-Walpolean politics – was soon dramatically demonstrated. In mid-April, to Newcastle's ecstatic delight,[1] Pitt defended the year's vote to employ Hanoverian troops as warmly as he had previously attacked them – and endured some not very damaging public obloquy, with pointed barbs from some hostile observers.[2] Yet Pitt and the other Cubs seemed more than content. Chesterfield might predict further difficulties from them but early in March Henry Fox reported a very amicable 'coalition dinner at Pelhams'.[3] Indeed, once Pitt became Paymaster General in May, he had all that he could reasonably expect as a first step. By then, the main lines of his role for the next eight years were established. In office of second rank – and sometimes now seriously handicapped by his apparently chronic ill health – he was to be at times a significant parliamentary spokesman for government foreign policy, often at the expense of his earlier stands. Complaisance, however, brought no further advance.

Henry Pelham was a worthy successor to Sir Robert Walpole, his gifts complementing those of his mentor. With Walpole's precedent of the management of power under the Hanoverians behind him, he could afford to give full rein to his instinct for conciliation. Even Granville came back into office in 1751 to the non-executive position of Lord President. With Pelham's equable temperament went considerable skills which ensured some constructive achievements, notably in financial management and reduction of the burden of debt. These won wide acknowledgement among MPs and, combined with a command of extensive patronage, melded the Old Corps into cohesive support for the now established Whig ideal of service to the Crown. Given the longevity of his brother, Newcastle, Pelham might well have gone further in recognition and control of new forces and issues in politics, both foreign and domestic, managing more smoothly than turned out to be the case the transition from the reign of George II to the era of George III and North.[4]

Opposition was greatly muted. In face of the hostility of the Old Corps and the king to the Tories – and despite the great upsurge of loyalty during the Forty-Five[5] which might have prompted some reconciliation – the broad-bottom experiment was not persisted with. So the Tories remained in opposition. Their numbers in parliament were further reduced in the 1747 election and they lacked consistent leadership. Attempts at alliance with them by the Prince of Wales from 1747 gave opposition greater purchase, especially as the king was in his late sixties. But the prince was politically inept and was caught by surprise by the early election of 1747, while Pelham's careful control of potentially divisive issues further weakened the opposition, even before the prince's sudden death in March 1751 robbed it of its figurehead. After 1751, Horace Walpole could justly remark that in 'the memory of England there never was so inanimate an age: it is more fashionable to go to church than to either House of Parliament'.[6]

Thus most political tensions in the Pelham years arose from personal strains within the administration, often over the still crucial issues of foreign policy – issues which Pitt's parliamentary activity had already identified as his major interest. Newcastle, with more than two decades of experience in the office behind him, was now the dominant Secretary of State. His fussy anxieties, timorous, almost pathological insecurity and constant need for reassurance – notorious to contemporaries and, through his voluminous papers, to generations of historians – disguised solid competence, conscientious hard work, good nature and skill in management of men. His personality compounded differences with his brother over policy by inventing a host of imagined slights. Pelham, too, was sensitive to the constant complaints. However, fraternal affection and the soothing skills of Lord Chancellor Hardwicke kept the tensions from coming to an open breach. Hardwicke was the third major figure in the administration, an able, eloquent lawyer of considerable reputation whose cool, sensible political judgement, while not profound, made him an essential ally of Newcastle throughout their long political dominance. Newcastle's quarrels with fellow Secretaries he found insufficiently submissive created further tensions. Chesterfield, the first to be eased out of office, in 1748, might disavow further politicking, but his successor, the much younger Duke of Bedford, a leading Whig peer, went into open opposition with his ally, the Earl of Sandwich, when forced out in 1751.

More serious frictions were created by the rising influence of the king's able younger son, the Duke of Cumberland, made Captain-General of the army by his father while still in his twenties and thus given an inevitable voice in foreign policy even if he could win victories nowhere else than at Culloden. This voice was generally not sympathetic to Newcastle, while both Pelham and Newcastle were uneasy about Cumberland's possibly exorbitant ambition. The king did more to exacerbate than to settle these tensions. Bedford was drawn into Cumberland's circle as his differences with Newcastle grew, while in Henry Fox, after his reluctant acceptance of the post of Secretary at War in 1746, Cumberland had an increasingly loyal and effective political lieutenant. Fox, an ex-Tory of already dubious personal reputation for his sexual and gaming exploits, had entered parliament at the same time as Pitt but, choosing to support the administration, had become one of 'Walpole's whelps', a minor officeholder from 1737 and a firm and valued Pelhamite from 1742.[7] The counterpoint of his career with that of Pitt was soon to become increasingly obvious as both sought to fish in the administration's sometimes troubled waters.

The reinforced administration had to cope first with a war situation which was increasingly gloomy, particularly in the Netherlands, so vital to British interests, where French success continued unabated. Peace negotiations, begun in August 1746, were prolonged in hope of better things, but by 1748 the fall of the United Provinces to the French seemed likely. Naval victories for Britain off the Spanish and French coasts in May and October 1747 pre-empted another invasion threat and gave Britain control of the Atlantic and the Channel – but too late to allow the highly popular capture of Louisburg to be capitalized on by the Canada expedition projected in 1746. So, in October 1748 the Peace of Aix-la-Chapelle was at last concluded largely on the basis of a return to the *status quo ante bellum.* Louisburg was exchanged, in part for Madras, which had fallen to the French East India Company in 1746, but even more for the French evacuation of the Netherlands – but Pelham's adroit early general election helped to defuse dissatisfaction. Not until 1750, in the Treaty of Madrid, were the Anglo-Spanish commercial disputes out of which war had begun in 1739 settled.

France's challenge to the post-Utrecht balance of power had been checked, but no fundamental issues had been resolved. In Europe, the Peace recognized the acquisition of Silesia by France's ally, Prussia, and gains by Bourbon Spain in Italy. Frictions in Franco-Spanish relations were small compensation for the manifest weakness of Britain's 'old system' of alliance with Austria and the Dutch. Beyond Europe, Anglo-Spanish disputes slipped into the background, but unresolved conflicts with France were intensifying all round the world. The clash of Companies in India, where French successes reached their height in 1750, might not yet excite much interest from government or public. Disputes over 'neutral' West Indian islands and border conflicts in North America were a different matter. The capture of Louisburg, particularly, had heightened awareness of the importance of the rapidly growing North American colonies to Atlantic trade, the most dynamic sector of British commerce. Yet, unchecked by either the government-sponsored military settlement at Halifax in Nova Scotia in 1749 or the negotiations of impotent commissioners appointed according to the peace terms, the French advanced their scheme to link the Great Lakes and Louisiana by a series of forts along the waterways, beginning on the Ohio and threatening to hem in the thirteen British colonies.

While Henry Pelham responded to the Peace with perhaps unwisely drastic financial retrenchment to reduce the burden of debt, foreign policy was effectively if not entirely in the hands of Newcastle, who in 1751 at last found a sufficiently pliable fellow Secretary in the Earl of Holderness. Newcastle recognized the significance of the conflicts beyond Europe;[8] but he also recognized that they could not be tackled unless France's power to threaten British interests in Europe was controlled, and he was naturally influenced by the king's continuing concern for Hanover and sufficiently a continentalist to become preoccupied with settling the French threat there.[9] Seeking to revivify the 'old system', he was drawn increasingly into a grandiose scheme to secure the election of Maria Theresa's son, Joseph, as King of the Romans and thus virtually guaranteed successor to his father, elected Emperor in 1745. While soundly conceived as an effort to bring peace to a crucial area, the scheme proved immensely complicated in execution and eventually ended in failure, even to the extent of alienating Austria and leaving Hanover open to Prussian attack.[10] Meanwhile, Pelham (with others) became alarmed at the considerable costs and the suspicions of subordination to Hanoverian interests which the scheme aroused.

. . .

PITT: PAYMASTER AND PARLIAMENTARIAN, 1746–54

Office as Paymaster gave Pitt some insight into eighteenth-century administration. His duties involved issuing the sums voted to pay regimental soldiers, the Chelsea military pensioners and army contractors, and remitting to their London agents the subsidies voted to foreign rulers. Pitt might well have left these duties largely to his deputy, as did some of his predecessors. Instead, he gave them energetic if hardly innovative attention – though whether more so than one of the calibre of Henry Pelham, Paymaster from 1730 to 1743, it is impossible to say.[11] In the longer run, Pitt showed some concern for the proper use of public money – and some humanity – by his successful bill of 1754, providing for payments in advance rather than arrears to the Chelsea pensioners which relieved them from the grip of money-lenders.[12] In the shorter term, he refused to accept the customary perquisites of office: the investment for personal benefit of the huge balances paid over by the Treasury well before they had to be expended, and the one-quarter per cent of foreign subsidies which usually went to the Paymaster. Pelham, too, had refused these perquisites. But others, notably Henry Fox, deliberately sought the office for the personal fortune that could be made from it. From Pitt's correspondence with deputies abroad, especially with Thomas Orby Hunter in 1747, he was kept informed about the military situation. He seems quickly to have won the respect of his subordinates and with one, Peregrine Furze, established a relationship of some warmth, even to the extent of Furze's reporting on the welfare of Pitt's wife, 'Lady Esther', in 1755.[13]

Pitt had been given office not for administrative ability but for his far more publicly visible parliamentary skills. Yet the administration had no lack of capable parliament-men. Pelham himself was a weighty and incisive debater and, among members of Pitt's generation, Henry Fox was a serious rival if only William Murray, the Solicitor-General, could match Pitt in compelling oratory while outweighing him in argument[14] – and Murray, like Fox, had been in office much longer. Moreover, the Pelhamite quietude made parliamentary sessions much less threatening, especially after the gadflies of the prince's opposition were silenced in 1751. These circumstances suggest that perhaps Pitt's silence was more important to the administration than any political speeches. Certainly, relatively few such speeches are recorded. Furthermore, Pitt's impetuosity could be a liability to government as well as to himself. This impetuosity was still very evident on a number of election petitions in 1747–8, when, in the case of his own constituency of Seaford, he earned a well-deserved public rebuke for treating a petition 'with great contempt' and turning it into 'a mere jest'.[15]

However, Pitt's ostensible wish, somewhat later, to be released from the 'oar of parliamentary drudgery',[16] together with hints of regular attendance, confirm the supposition that he contributed more to routine parliamentary business than the sparse records of political occasions allow. Moreover, he could also justly claim to have given his 'most zealous endeavours in parliament, on the points that laboured the most', questions of military discipline and foreign affairs.[17] He took an immediate part against the new opposition and particularly helped to counter attacks on the annual mutiny bills which became a feature of the Earl of Egmont's leadership of the Prince of Wales's party.[18] As a second-rank office-holder Pitt was not of the inner circle of policy makers, but, on his major interest, foreign affairs, he signalled his acquiescence in the administration's policies by both speeches and silence, despite their variance from his earlier views. On occasion, most notably in the only session in which he was particularly active, that of 1751, 'Pitt the Thunderer'[19] could be so useful as to rank as a major government speaker.

Pitt's deviations from his earlier views in service to the administration were immediately evident, of course, in his support for Hanoverian troops in April 1746. This he defended on political grounds: he 'was now with a set of men with whom he should ever think it an honour to act, and that he should not act with them falsely, hollowly, or coldly', he declared; at the same time he was contemptuous of the opposition, 'putting them on the foot of children and idiots'.[20] But in February 1750, when taxed with his formerly more aggressive attitude after he had defended the Peace as a remarkable achievement 'when our condition and the situation of our allies was so bad', he frankly admitted his changed views. He acknowledged 'that upon some former occasions I have been hurried by the heat of youth, and the warmth of debate, into expressions which, upon cool reflection, I have deeply regretted'.[21]

Pitt adopted a similar justification the next year, when he took the lead in successfully defending the Treaty of Madrid with Spain against vigorous attack in the address-in-reply debate. In face of the treaty's abandonment of virtually all that the opposition to Walpole had demanded of war with Spain, Pitt 'frankly acknowledged' the 'errors' of his earlier opinions. 'I was then very young and sanguine', he said. 'I am now ten years older, and have had time to consider things more coolly.' He added some substantial if specious argument that 'by the conditions of the treaty, British commerce had acquired greater advantages than had been enjoyed for many years'. The address was approved by 203 votes to 74.[22]

The most fully attested and striking aspect of Pitt's views on foreign policy in the Pelham years, however, is his whole-hearted support for Newcastle's European negotiations. In a lengthy correspondence over the summer of 1750, Pitt complimented Newcastle on having 'advanced the great work of the election of a King of the Romans far beyond my most sanguine expectations', although expressing 'the highest satisfaction' that 'new subsidiary engagements' were confined to Bavaria only.[23] More to the point for the administration, in debates in the House in January and February 1751, Pitt publicly 'made a great panegyric on the Duke of Newcastle's German negotiations', giving them substantial and cogent justification. He

> applauded the care of his Majesty for the preservation of tranquillity; expatiated on the danger, which must arise from a new vacancy in the imperial throne; and argued that the Bavarian treaty was justifiable, on every principle of sound policy, as a proceeding subservient to that end, and to the important purpose of detaching Bavaria from the French interest.

Intervention in European affairs by subsidy arrangements, even in peacetime, was justifiable, he argued, on grounds of preservation of the balance of power against France's attempts at subversion, and the importance of uniting in the preservation of peace with 'our most proper, our most natural allies', 'the Dutch, and the empire of Germany'.[24] By the next year, 1752, the complex electoral negotiations were running into difficulties. When a further subsidy treaty with Saxony came before the House in January, Pitt was privately more cautious about 'foreign expenses, and . . . entanglements abroad'. But by then he was ill and reservations were expressed publicly only by Richard Grenville, now Lord Cobham, seen by hostile observers as his 'absolute creature'.[25] Friendly exchanges with Newcastle over European policy still went on for some time, and in September 1753 Pitt was happy enough with a projected subsidy treaty with Russia if savings could be made elsewhere.[26]

Moreover, Pitt did not continue the emphasis on maritime and colonial war he had adopted in late 1745. When in April 1746 he 'pressed the case for a strong navy', he was simply supporting the promise in the King's Speech of particular attention to naval war.[27] There is no evidence that he played any part in the plan to follow up the capture of Louisburg by an expedition into French Canada or that he supported its retention in the peace negotiations. Newcastle, rather than Pitt, supported the Canada expedition as one way to strengthen Britain's position while maintaining public support for the war.[28] Newcastle, too, was firm on North American questions through the negotiations of 1746–48. Pitt showed no interest in continuing public discussion of these issues, and it was left to Dr George Lee, for the opposition, to claim in the debate on the address in November 1748 that by proper use of British sea power all the French colonies in America and the West Indies could have been conquered.[29] Pitt seems to have been consistently on the side of those who saw an early peace rather than attempts to strengthen Britain's position as the only way out of the gloomy foreign situation.[30] And, although in 1751 he was to praise Pelham's financial reforms as grounds for hope 'that England would make as great a figure, in a few years, as it had done in any age',[31] there is nothing to suggest that he saw any more need than did others in the administration to do more than hold the peace.

Nor was Pitt particularly assertive over the situation in North America in the early 1750s. In correspondence with Newcastle in the summer of 1750, he demanded firm protests over an incident there in which French officials stirred up French settlers in British Nova Scotia. But, when Newcastle's replies showed that he had 'not neglected the immediate interests of Great Britain' in this case, Pitt was apparently placated, and did not take up Egmont's comments on French encroachments in North America at the beginning of the next session of parliament.[32] Nor did he soon return to the escalating North America issues. Rather, in August 1753, he was concerned about 'clouds' over 'the calm of Europe', and in September he indicated '*Dunkirk* and the *West Indies*' as 'our points with France' to be adhered to.[33]

Nor was there much consistency in Pitt's attitudes to Prussia, still France's ally. By this time, he was arguing the need for the support of a Russian army to help restrain Prussia. Earlier, in the last stages of the war and peace negotiations, he, like others in the ministry, had been strongly in favour of agreement with Prussia in order, as Pitt put it in December 1747, 'to see Europe pacified, and France contained within some bounds'. But neither when Henry Legge was sent to Berlin in 1748 nor later did Pitt continue to press this possible but by no means obviously easy alternative to the 'old system'.[34]

There were powerful political considerations behind Pitt's warm support for Newcastle's foreign policy. From the 1747 election, he was indebted to Newcastle for his seat in parliament for Seaford – Thomas Pitt, electoral agent of the Prince of Wales, had other uses for Old Sarum – and the relationship was warm enough by 1750 for Newcastle to invite Pitt to open a private correspondence with him when he went to Hanover with the king and to give Pitt 'full power' to act for him in his increasingly difficult relations with Pelham. This invitation led to an extensive correspondence over the next few months.[35] Pitt naturally hoped to exploit this opportunity both to improve his relations with the king and to raise his profile in the administration.[36]

However, Pitt also readily granted that experience had changed his mind over major issues, pointing out that others, too, had changed theirs.[37] He developed substantial arguments to support his new views, which make it difficult to dismiss them as pure sycophancy. The conclusion seems clear: Pitt's continuing education in and increasing grasp of the complexities of foreign policy had made him something of a continentalist by conviction. He had, of course, never been as committed as Cobham or other Cobhamites to disengagement from Europe, and it is significant that by 1750 he had broken his reportedly close relations with Bedford, just at the time when Bedford was moving to oppose the granting of subsidies in peacetime.[38] Certainly, a thread of concern about expense runs through Pitt's correspondence with Newcastle; he was perhaps developing some scepticism about grand schemes, and he kept his conviction that British interests should be paramount. But, equally certainly, he also argued that involvement in the affairs of the 'empire of Germany' could serve Britain well.

. . .

STALLED AMBITION, 1751–55

Even before the sterling parliamentary service of 'Pitt the Thunderer' on foreign policy in 1751, Pelham had recognized him as 'the most able and useful man we have amongst us; truly honourable and strictly honest. He is as firm a friend to us, as we can wish for, and a more useful one there does not exist.'[39] However, recognition of service did not bring Pitt the advancement he might reasonably have expected. In 1748, it was too early to hope to replace Chesterfield as Secretary of State,[40] but by 1750–51 Pitt's obvious ambition to take Bedford's place was more reasonable.[41] Instead, Pelham, in the same breath as acknowledging Pitt's usefulness, objected again to a Secretary of State in the Commons as he had in 1748,[42] and, when Bedford finally went in June, Pitt was again passed over for the much younger Holderness. Holderness, like Bedford – also younger than Pitt but the holder already of two first-rank offices – had the advantage of being a peer.

By 1750–51 Pitt was renewing contacts with the Prince of Wales – until they were cut short by the prince's death on 20 March. Just what lay behind these negotiations, which Pitt conducted together with the other 'Cobhamites' and probably in collusion with Newcastle, who was also courting the prince,[43] is far from clear. It was wise to be in touch with the heir to the throne. Horace Walpole, linking these negotiations with Pitt's unexpected opposition to the decreased number of seamen, suggested that Pitt intended to go further, to the extent of breach with the Pelhams, and take advantage of the gathering momentum of the prince's opposition to push once again for advancement 'by storm' in the Commons.[44] This seems unlikely. Pitt had recently urged Newcastle to 'cordial intercourse' with his brother, in order to preserve 'that union which alone can inform and maintain a solid system for carrying on our business'.[45] At this very time, he was zealously defending the administration's foreign policy and he was soon carefully mending his bridges with Pelham. For their part, Newcastle sought to soothe the ruffled feelings of the Old Corps over Pitt's behaviour, while the next year Pelham proposed an increase to 10,000 seamen, reportedly so that 'the Pitts and the Lytteltons' would be 'cajoled'.[46]

More probably, Pitt was driven both to Leicester House and to much greater parliamentary activity during this session by widely shared concern over the growing power of the Duke of Cumberland and his influence with the king[47] – which gave Pitt good reason to stay with the Pelhams. Certainly, 'the long-smothered rivalship'[48] between Pitt and Cumberland's lieutenant, Fox, now became obvious, not only over the seamen, but also over an unsuccessful bill to facilitate the naturalization of foreign Protestants, which Pitt supported and Fox initially opposed, and most remarkably over moves to call the MP and former Governor of Minorca, General Anstruther, to account by parliamentary enquiry for allegedly vindictive harshness in the conduct of courts martial. There was some force in Pitt's argument for improvements in courts martial, and he was often to assert in diverse circumstances the right of parliamentary enquiry (in this case saying to Pelham after the debate that 'he would never consent to lop the bough on which he stood'). However, he pushed his argument with grave indiscretion, not only in heated exchanges with Fox, but also against Pelham's wishes and, most importantly, with great offence to the king, who regarded army affairs as matters of prerogative.[49] This offence was grossly compounded in debates on the Regency Act, made necessary with a minor, Frederick's son, George, now heir to the throne. Pitt, again in competition with Fox, not only extravagantly bewailed 'the loss of the most *patriot* prince that ever lived', he also played offensively on growing prejudice against Cumberland by referring to 'dangers' from 'the great person who might have become sole regent' and gibing at 'any ambitious person' who might, in the future, 'think less of protecting the Crown, than of wearing it!' Well might Fox exclaim on one occasion, 'He is a better speaker than I am, but thank God! I have more judgment'.[50]

In this session, Pitt was undoubtedly flexing his muscles, perhaps against Pelham, certainly against Fox and Cumberland. However, over the next three years and more, Pitt's political activity was seriously constrained by his first prolonged bout of illness.[51] He remained close, even more obsequious, to Newcastle, it seems, although their correspondence was reduced to a trickle.[52] When he returned briefly to parliament in November 1753, he supported Pelham's decision to repeal the Act to facilitate Jewish naturalization, passed in May, over which an indignant popular outcry had been fanned by the Bedford group – the one issue that broke the quiet of these three years.[53] Pitt, like Pelham, supported the repeal on pragmatic grounds. Yet, as on the 1751 bill on the naturalization of foreign Protestants, he revealed his tolerant Whig religious principles by defending the Act for modifying 'our persecuting unChristian laws relating to religion' and regretting that the 'old High Church persecuting spirit' had taken hold of the people.[54]

Virtual silence in the House over these three obscure years had diminished Pitt's chief political strength, his now mature oratory. Although praised less for substance than for 'ornamental eloquence', '[b]itter satire' and 'ridicule', by 1751 he was widely recognized as 'beyond comparison' (except with the Solicitor-General, William Murray) the best speaker in the Commons, enjoying an easy supremacy over all who might challenge him.[55] But oratory alone had not helped Pitt overcome his greatest political handicap, the hostility of the king, which Newcastle and Pelham had manifestly failed to ameliorate. Rather, the king gloated over Pitt's 'indiscretions'.

Moreover, Pitt continued to provoke the resentment of the Old Corps.[56] He might have cast his lot with them, but he was never seen to belong wholeheartedly with them. To the generally reliable support from the Grenville–Lyttelton 'faction of cousins' Pitt had added a valuable new ally, Thomas Potter, the able, lively, but dissolute son of the last Archbishop of Canterbury, a very good speaker. Pitt had also developed some contacts with another younger politician, well experienced in office and entrenched in the Old Corps, Henry Bilson Legge.[57] But such a tiny connection, even when coupled with oratory and sterling parliamentary service, scarcely offset Pitt's handicaps, especially when matched against the legal and parliamentary service of William Murray and the experience, debating weight and princely and aristocratic connections of Fox.

And matched they were very soon to be. On 6 March 1754, the political world was thrown into turmoil by the quite unexpected death of Henry Pelham. In fact, once Newcastle decided to take the Treasury, an administration satisfactory to the king was easily reconstructed. Sir Thomas Robinson, a holder of household office with diplomatic experience, joined Holderness as Secretary of State, and Legge took Pelham's other office of Chancellor of the Exchequer. The administration, to which Newcastle brought long experience, conscientiousness and some judgement, the firm loyalty of the Old Corps and good relations with the king, promised competence – especially when soon strengthened by a decisive general election victory, in which Pitt was once again beholden to Newcastle's patronage, this time in Aldborough. Whether the ministerial stability Walpole and Pelham had constructed could be maintained or not would depend on the containment of divisive issues and on Newcastle's ability to manage a House of Commons which had grown used, over more than 30 years, to the presence in it of the leading minister. Newcastle's pathological lack of self-confidence was likely to inhibit a working relationship with the able spokesman he needed in the Commons; even Pelham, after all, had been wary of a Secretary of State in the Commons as a possible rival. And indeed, so limited was the initial offer Newcastle made to the most obvious candidate, Fox, that it was refused, and the 'lead' fell instead to Robinson, a parliamentary lightweight.

Pitt still found advancement elusive.[58] Like Fox, he was of a similar age to Walpole when he seized the great opening of his career; unlike Fox, Pitt's fitness for office was thrown in doubt by his seemingly chronic ill health.[59] He was entirely passed over in the initial reconstruction, though George Grenville and George Lyttelton got some crumbs of advancement.

Now, however, Pitt was newly determined to press his case.[60] Serving under someone of Pelham's stature was one thing – and Pitt was genuinely upset at Pelham's death and concerned about its public consequences.[61] Being passed over for Fox and Robinson was quite another. Pitt began with uncharacteristic caution, born perhaps of awareness of his weakness. He sought to exploit Newcastle's 'own fears and resentments' against Cumberland and Fox by negotiation within the administration. However, despite hints of retirement, his expectations were clear. He wanted 'marks of Royal favour, one of the connection' – more specifically, himself either as Chancellor of the Exchequer or Secretary of State – 'put into the Cabinet, and called to a real participation of councils and business'.[62] No longer would he defend policies he had no share in making. And, in his seemingly respectful letters to Newcastle and Hardwicke, there was a growing resentment at the humiliation of the king's 'negative personal to me' while others were promoted, and an unwillingness to wait any longer in the 'general hope' that it might eventually be removed.[63] Well aware of his group's parliamentary service to the administration, he ominously reminded Newcastle that 'the inside of the House must be considered in other respects besides merely numbers, or the reins of government will soon slip or be wrested out of any minister's hands'. And there were half-formed hints of alternative strategies for his own advancement – remarks that, if 'royal favour' did not give it, 'consideration' in the House could also come from 'weight in the country, sometimes arising from opposition to public measures' and reiterated professions of 'attachment' not only to the '*King's* government' but also to 'the future plan *under the Princess*' (mother of the Prince of Wales).[64]

The test of Newcastle's arrangements came when the new parliament assembled in November 1754. Soon Pitt was showing his old brilliant form. In uneasy partnership with Fox born of shared dissatisfaction,[65] he took advantage of debates on election petitions and the army vote to show up Robinson's inadequacies, embarrass Murray over his Jacobite past, and (forgetting his own levity of 1747–48) to thunder rebukes to the House for levity on 'the topics of bribery and corruption'. He even gibed at Newcastle (his own electoral patron) for seeking to reduce the House merely to registering '*the arbitrary edicts of one too powerful a subject*'.[66] Newcastle had recently told the Sardinian envoy in London that only Pitt could manage the government's affairs. Yet Fox rather than Pitt was bought off in December with the offer of a cabinet place, while Pitt was threatened with dismissal.[67] Pitt went on alone to incipient 'patriot' stands later in the session, with 'spirited declamations for liberty' which attracted some attention but were no real embarrassment to the administration.[68]

Still preoccupied with 'his Majesty's irremovable displeasure', Pitt had intended to apply pressure, not to precipitate a breach with either Newcastle or Fox. However, by late April, Fox and his patron, Cumberland, had been appointed to the Council of Regency to preside over government while the king was in Hanover, while Pitt's 'state with the King' had not been brought 'to an explicit point' in further overtures from Newcastle. Encouraged by tentative contacts with Leicester House – where the young Prince of Wales's mother and the Scots Earl of Bute (recently returned to favour there) were alarmed at Cumberland's growing influence – Pitt was provoked to a decisive if ill-considered breach with Fox. By now his impatience with Newcastle was also reaching breaking point.[69]

. . .

MARRIAGE, 1754

At this crucial point in his career – at the beginning of perhaps the most important three years of his life – Pitt's confidence had been reinforced by a dramatic change in his personal life. In September 1754, while on his usual summer sojourns with his friends, he had fallen in love with Lady Hester, the young sister of the Grenvilles, whom he had known since girlhood; in October, they were engaged; the wedding took place on 16 November, 'the day on which I shall date all the real honour and happiness of poor life'.[70] It was an unusual match, he at 46 twelve years her senior, both of them old by the standards of any time. However, their correspondence over many years amply testifies to their intense mutual devotion and delight in the happy family life brought by the five children born over the next six years. Pitt had good reason to be grateful to Hester for joining 'part of her best days to a very shattered part of mine'.[71] The marriage, greeted ecstatically by all the brothers, initially strengthened his ties with them, bringing generous financial support from Richard, now Earl Temple, when Pitt lost office a year later.[72] It must also have contributed to the surge of energy that was to drive Pitt over the next seven years of high achievement. And indeed, without Hester's unstinting devotion and skills of family management, Pitt's chronic ill health, financial irresponsibility and personal arrogance might well have wrecked, rather than merely hampered, his later career. However, whether that career was in fact enhanced by unquestioning, cosseting adulation which widened the already developing gulf between the public and the private man is another question.[73]

. . .

THE CHANCES OF WAR, 1755–56

As yet, Pitt had not sought to embarrass Newcastle over any major issue of policy. However, the situation abroad was deteriorating in ways which provided potentially divisive issues. In America, disputes with France were coming to a crisis. In 1754, the defeat of a Virginian force sent to check the French on the Ohio led to the dispatch of British troops under General Braddock in December. It was this need for military measures that brought Cumberland into the cabinet, and eventually the regency, which in May 1755 took a further step towards war when it dispatched a squadron under Admiral Boscawen to intercept French reinforcements for America. With Austria and the Dutch less reliable than ever as allies, over the summer new subsidy treaties were negotiated with Hesse-Cassel and Russia to discourage French reprisals on Hanover or the Netherlands in the event of open war.[74]

The growing public interest in North America had already led to parliamentary debate in 1754, but neither Pitt nor Fox took up the issue. Instead, as Walpole pertinently remarked, their warm campaign diverted attention and 'quite put the Ohio upon an obsolete foot'.[75] Pitt's role in policy making remained negligible. He was consulted over the sending of troops to America only late in the deliberations of 1754 and his enthusiasm then for vigorous measures was probably shaped by his mounting distrust of Newcastle.[76] Not until the late summer of 1755 did issues of foreign policy have an impact on politics beyond the cabinet. Then, however, subsidy treaties, with their controversial implications of expensive continental involvement and subordination to Hanover, raised major concerns. And the need to defend them in parliament brought greater urgency to the question of an effective lead in the Commons.

A 'system for the House of Commons' was the issue in negotiations with Pitt between July and September 1755.[77] For the first time Pitt clearly stated his terms to Newcastle. As a condition for active assistance in getting 'the great wheels of the machine' of the House moving again, he demanded not just the call to the cabinet that the king had reluctantly agreed to, but '*an office of advice* as well as of *execution*' concerning the measures he was expected to support. Newcastle had no doubt he meant a Secretaryship.[78] About policy, in these conversations Pitt was chary about any 'general plan for the Continent' or 'subsidiary system', while concurring in 'a national war' and coming 'roundly into' the 'maritime and American war'.[79] He was cautious about further offence to the king to the extent that he promised – and generally showed – restraint on the issue of Hanover. Nevertheless, he advanced substantial grounds for opposition to subsidy treaties, fearing both that they would be inadequate to defend Hanover and that their cost would compromise the maritime and American war. He seemed prepared to accept the Hessian treaty on the grounds that it was useless anyway, but not the Russian treaty, despite his earlier support for a similar measure.[80] Yet Legge rather than Pitt had first begun to exploit the subsidies issue, and there is little doubt that Pitt could have seen both treaties as acceptable and necessary, had his political objectives been met.[81] Percipient observers recognized his tactics as chiefly intended 'colourably to raise the terms for himself'.[82] Undoubtedly he was encouraged by his now openly avowed connection with Leicester House, where the king's unwelcome proposal of a marriage for the Prince of Wales had widened the breach caused by Cumberland's advance.[83]

By late September, Newcastle – not yet 'sufficiently intimidated to make any Man a Minister who had frankly told him, he *would not be directed*'[84] – had closed with Fox rather than Pitt. Fox, it was agreed, should be leader in the House with full authority and, after he had faced the opening of parliament, also Secretary of State. Outmanouevred in ministerial negotiations, Pitt was forced to other tactics: to continue, with the help of Leicester House, to build support, even among the Tories he had excoriated less than a year before, for a parliamentary opposition and to stand forth as its leader in November.[85]

Then Pitt – 'haughty, defiant, and conscious of injury and supreme abilities' – magnificently revived on a broad scale the patriot argument on foreign policy. In the great night-long address-in-reply debate, Pitt's 'eloquence, like a torrent long obstructed, burst forth with more commanding impetu-osity'. Not only did he attack the subsidies as 'incoherent, un-British measures', likely to lead to a general war in Europe and waste away British resources; he also attacked the peace he had hitherto defended and spoke clearly for a war 'under-taken for the long injured, long neglected, long forgotten people of America', a war in British interests to be fought by 'our proper force', the navy. Unusually restrained in its references to Hanover, the speech was embroidered with the famous mocking comparison of the union of Fox and Newcastle to the confluence of the Rhone and Saône.[86] With George Grenville and Legge, Pitt reaped his reward in sum-mary dismissal from office.

Pitt's arguments, foreshadowed in the summer nego-tiations, were reiterated in later debates before and after Christmas. 'This waste on Hessians' (brought to England with Hanoverian troops to meet the threat of French invasion) 'would have conquered America', Pitt proclaimed – unconvin-cingly – early in May.[87] He also joined in pressing the admin-istration closely on the question of new taxes and deployed standard patriot arguments to support Lieutenant-Colonel George Townshend's proposal for a reformed militia, pre-senting it as an alternative to the ignominy of paying others for Britain's defence and as a support to the constitution.[88] And through the whole campaign ran an attack on a ministry 'disjointed . . . united only in corrupt and arbitrary measures', 'an unaccording assemblage of separate and distinct powers with no system . . . driving a go-cart on a precipice'.[89]

However, there was no sign yet that Pitt's attempt to re-claim the patriot ground – with all its attendant risks – could overcome the disillusionments of the 1740s. His reversion to aggressive oratory in parliament had little success. The administration was forced to allow the militia bill through the Commons, but otherwise only occasionally did the opposi-tion vote rise above 100.[90] Pitt's vehemence aroused sus-picion and his support amounted to 'little more than his own family, the Grenvilles, 2 Townshends [George and his brother Charles], and the Tories' – and the latter were as yet lukewarm and unreliable. Fox could show up the hypo-crisy of Pitt's attacks on an administration of which he had been a part and could, in the new year, credibly claim 'a complete *conquest*' over Pitt's 'violent speeches'.[91] As the situation slipped towards open war with France it was generally felt that Newcastle's policies were appropriate.

However, the misfortunes of war were on Pitt's side. On 6 May, news arrived that a French force had landed in Minorca, a highly valued British naval base in the Mediterranean. A British force, perhaps too cautiously commanded by Admiral Byng, proved unable to prevent its fall, news of which reached London on 14 July. On his return, Byng was arrested. For more than four months from June, the question of responsibility for this humiliating disaster was vigorously debated in an outburst of public indignation even more intense than the clamour over the excise or that accompanying the fall of Walpole. Fuelled by the interaction of press propaganda with formal expressions of opinion to crown and parliament, the outburst seemed indeed to have 'opened every sluice of opposition, that have been so long dammed up'.[92] In mid-October, its effects were brought to the heart of politics when fear of being left 'as the only figure of a Minister' in the Commons to 'draw all the Odium on me' helped to shape Fox's decision to resign.[93]

Suddenly, with the meeting of parliament only weeks away, the lead in the Commons became an urgent concern again. With Murray determined on the vacant position of Chief Justice which would take him to the Lords, Newcastle insisted that the king allow another approach to Pitt. However, although he was offered the Secretary's seals, Pitt's terms had hardened beyond stipulating policy. Now convinced both that Newcastle 'had so engrossed the King's confidence that he could expect no share in it' and that Newcastle was responsible for the 'mistakes' and 'ill successes' in the war that had 'incensed' the nation, he refused point blank to serve with him.[94] When Newcastle, his nerve shaken and unable to make alternative arrangements for the Commons, declared he could no longer continue, Pitt went on to refuse to serve with Fox. By mid-November, the king had been forced to agree to a ministry with the independent but inexperienced Whig peer, the Duke of Devonshire, at the Treasury, Pitt as Secretary of State and his followers in major positions.

The temerity of 'mad' Pitt's terms startled the political world.[95] Driven first by utter disillusionment with Newcastle, he was further emboldened by the support of Leicester

House – though he went into negotiations ostentatiously alone[96] – and above all by the swell of indignation over Minorca. When negotiations began, public attention had turned tentatively to him.[97] Now, unlike Pulteney, he came at last to high office apparently true to the patriot role for which he had laid the basis in the last two sessions and now clinched in his terms of negotiation – at least to the extent of demanding a militia bill and enquiries into failures abroad.[98]

. . .

HIGH OFFICE WON, LOST, SECURED, 1756–57

But would Pitt be able to ride the crest of the patriot wave? The great enthusiasm from Tories, City of London and wider opinion which greeted the new administration obviously expected far more than he had promised.[99] Yet, clearly lacking the confidence of the king, the administration could hardly be supported in parliament by Pitt's 'fifteen or sixteen' personal followers – 'one single family against the united force of the principal nobility', as one observer had it[100] – and depended on the forbearance of Fox and Newcastle, many of whose supporters remained in office. Pitt's rashness seemed merely to have produced impotence – especially when illness kept him much of the time from court, parliament and even his office.[101] It is hard to see what he hoped to gain from office in such circumstances.

Furthermore, the foreign situation was threatening on every side. In America, on top of Braddock's defeat and death and Boscawen's failure to intercept the French fleet in 1755 had come the loss in 1756 of Fort Oswego, an important trading post on Lake Ontario, while in India the East India Company had lost Calcutta to Indian forces. Much more serious, in Europe Newcastle's subsidy diplomacy in defence of Hanover had precipitated a reversal of alliances which, in immediate consequences anyway, was hardly favourable to Britain. Prussia, alarmed by the threat of Russian intrusion into Germany, at last responded to overtures from Britain from which came the Treaty of Westminster in January 1756, guaranteeing German neutrality. Prussia's desertion stung France into accepting advances from Austria in the defensive Treaty of Versailles, soon joined by Russia.

When, in September 1756, Frederick the Great of Prussia once again launched a war by rashly invading Saxony, Hanover was left exposed to the vengeance of his enemies and Britain's new ally seemed a distinct liability rather than an asset. As Pitt well knew from his previous experience, the blue-water patriot programme's stark alternatives of 'a Continent war' or 'a truly British war, by sea'[102] provided no strategy to meet this dire situation.

The foreign situation was handled with some address. When parliament opened on 2 December, the King's Speech, shaped by Pitt, promised the 'succour and preservation of America', and Pitt was soon energetically planning further ambitious reinforcements there, as well as sending a further small squadron of ships to aid the East India Company and encouraging an expedition to the West African coast. Here was fresh vigour, if not new policies. But the speech also referred to the 'new and dangerous crisis' in Germany, and Pitt's speech spoke of help to the continent when everything had been done 'for yourselves', acknowledging that 'the interests of this country were combined with those of the Powers on the continent'. Observers saw little change in policy here – and, indeed, the other Secretary, Holderness, had already assured Prussia to this effect. Others heard only a sterling call to 'strain every nerve in this important contest with France';[103] and when, more than two months later, Pitt next appeared in the Commons, he came to ask for extraordinary supplies to support an 'army of observation' of mercenary troops for the defence of Hanover, in fulfilment of obligations to Prussia.[104] Less than a year earlier (when circumstances were very different), Pitt had resoundingly declared of the Treaty of Westminster that he 'would not have signed it for the five great places of those who had signed it'; he now replied to gibes from Fox by distinguishing 'moderate sums' for 'a continent war' from squandering 'millions' – and £200,000 was granted.[105]

Domestic policy was more problematic. In the chequered but eventually successful progress of a militia bill Pitt played no part. He was similarly cautious on the question of the enquiries into failures abroad, which proceeded lethargically and eventually produced an innocuous (and fair) result. The novel and supposedly popular financial measures of the administration were miserable failures. But most compromising was the administration's record after Admiral Byng was sentenced to death by court-martial for failing to do everything possible to defeat the French fleet, but with a strong recommendation for mercy. As part of moves to save him prompted by this strange verdict, Pitt spoke twice in the Commons and, with Richard Grenville, now Earl Temple, the First Lord of the Admiralty, made representations to the king. There were good political reasons for not wanting all public indignation diverted from the previous ministers. But the tide of opinion was overwhelmingly hostile to Byng, and he was executed on 14 March. Pitt reaped bitter criticism for his efforts, while their failure added to the impression of ministerial weakness.[106]

This impression and his ill health compounded weakness at court. By February and March, the king, further antagonized by representations on Byng's behalf, was putting out constant feelers for a change. Early in April, with Cumberland unwilling to leave to command the army of observation without a change,[107] Temple and Pitt were dismissed. Legge, George and James Grenville and Thomas Potter resigned in protest.

Pitt's pretensions seemed thus duly chastened. Yet in fact, the very circumstances of his dismissal helped Pitt escape the ignominy of failed patriotism by making him appear the victim of the 'old junto'. Casting of him in this role had already begun, in reaction against the very pungently written Foxite essay paper, the *Test*, which, from November, had amplified to a wider audience the attacks on Pitt's inconsistency, illness and inertia made privately and in parliament. The *Test* had been founded to answer the established but less effectively written paper, the *Monitor*, which had come over to Pitt at the beginning of his ministry with its patron, the Tory Alderman and City of London MP, William Beckford. More tangible expressions of support came in the 'rain' of gold boxes, conferring the freedom of a dozen cities on Pitt and Legge as a mark of protest at their exclusion from office. Most were, in fact, produced by the manoeuvres of Pitt's supporters and the Tories but, orchestrated by the press, they helped to produce the impression of overwhelming public support.[108]

Pitt turned this clamour to political advantage by parading his patriot zeal in the House just sufficiently to suggest the trouble he might cause, without at the same time antagonizing potential allies. Late in April, he made another theatrical appearance as an invalid to speak strongly for enquiries (on which Grenville took the lead) without pressing charges home. In May, on a motion to ask for a vote of credit of £1,000,000 for war expenses, Pitt professed his readiness to consent 'if it was to be confined to Great Britain and America', rather than supporting 'the troops of Hanover', while adding 'some hints of his own popularity, and on the independence of the country gentlemen who favoured him'.[109]

Thus, in time of crisis, Pitt could make himself seem essential in managing the House of Commons if potentially divisive opposition was to be contained while the deteriorating war situation was faced.[110] Fortunately for him, in extraordinary circumstances, the very appearances that strengthened him weakened powerful rivals. Fox's now inveterate rivalry with Pitt and the general hostility to Cumberland undermined the otherwise viable alternatives they offered the king. Pitt's relations with Leicester House now restored, his cause was helped by the promise of reconciliation in the royal family and – if not always unequivocally – by the determination of the Earl of Bute, now ensconced as the prince's Groom of the Stole and confidant, to demonstrate his influence. Newcastle, whose Old Corps could anchor a ministry, preferred to have the necessary leader in the Commons provided by Leicester House's 'reversionary' interest rather than Cumberland's military one. The king, robbed of alternatives in the midst of war, was now, at last, by force of necessity, not implacably averse to Pitt if he was restrained in a coalition. In fact Pitt, still afraid of Newcastle's 'engrossing chicanery',[111] did most to keep the country with only a caretaker administration for virtually three months in the midst of unsuccessful war. Only when he was persuaded to moderate his terms could the Newcastle–Pitt coalition at last kiss hands on 29 June.[112]

. . .

ON THE THRESHOLD OF POWER, 1757

At the end of perhaps the three most important years of his political life, Pitt had apparently achieved what he had set out for in 1754 – and more than he could have hoped for had Pelham lived. True, the king was only reluctantly reconciled; Newcastle had not been excluded. But no longer was he Pitt's patron; after re-appointment to office as Secretary of State, Pitt was returned for Bath, elected by its thirty-member corporation. The duel with Fox had been decisively concluded, as Fox – probably as able as Pitt and a better dealer with men – threw away his great chance in finely balanced politicking behind the facade of public encounter, while safeguarding his opportunities to make money in his long-desired office of Paymaster General. At least as important, the king and Leicester House were now reconciled. Thus the coalition was so broad as to offer hopes of easy containment of opposition. Although none was given office, there was even some prospect of Pitt holding the Tories he had courted with such shameless opportunism[113] – and hence of some further attenuation of the party divisions earlier so marked in Hanoverian politics. This satisfactory outcome owed something to Pitt's sometimes shrewd tactical skill and nerve. But without the misfortunes of war and the mistakes, lack of nerve and changing ambitions of Fox and Newcastle – who could well have survived in 1756 – Pitt's rashness could have left him fulminating on the opposition benches in this war as in the last.

However, the turns of fortune had now made him, quite suddenly, something more than a parliamentary orator and aspiring politician. He had felt, for the first time for himself, the force that wider opinion could exert on the politics of court and parliament, at least in times of crisis and division. This time the interconnection of opinion and high politics was more powerful even than in the events of the late 1730s and early 1740s and working for rather than against a major politician. More by luck than skill or substance, Pitt had successfully defended his revived 'patriotism' and, in so doing, turned to good effect his ambivalent relationship with the Old Corps. He thus added a new dimension to this interconnection – the possibility that wider opinion, and the tangible support it could give (for example in the City of London and among groups of Tories) could be used as part of the armoury of a politician in power, aided by the perception that at last the forty-year grip of 'corrupt' Walpole–Pelhamite politics might be broken. Pitt was hardly yet, as Johnson was later to say, 'a minister given by the people to the King'. But 'the popular

Cry without doors . . . violent in Favor of Mr Pitt' had given him a new strength.[114]

It was, however, a vulnerable strength. While many kept their new expectations of Pitt, other admirers, more percipient perhaps, had already been disillusioned by his vehement opposition and rampant ambition.[115] More recently, the very formation of the coalition, and especially the return to the Admiralty of Admiral Lord Anson, who had dispatched Byng's expedition, was said to have 'ruined the popularity of Mr Pitt and his party' and had offended some important recent allies.[116]

Moreover, if popular mood or circumstances changed, the king could well still undermine Pitt. The Old Corps were hardly reconciled to him, and his own connections had been weakened, if anything, in the struggle for power. George Lyttelton – gifted but too amiable and high-minded for the ruthless business of politics – had refused to follow Pitt into renewed opposition in 1755, thinking it unjustified. Relations were strained with the prickly, ambitious George Grenville when Pitt grew close again to Legge over the subsidy issue and promoted him as Chancellor of the Exchequer.[117] Newcastle still held most of the cards – control of the Commons majority, the ear of the king (likely to be only temporarily estranged from him), the Treasury. Although Newcastle needed Pitt as leader in the Commons, could the embittered relationship between them be satisfactorily mended? It was by no means certain yet that the modification of the Walpole–Pelham model the coalition represented would resolve the dangerous crisis of ministerial and parliamentary instability and contain the threat of revived anti-Hanoverianism so obvious in the negotiations as well as in the public debate surrounding its formation.[118]

Above all, the coalition had still to face the strains of unsuccessful war. Just what Pitt would contribute to this task was far from clear. True, in giving voice to the swelling sense of injured national interest, Pitt had been identified with a 'patriot' foreign policy – '*Whig* and *English*' in one formulation, 'our insular policy', he called it himself.[119] Devonshire, for one, with some foundation and like Horatio Walpole earlier, thought him 'averse to continental extravagance . . . attentive to the interest of his country'.[120] However, Devonshire also assured the king in June 1757 that if Pitt saw 'his way in the closet' he would 'go as far as another' towards the continental policy the king wanted, and Pitt's flexibility over Prussia supported his view. More sceptically still, the courtier Earl Waldegrave pointed out that Pitt's 'former Violence against Hanover' would not

> be any kind of Obstacle, as he had given frequent Proofs that he could change Sides whenever he found it necessary, and could deny his own words with an unembarrass'd countenance.[121]

Much more certain than Pitt's commitment to policy and long obvious to contemporaries was 'his passion' for 'power', his ambition.[122] Equally recognized were his boldness and resolution, his 'independent spirit and energy of character', which made him, in Fox's words, 'single, imperious, proud, enthusiastick', but also 'capable of over-ruling the wavering counsels of a divided cabinet' and likely to exercise power with more 'vigour and effect' than either Fox or Newcastle.[123] Whether more solid abilities undergirded this vigour remained to be seen. Horatio Walpole and Devonshire thought so; a junior colleague saw 'greatness of mind' and 'nobleness of . . . spirit', and those more distant from power 'eminent Faculties'. However, the king and Granville (still in the cabinet) thought him 'impracticable'.[124]

Pitt's single-minded ambition for power, so evident in these three years, widened the gap between the public and the private man. At their beginning, the lively, personable young man was still to be glimpsed in middle age – 'surprisingly well and grown fat' – in a tea party with horn music and a five-day tour of Sussex, organized to relieve the dullness of taking the waters at Tunbridge. Service to a friend was 'given with a grace that few know how to put into any action'. There was warm family affection.[125] But then came the bitter breach with Lyttelton, his oldest friend, and the tensions with his brother-in-law. As emotional solace came more and more from marriage, Pitt's already scarred personality developed a hard crust in his more public dealings, accentuated by the burden of illness. At the same time, a tendency to histrionic pronouncements, suggestive at least of self-dramatization, perhaps of self-deception, became more obvious. 'I am sure I can save this country, and nobody else can', were his famous reported words to Devonshire in November 1756, perhaps echoing those Charles Lyttelton wrote to him, 'If this poor country can be rescued from destruction you alone can do it'. His private reply was more ambivalent, if no less self-important and melodramatic: with 'feeble hand' and 'heavier heart', he wrote, he would 'crawl' to embark on his task, 'in all senses unfit, for the work'.[126]

In Pitt's private and public life, as in British politics and foreign policy, these years indeed were a turning point. As the coalition began to face its responsibilities, it remained to be seen whether the personality and political base shaped in these years could sustain the high expectations now thrust on Pitt.

. . .

NOTES

1. William Coxe, *Memoirs of the Administration of the Right Honourable Henry Pelham* 2 vols (1829), I, p. 309; cf. below, p. 53.
2. It is easy to exaggerate the public obloquy – Basil Williams, *The Life of William Pitt Earl of Chatham* 2 vols (1913), I, pp. 147–8, and Jeremy Black, *Pitt the Elder* (Cambridge, 1992), p. 74, mention the same three examples – although it did permeate the press more widely (Robert Harris, *A Patriot Press. National Politics and the London Press in the 1740s*, Oxford, 1993, pp. 77–8), and lingered on (e.g. *London Evening Post*, 18–20 April 1747, p. 4) as part of the wider disillusionment of which Pulteney was the prime target. Among observers, see e.g. Walpole to Mann, 15 April 1746, *Correspondence*, XIX, p. 247; *Memoirs George II*, I, pp. 4, 5.
3. Chesterfield to Newcastle, 27 Feb. 1746, in Richard Lodge (ed.), *Private Correspondence of Chesterfield and Newcastle 1744–46* (1930), p. 114; Fox to Ilchester, 4 March 1746, in Earl of Ilchester, *Henry Fox, First Lord Holland, His Family and Relations* 2 vols (1920), I, p. 131.
4. Reassessment of Pelham is hampered not only by his early death but also by the disappearance of his papers.
5. Harris, *A Patriot Press*, ch. 6, pp. 193ff.
6. *Correspondence*, XX, pp. 357–8 (1753).
7. Recently he had clandestinely married Lady Georgiana Caroline Lennox, daughter of the Duke of Richmond and great-granddaughter of Charles II.
8. T.R. Clayton, 'The Duke of Newcastle, the Earl of Halifax, and the American origins of the Seven Years' War', *Historical Journal* 24 (1981), pp. 571–603.
9. See e.g. Newcastle to Hardwicke, 2 Sept. 1749, in Philip C. Yorke, *The Life and Correspondence of Philip Yorke Earl of*

Hardwicke Lord High Chancellor of Great Britain 3 vols (Cambridge, 1913), II, pp. 22–3.

10. Jeremy Black, *A System of Ambition? British Foreign Policy 1660–1793* (1991), pp. 182–3; Paul Langford, *The Eighteenth Century 1688–1815* (1976), pp. 130–2.

11. Williams, *The Life of William Pitt*, I, pp. 152–7, gives a reasonably balanced account, largely based on the correspondence from Pitt's subordinates in the Chatham Papers and *Chatham Correspondence*, I, pp. 5–22 (on which the following outline also draws).

12. *Chatham Correspondence*, I, pp. 110–11 and n.; Newcastle to Hardwicke, 2 Oct. 1754, Newcastle Papers, Add. MSS 35414, f. 197; *Parl. Hist.*, XV, cols 374–5.

13. Furze to Pitt, 8 Aug. 1755, PRO 30/8/32, f. 339.

14. Chesterfield to his son, 11 Feb. 1751, in B. Dobrée (ed.), *The Letters of Philip Dormer Stanhope, fourth Earl of Chesterfield* 6 vols (1932), IV, pp. 1678–9.

15. *Parl. Hist.*, XIV, col. 103; Williams, *The Life of William Pitt*, pp. 162–3; Black, *Pitt the Elder*, p. 79. Ill-judged impetuosity was even more noticeable in the 1751 session; see below p. 58.

16. Pitt to G. Lyttelton, 4 April 1754, in Robert J. Phillimore (ed.), *Memoirs and Correspondence of George, Lord Lyttelton, from 1734 to 1773* 2 vols (1845), I, p. 467.

17. Pitt to Newcastle, 24 March 1754, Add. MSS 32734, f. 323.

18. Hume Campbell to Marchmont, 22 Jan. 1747, HMC, *Polwarth*, V, p. 169; *Parl. Hist.*, XIV, cols 397, 622, 664–6, 973 (1749–51); Romney Sedgwick, *The House of Commons 1715–1754* 2 vols (1971), I, p. 58.

19. Black, *Pitt the Elder*, p. 83 (17 Jan. 1751).

20. Fox to Ilchester, 12, 15 April 1746, in Ilchester, *Henry Fox*, I, pp. 134–5.

21. *Parl. Hist.*, XIV, cols 692–6 (quotation), 721–3; [John Almon], *Anecdotes of the Life of the Right Honourable William Pitt, Earl of Chatham* 3rd edn, 3 vols (1793), I, pp. 245–6; *Parl. Hist.*, XIV, col. 695. The opposition had attacked the government for failing to enforce provisions for the dismantling of the fortifications at Dunkirk.

22. *Parl. Hist.*, XIV, cols 799–802 (17 Jan. 1751).

23. Pitt to Newcastle, 13 July 1750, Add. MSS 32721, f. 354; cf. Pitt to Newcastle, 24 Aug. 1750, *Chatham Correspondence*, I, pp. 34–44.

24. *Memoirs George II*, I, p. 5, Coxe, *Pelham*, II, p. 140 (both 17 Jan. – quotations); *Parl. Hist.*, XIV, cols 802–4 (17 Jan.), 963–70 (22 Feb. 1751 – latter quotations col. 965).

25. Pitt to Horatio Walpole, [Feb. 1752], *Chatham Correspondence*, I, p. 64, cf. pp. 63–4n.; *Memoirs George II*, I, pp. 165, 90.
26. Newcastle to Pitt, 29 Sept. 1752, Pitt to Newcastle, 14 Aug. 1753, and even 22 April 1754, Add. MSS 32729, ff. 386–7, 32732, ff. 460–1, 32735, ff. 143–4; Black, *Pitt the Elder*, p. 89.
27. Black, *Pitt the Elder*, p. 76, citing Sir Roger Newdigate's diary; *Parl. Hist.*, XIII, cols 1396–7.
28. Marie Peters, 'The myth of William Pitt, Earl of Chatham, great imperialist. Part I: Pitt and imperial expansion', *Journal of Imperial and Commonwealth History* 21 (1993), pp. 37–8 and nn. 61–2; Black, *A System of Ambition?*, p. 188.
29. Peters, 'Myth', p. 38 and nn. 63, 64; Harris, *A Patriot Press*, pp. 222–33, 242–4; Black, *A System of Ambition?*, p. 176.
30. Black, *Pitt the Elder*, pp. 77, 78; Pitt to Newcastle, 5 Dec. 1747, Add. MSS 32713, ff. 517–18; Philip Yorke's notes, 14 Feb. [1748], on a conversation with his father, in Yorke, *Hardwicke*, I, p. 631; Pitt to G. Grenville, 26 April 1748, in William James Smith (ed.), *The Grenville Papers* 4 vols (1852–53), I, p. 73.
31. Stone's account of the debate on the Bavarian subsidy, [22 Feb. 1751], Add. MSS 32724, f. 133.
32. Pitt to Newcastle, 19 June, 6 July, Newcastle to Pitt, 26 June/ 7 July, 4/15 July 1750, Add. MSS 32721, ff. 129–30, 283, 192–3, 251 (quotation); Coxe, *Pelham*, II, p. 139 (Egmont).
33. Pitt to Newcastle, 14 Aug. 1753, Add. MSS 32732, f. 461; Black, *Pitt the Elder*, p. 89.
34. Black, *Pitt the Elder*, p. 89; Pitt to Newcastle, 5 Dec. 1747, 25 Jan. 174[8], Add. MSS 32713, f. 517, 32714, f. 69; Newcastle to Pitt, 19 Jan. 1748, *Chatham Correspondence*, I, p. 27. Cf. Black, *A System of Ambition?*, pp. 179–80, 183–5.
35. Pitt to Newcastle, 19 June, Newcastle to Pitt, 26 June/7 July 1750, Add. MSS 32721, ff. 129, 192; cf. Newcastle to Pitt, 31 March, 4/15 July, 12/23 Aug., 9/20 Sept., Pitt to Newcastle, 24 Aug. 1750, *Chatham Correspondence*, I, pp. 31–44, 47–8, 44–5, Pitt to Newcastle, 2 April, 13 July, 28 Sept 1750, 1 Jan, [25 Feb.] 175[1], Add. MSS 32720, ff. 177–8, 186–7, 32721, ff. 351–4, 32723, f. 45, 32724, ff. 3, 143.
36. Newcastle to Pitt, 9/20 Sept. 1750, *Chatham Correspondence*, I, p. 47; Pitt to Newcastle, 28 Sept. 1750, Add. MSS 32723, f. 45.
37. *Parl. Hist.*, XIV, col. 721.
38. Newcastle to Chesterfield, 18 Feb., 5 March 1746, in Lodge (ed.), *Private Correspondence*, pp. 108, 119; Walpole to Mann, 2 April 1753, *Correspondence*, XX, p. 138; Pitt to Newcastle, 19 June, 28 Sept. 1750, Add. MSS 32721, f. 130, 32723, f. 45.
39. Pelham to Newcastle, 3 Aug. 1750, Add. MSS 32722, f. 33.

40. His name was mentioned by observers, for example, by the Earl of Marchmont (memorandum, 5 Feb. 1748, HMC, *Polwarth*, V, p. 271), and he and Lyttelton opposed Bedford's appointment (Philip Yorke's note, 14 Feb. 1748, in idem, *Hardwicke*, I, p. 630).

41. Walpole to Mann, 19 Nov. 1750, *Correspondence*, XX, p. 202 and n.; *Memoirs George II*, I, pp. 8, 109.

42. Pelham to Newcastle, 3 Aug. 1750, Add. MSS 32722, f. 33; Marchmont, memorandum, 5 Feb. 1748, HMC, *Polwarth*, V, p. 271.

43. Sedgwick, *The House of Commons*, I, pp. 59–60; *Memoirs George II*, I, pp. 8, 55; William Coxe, *Memoirs of Horatio, Lord Walpole* (1802), pp. 413–14; Black, *Pitt the Elder*, p. 88.

44. *Memoirs George II*, I, p. 8; Walpole to Mann, 9 Feb. 1751, *Correspondence*, XX, p. 223.

45. Pitt to Newcastle, 19 June, 13 July 1750 (quotation), cf. 2 April 1750, 14 Aug. 1753, Add. MSS 32721, ff. 129, 351–3, 32720, ff. 186–7, 32732, ff. 460–1.

46. Philip Lawson, *George Grenville. A Political Life* (Oxford, 1984), p. 64; *Memoirs George II*, I, pp. 12, 42, 142; Newcastle to James Pelham, 30 Jan. 1751, Add. MSS 32724, f. 105; Coxe, *Pelham*, II, p. 144.

47. *Memoirs George II*, I, p. 8, cf. Walpole to Mann, 23 March 1749, 22 April 1751, *Correspondence*, XX, pp. 38, 249.

48. Walpole to Mann, 13 March 1751, *Correspondence*, XX, p. 230.

49. *Memoirs George II*, I, pp. 43, 64 (naturalization bill, 8 March, 16 April), 39, 40–1, 42 (quotation), 66, 74–5 (Anstruther, 4, 5 March, 18, 24 April 1751).

50. Ibid., pp. 91–2 (Regency Act, 16 May), 43; John Carswell and Lewis Arnold Dralle (eds), *The Political Journal of George Bubb Dodington* (Oxford, 1965), p. 121 (16 [May] 1751).

51. Black, *Pitt the Elder*, pp. 91–5.

52. See letters 29 Aug., 29 Sept. 1752, 10, 24 March, 26 July, 9, 14 Aug. 1753, Add. MSS 32729, ff. 250–1, 386–7, 32731, ff. 244–5, 298, 32732, ff. 357–8, 433–4, 460–1 (this last hinting some resentment at the unimportance of his views on public affairs). The obsequiousness felt necessary to retain his seat is illustrated in letters of 6 and 13 Oct. 1753 (offering thanks for 'such very obliging remarks of your goodness to me', the 'honour' of which 'I have but too much reason to be sensible how little I can merit'), and even 2, 20, 22 April 1754, if then with touches of sarcasm: Add. MSS 32733, ff. 26–7, 63–4, 32735, ff. 14–15, 139–40, 143–4.

53. Paul Langford, *A Polite and Commercial People. England 1727–1783* (Oxford, 1989), pp. 224–5.

54. *Parl. Hist.*, XV, cols 152–3; *Memoirs George II*, I, pp. 244–5. Pitt also assisted in opposing the repeal of an older provision allowing Jewish naturalization in the colonies.

55. *Memoirs George II*, I, p. 64; Chesterfield to his son, 11 Feb. 1751, in Dobrée (ed.), *Letters*, IV, pp. 1678–9; Williams, *The Life of William Pitt*, I, p. 149; Coxe, *Lord Walpole*, pp. 411–12 and nn.

56. Walpole to Mann, 2 April 1750, 9 Feb. 1751, *Correspondence*, XX, pp. 138, 223; *Memoirs George II*, I, pp. 75, 42; Coxe, *Pelham*, II, p. 144; Carswell and Dralle (eds), *Dodington*, p. 211.

57. Sir Lewis Namier and John Brooke, *The House of Commons 1754–1790* 3 vols (1964), III, p. 310; Legge to Pitt, 8 Jan., 10/21 May, 10 July 1748, *Chatham Correspondence*, I, pp. 24–6, 28–31, PRO 30/8/48, ff. 79–80. W.H. Lyttelton had joined the cousins in 1748 as a protégé of Pitt (Pitt to Sir Thomas Lyttelton, 8 June 1748, in Phillimore (ed.), *Lyttelton*, I, pp. 264–5), but Richard Grenville, now Lord Cobham, sometimes took an independent line (*Memoirs George II*, I, p. 151).

58. For this account of Pitt's tactics in 1754–57, cf. Marie Peters, *Pitt and Popularity. The Patriot Minister and London Opinion during the Seven Years' War* (Oxford, 1980), chs 1, 2, Richard Middleton, *The Bells of Victory. The Pitt–Newcastle Ministry and the Conduct of the Seven Years' War 1757–1762* (Cambridge, 1985), ch. 1 (especially for 1756–57), Black, *Pitt the Elder*, pp. 98–149, and, in much greater if not always convincing detail, J.C.D. Clark, *The Dynamics of Change. The Crisis of the 1750s and English Party Systems* (Cambridge, 1982), passim.

59. *Correspondence*, XX, p. 411; Carswell and Dralle (eds), *Dodington*, p. 279 (10 June 1754); Pitt to Newcastle, 5 April 1754, *Chatham Correspondence*, I, p. 101, and cf. below, n. 60. On Pitt's ill health see above, p. 10.

60. A series of letters give a unique insight into his views at this time. They are listed in Williams, *The Life of William Pitt*, I, p. 249, with locations in printed works in most cases.

61. Pitt to Lyttelton and the Grenvilles, 7 March 1754, in Smith (ed.), *Grenville Papers*, I, p. 106.

62. Pitt to Temple, 11 March, to Lyttelton and the Grenvilles, 7 March 1754, in Smith (ed.), *Grenville Papers*, I, pp. 112–13, 110; Pitt to Newcastle (draft), 5 April 1754, *Chatham Correspondence*, I, pp. 100–1.

63. Pitt to Newcastle, 24 March, 5 April (first quotation), to Hardwicke, 6 April 1754 (second quotation), Add. MSS 32734, f. 322, *Chatham Correspondence*, I, pp. 102, 105.

64. Pitt to Newcastle, 24 March, to Lyttelton, 10 March, to Temple, 11 March 1754, Add. MSS 32734, f. 325, Yorke, *Hardwicke*, II, p. 20.

65. *Memoirs George II*, II, p. 14; Carswell and Dralle (eds), *Dodington*, p. 292 (8 Oct. 1754).
66. *Memoirs George II*, II, pp. 24–6, 27–8.
67. Ibid., p. 30; Hardwicke to Newcastle, 15 Dec. 1754, in Yorke, *Hardwicke*, II, pp. 221–2; Black, *Pitt the Elder*, pp. 102, 106.
68. *Memoirs George II*, II, pp. 39–40, 45; *Parl. Hist.*, XV, cols 500–4.
69. Draft in Pitt's hand, [late April 1755], PRO 30/8/1, ff. 196–7 (quotation), wrongly connected in *Chatham Correspondence*, I, pp. 134–7, with the preceding correspondence with Fox, which in fact took place in Dec.; 'Mr Grenville's narrative', in Smith (ed.), *Grenville Papers*, I, pp. 432–3; Sir George Lee's memorandum, quoted by Clark in *The Dynamics of Change*, pp. 162–3; Coxe, *Lord Walpole*, p. 440; Carswell and Dralle (eds), *Dodington*, pp. 295–6 (9, 15 May), 309–10 (16 July 1755); cf. Yorke, *Hardwicke*, II, pp. 228, 230. Significantly, there is no correspondence with Pitt in the Newcastle Papers between April 1754 and 1757.
70. Pitt to G. Grenville, 27 Oct. 1754, in Smith (ed.), *Grenville Papers*, I, p. 128.
71. Williams, *The Life of William Pitt*, I, pp. 238–48, Vere Birdwood (ed.), *So Dearly Loved, So Much Admired. Letters to Hester Pitt, Lady Chatham, from her Relations and Friends 1744–1801* (1994), ch. 2; Pitt to Ann Pitt, 21 Oct. 1754, Dropmore Papers, Series II, Add. MSS 69289, no. 39.
72. PRO 30/8/34, f. 11, vol. 35, f. 8, vol. 61, ff. 9–12; Smith (ed.), *Grenville Papers*, I, pp. 149–52.
73. See below, pp. 244–5.
74. Black, *A System of Ambition?*, pp. 188–92.
75. Simmons and Thomas, I, pp. 3–23 (15 Nov. 1754); Walpole to Mann, 1 Dec. 1754, *Correspondence*, XX, p. 455.
76. Newcastle to Hardwicke, 2 Oct. 1754, Add. MSS 32737, f. 24; Carswell and Dralle (eds), *Dodington*, p. 292 (8 Oct. 1754), cf. Clark, *The Dynamics of Change*, pp. 101–2.
77. Yorke, *Hardwicke*, II, pp. 196–7, 227–49 (quotation, p. 238).
78. Newcastle to Hardwicke, 3 Sept. 1755, in ibid., p. 238.
79. Ibid., pp. 240, 236, 230.
80. Ibid., pp. 240–1, 231; cf. above, p. 54.
81. *Memoirs George II*, II, p. 57; Hardwicke to Newcastle, 4 Sept. 1755, cf. 29 Aug. 1756, in Yorke, *Hardwicke*, II, pp. 245–6, 310, cf. Smith (ed.), *Grenville Papers*, I, pp. 139, 145.
82. Hardwicke to Newcastle, 9 Aug. 1755, in Yorke, *Hardwicke*, II, p. 233; cf. Horatio Walpole to Devonshire, 6 Sept. 1755, quoted in Clark, *Dynamics of Change*, p. 197 and J.C.D. Clark, *The Memoirs and Speeches of James, 2nd Earl Waldegrave* (Cambridge, 1988), pp. 167–8.

83. James Lee McKelvey, *George III and Lord Bute. The Leicester House Years* (Durham, NC, 1973), pp. 22–3.
84. Clark, *Waldegrave*, p. 168.
85. McKelvey, *George III and Lord Bute*, p. 24; Peters, *Pitt*, p. 39; Hardwicke to Newcastle, 12 Aug., Newcastle to Hardwicke, 22 Aug. 1754, in Yorke, *Hardwicke*, II, pp. 233, 234–5; Linda J. Colley, 'The Loyal Brotherhood and the Cocoa Tree: the London organization of the Tory Party, 1727–1760', *Historical Journal* 20 (1977), p. 90. On Pitt's 27 Nov. 1754 attack on Oxford for Tory Jacobitism, see *Memoirs George II*, II, pp. 27–8.
86. *Memoirs George II*, II, pp. 69–72 (13 Nov. 1755).
87. Ibid., e.g. pp. 76–7, 79, 84, 85, 99–101, 111–13, 125–6, 140–2 (quotation). On this session, cf. Black, *Pitt the Elder*, pp. 109–17, Lawson, *George Grenville*, pp. 82–94 (from Grenville's point of view).
88. *Memoirs George II*, II, pp. 87, 92–3, 136.
89. Ibid., pp. 123, 142–3, 145.
90. Peters, *Pitt*, pp. 40–1.
91. Black, *Pitt the Elder*, pp. 112–14; H. Digby to Hanbury Williams, 23 Dec. 1755, Add. MSS 69093, f. 3, cf. Peters, *Pitt*, pp. 42–3; *Memoirs George II*, II, pp. 77–9, 87–8; Fox to Devonshire, 31 Jan. 1756, Chatsworth, Devonshire Papers, 330.115.
92. Peters, *Pitt*, pp. 47–56; Walpole to Mann, 29 Aug. 1756, *Correspondence*, XX, p. 585.
93. Fox to Devonshire, 31 July 1756, Devonshire Papers, 330.156; cf. Hardwicke to Newcastle, 14 Oct. 1756, in Yorke, *Hardwicke*, II, p. 320.
94. Newcastle to Hardwicke, 15 Oct., Hardwicke to Royston, 21 Oct., 'Relation of my [Hardwicke's] Conference with Mr Pitt, 24 Oct.', Hardwicke to J. Yorke, 31 Oct. 1756, in Yorke, *Hardwicke*, II, pp. 321–4, 328–9, 277–9, 331 (quotations); R[igby] to Gower, 21 Oct. 1756, Granville, Papers, PRO 30/29/1/14, no. 9 (quotation); cf. Samuel Martin's memorandum, 1756, Martin Papers, Add. MSS 41356, pp. 8–10, 11–12. Private letters (in Smith (ed.), *Grenville Papers*, III, pp. 165, 168) confirm Pitt's conviction of the Newcastle administration's incompetence.
95. R[igby] to Gower, 28 Oct. 1756, PRO 30/29/1/14, no. 1.
96. Peters, *Pitt*, pp. 59–62; Walpole to Mann, 4 Nov. 1756, *Correspondence*, XXI, pp. 12–13.
97. Peters, *Pitt*, pp. 56–7, 59–60.
98. Ibid., pp. 60, 61.
99. Ibid, pp. 63–5; Peters, 'Myth', pp. 41, 43; Add. MSS 41356, pp. 14–15.

100. Walpole to Mann, 4 Nov. 1756, *Correspondence*, XXI, p. 12; Rigby to Gower, 14 Nov. 1756, PRO 30/29/1/14, no. 14.
101. Black, *Pitt the Elder*, pp. 130, 134–5.
102. Frances Boscawen to Elizabeth Montagu, 13 Nov. 1754, HL, Montagu Papers, MO505.
103. *Parl. Hist.*, XV, col. 772; Peters, *Pitt*, p. 69, 'Myth', p. 42; H. Digby to Lord Digby, 7 Dec. 1756, HMC, *Eighth Report*, Appendix, Pt 1, p. 223; Elizabeth Montagu to Sarah Scott, 2 [Dec. 1756], HL, MO5763.
104. *Parl. Hist.*, XIV, cols 782–803 (17 Feb. 1757); Michell to Frederick, 22 Feb. 1757, in J.G. Droysen *et al.* (eds), *Politische Correspondenz Friedrichs des Grossen* 39 vols (Berlin, 1879–1935), XIV, p. 344.
105. *Memoirs George II*, II, p. 145; Black, *Pitt the Elder*, p. 135.
106. Peters, *Pitt*, pp. 67–71; cf. Lawson, *George Grenville*, pp. 100–3.
107. Cf. Michell to Frederick, in Droysen *et al.* (eds), *Correspondenz*, XIV, pp. 501–2.
108. Peters, *Pitt*, pp. 13–15, 63, 65–6, 72–8.
109. *Memoirs George II*, II, pp. 253, 257–8; Lawson, *George Grenville*, p. 105.
110. Cf. Black, *Pitt the Elder*, pp. 145–7.
111. *Memoirs George II*, II, p. 256.
112. On the negotiations see Peters, *Pitt*, pp. 80–1, Middleton, *Bells*, pp. 15–18; Black, *Pitt the Elder*, pp. 138–49.
113. Sir J. Philipps to Pitt, 6 Aug. 1757, PRO 30/8/52, f. 89.
114. G.B. Hill and L.F. Powell (eds), *Boswell's Life of Johnson* 6 vols (Oxford, 1934–50), II, p. 196 (1772); Clark, *Waldegrave*, p. 205.
115. Sir John Philipps to Pitt, 6 Aug. 1757, PRO 30/8/52, f. 89, cf. Peters, 'Myth', pp. 42–3 and n. 109; contrast the change of tone (admittedly shaped by her friendship with Lyttelton) very evident in Elizabeth Montagu's letters, e.g. to Frances Boscawen, 29 Oct. 1755, to Sarah Scott, 30 March 1756, to Edward Montagu, [Dec. 1756], HL, MO568, 5751, 2331.
116. Devonshire to Cumberland, 28 June 1757, Devonshire Papers, 260.239; cf. Calcraft to Loudoun, 8 July 1757, Lord Chatham's Letterbook, PRO 30/8/86, f. 349; Peters, *Pitt*, pp. 83–7.
117. Phillimore (ed.), *Lyttelton*, II, pp. 477–81, 488–91; Yorke, *Hardwicke*, II, pp. 232, 235, 239; Lawson, *George Grenville*, pp. 81, 97.
118. See e.g. Clark, *Waldegrave*, p. 206.
119. Add. MSS 41356, p. 9 (Martin); Pitt to Grenville, [Dec. 1755], in Smith (ed.), *Grenville Papers*, I, p. 152.
120. K. Schweizer, 'Some additions to the Devonshire Diary', *Notes and Queries* 231 (1986), p. 66; Coxe, *Lord Walpole*,

p. 439 (mid-1755). Horatio, an experienced diplomat, was Sir Robert's brother.

121. Devonshire to Cumberland, 21 June 1757, Devonshire Papers, 260.236; Clark, *Waldegrave*, p. 206; cf. Newcastle to Hardwicke, 4 Jan. 1757, Add. MSS 32870, f. 23.

122. Carswell and Dralle (eds), *Dodington*, p. 278; cf. p. 184, Coxe, *Lord Walpole*, p. 412, Hartington to Devonshire, 8 Nov. 1755, Devonshire Papers, 260.181, Hardwicke to Newcastle, 29 Aug, to J. Yorke, 31 Oct. 1756, in Yorke, *Hardwicke*, II, pp. 310, 331, *Memoirs George II*, II, p. 179, III, pp. 1–2, Clark, *Waldegrave*, p. 206.

123. Coxe, *Lord Walpole*, p. 440; Fox to Hanbury Williams, 26 Dec. 1756, Add. MSS 69093, f. 13; cf. Clark, *Waldegrave*, p. 206, Peters, 'Myth', p. 42, n. 108.

124. Add. MSS 41356, pp. 9, 10 (Martin); Frances Boscawen to Elizabeth Montagu, 9 Jan. 1757, HL, MO510; Devonshire to Cumberland, 5 May 1757, Devonshire Papers 260.223; Williams, *The Life of William Pitt*, I, p. 307 (Granville).

125. Elizabeth to Edward Montagu, 8 [July], [July 1753], 13 April [1754], to Frances Boscawen, 24 [April 1754], HL, MO2277, 2286 (quotation), 2305, 565 (quotation); Pitt to John Pitt, 31 July 1753, in Georgiana, Lady Chatterton (ed.), *Memorials . . . of Admiral Lord Gambier* 2 vols (1861), I, pp. 61–2. Pitt's letters to John in this collection are warmly affectionate.

126. *Memoirs George II*, III, p. 1; C. Lyttelton to Pitt, 16 Nov., PRO 30/8/48, f. 239; Pitt to Lyttelton, 19 Nov. 175[6], Add. MSS 69288, no. 28.

Chapter 3

WAR MINISTER AND GREAT COMMONER, 1757–61

In little more than two years from the difficult inception of the Pitt–Newcastle coalition, the early disasters in war were totally reversed. Pitt came to be hailed as the great war minister, 'that Genius', whose leadership in diplomacy and strategy 'first raised the abject Spirits of the Nation and . . . conducted them to Glory and Conquest'.[1] This remarkable transformation of Pitt's fortunes concurrently with those of Britain gave him an enduring reputation which profoundly affected his future career. Yet this outcome was hardly imaginable in July 1757 as the new coalition, in which his position was so weak, turned its attention to the dire war situation. How the transformation was wrought and how far he deserved the credit given him for Britain's success – these are the central questions of this chapter and, indeed, the most important questions about his whole career.

. . .

NEW ISSUES OF DIPLOMACY AND STRATEGY

The Seven Years War presented novel problems of diplomacy and grand strategy for Britain, about which more than half a century's experience as a great power provided little guidance. The war was the first in which non-European theatres remained the chief focus of interest: Britain confronted France in open war from the beginning, not so much now as a challenge to the balance of power in Europe but as the major competitor in the contest for advantage in the New World. Over the long term, this situation was the natural result of that fluctuating yet substantial growth of Britain's trans-oceanic commerce for more than a century which had given Britain commercial aims in all the major wars marking her emergence as a great power, led the state dominated by a landed elite to recognize the importance of trade, and shaped among the wider political nation a perception of itself as a peculiarly commercial people. These developments came to a climax in the mid-eighteenth century, when growing interest in regions outside Europe came to be concentrated on Britain's mainland colonies in North America. In part, attention was drawn to those colonies – away from the sugar-producing Caribbean, the slave trade which sustained its plantations, and traditional dreams of gains from the Spanish empire – by their dramatic tenfold increase in population since 1700 and growing prosperity, which created a thriving market for British goods and diversified Britain's growing 'Atlantic economy'.[2] Even more important, North America was also the area where competition with France outside Europe had become most intense. Conviction of the importance of the American colonies in international rivalry not only brought British regular troops to the Ohio in support of the colonists in the immediate colonial origins of the war; it also made the security of those colonies Britain's paramount war aim.

To many contemporaries, of course, the 'patriot' policy of reliance on maritime rather than continental war clearly answered the question of how such a war should be fought. And, arguably from the later seventeenth century, Britain's growing commercial strength had indeed shaped general agreement on a 'blue-water' grand strategy of reliance on the navy rather than a large army to defend her interests.[3] But a blue-water strategy did not necessarily give Britain a decisive advantage. Britain might have the edge, but France, too, was a formidable naval power and a renewed 'family compact' with Bourbon Spain would decisively change the balance. Unrealistic expectations of naval power also consistently underestimated the constant attention necessary to mobilize resources, especially manpower, let alone the difficulties created by hazardous weather and uncertain communications.[4] Nor did a blue-water strategy automatically decide crucial questions of deployment of over-stretched resources in favour of objectives beyond Europe. The French invasion threat of 1756 reinforced the priority of home defence, while the seizure of Minorca drew attention to the needs of Mediterranean trade. Reconstitution of a 'western squadron' which could deny the Channel and Atlantic approaches to French ships was vital if Britain and her trade were to be protected while war was waged overseas. But unsuccessful early attempts at such a reconstitution indicated substantial practical problems in keeping ships at sea in the right place for long periods: the French were still able to get substantial reinforcements to America.[5]

Moreover, Britain also had interests in Europe which could not be ignored. Her European trade to north and south was still the most substantial, if relatively stagnant, sector. Even without her connection with Hanover, Britain would have been concerned – as in the last war – about the threat of French dominance in the Netherlands posed by France's alliance with Austria.[6] The Hanover link and Hanover's openness to French attack intensified British vulnerability – and to follow Pitt's hint of 1755 that Hanover might be abandoned, to be bought back in a peace settlement, might well prove too costly of valuable conquests elsewhere.

Furthermore, such a course of action would undoubtedly offend the king. His considerable interest in foreign policy and particular concern for his electorate – at least to keep it out of the war zone, at best to secure territorial gains – drew Britain further into Europe in ways soon to be demonstrated, ways that British ministers could not easily control. Pitt's clear preference for the northern Secretaryship[7] illustrates the primacy the king's interests tended to give to German affairs, while his denial of Pitt's wish emphasizes an influence that went far wider. The king took a keen interest in appointments, especially in the army, and the final sanction he gave to administrative, diplomatic and military instructions issued in his name was no mere formality. It often had to be won by argument in the closet.

So when Newcastle's attempts to 'keep the war out of Germany' were subverted by Prussia in 1756 and the European situation became even more volatile, Britain could not simply abandon her only possible ally. Yet she had few resources to add to the subsidized foreign troops and Hanoverians in the army of observation Cumberland commanded in 1757. Her navy was already stretched, her troops numbered tens of thousands, rather than the hundreds of thousands continental powers could raise, and at least half were deployed overseas.[8] Against France's much greater population and strong military tradition, Britain could set only her sounder ability to raise money.

Success in the war so disastrously begun turned on these major problems of conception and execution of policy, problems requiring a balance between developing, for British as well as Hanoverian interests, an effective new relationship with Prussia and directing major resources to the war beyond Europe. Yet to them Pitt initially brought neither direct experience of foreign affairs nor any special wisdom. Policy questions were certainly not discussed in the coalition negotiations. Pitt's short ministry in 1756–57 had suggested little more than basic agreement with the policy followed by Newcastle, while his proposal of the utterly inexperienced Temple for the Admiralty and his own wish for the northern Secretaryship hardly suggest particular sympathy for the war overseas.[9]

His role in coalition policy making had yet to be determined.[10] As Secretary of State for the Southern Department he certainly held a leading office. With Holderness, the other Secretary, he conducted diplomatic correspondence and shared domestic responsibilities, and they also had the formal task of transmitting the king's orders, when necessary, to executive departments and military commanders. It was not unusual for one Secretary to be dominant, and Newcastle was soon commenting that '[p]oor Holderness is a greater cipher than ever'.[11] But according to eighteenth-century constitutional convention, always suspicious of overweening ministers, such domination did not extend to oversight of other departments to which orders might be transmitted. Their heads were, like the two Secretaries, responsible directly to the king, the important ones dealing individually with him in the closet on their normal business. In any case, the cumbersome methods and machinery of administration hindered any effective oversight.

Furthermore, while the Secretaries might transmit the king's orders, they did not determine them. The necessary co-ordination, especially of foreign and military affairs, was achieved informally through discussion in the king's closet and especially in cabinet – the meeting together of the king's leading ministers.[12] During the coalition negotiations Pitt and Newcastle had explicitly agreed on the need for such a body, and it continued to meet frequently, comprised – as under the Newcastle and Devonshire–Pitt ministries – of a varying group of people determined partly by office and the business under discussion, partly by political standing. Of course, a minister might come to exercise a predominant influence in closet or cabinet, but that would depend, not on constitutional or administrative position, but on political weight – and initially in both venues Pitt was weak. No wonder he took up 'this bitter, but necessary cup' of coalition with 'foreboding', fearful that 'a mutilated, enfeebled half-formed system'[13] would compromise the power and voice in policy he had fought for over the last three years.

Nevertheless, Pitt's status and office gave him an assured place in cabinet, while the Secretary's extensive correspondence, which, despite prolonged spells of debilitating illness, he tackled energetically,[14] provided other opportunities. He handled the major theatres of war overseas, especially in America, and the process of turning cabinet minutes into detailed orders gave room for a personal imprint. Furthermore, while diplomatic correspondence with France lapsed in wartime and much of the rest was predominantly inwards or obviously delegated to clerks, this personal imprint could be evident here also, notably in dealings with Spain – for example, in an early abortive attempt to buy an alliance with the return of Gibraltar.[15]

. . .

THE GERMAN WAR, 1757–58

Much about the internal politics of the coalition remained to be determined as the new ministers turned from politicking to the business of war. In Germany, they faced a rapidly deteriorating situation. France and Austria had signed a second, offensive, alliance at Versailles in May. Prussia was under pressure on all sides: forced to reverse a hitherto triumphant advance into Bohemia by a bad defeat at Kolin in June, exposed in East Prussia by a Russian victory in August, and threatened by both Russians and Swedes in the Baltic. Meanwhile, and most worrying for Britain, Cumberland's army of observation was forced into retreat by the French, and he could not stop them advancing into and across Hanover. On 10 September, he signed with them the

Convention of Klosterseven, by which the army of observation was disbanded and Hanover virtually abandoned to the French. Prussia, with its western flank thus opened to the French, began overtures for a separate peace with France. At home, riots over the high price of corn and disturbances provoked by attempts to implement the supposedly popular Militia Act created dangerous tumult. The early weeks of the coalition were indeed ones of black crisis – not least for the Secretaries of State.

If the German theatre was not to collapse entirely, a new Anglo-Prussian agreement had to be negotiated to meet changed circumstances. But the dire German situation threw into stark relief the divergent expectations of Britain and Prussia. Each wanted to receive, not give, aid, Prussia chiefly against the obvious territorial designs of Russia and Austria, Britain to contain the French threat in Europe while she concentrated on defeating them overseas – while Hanover wanted above all to keep out of the war.[16] Tortuous negotiations stretched over nine months before a new relationship was settled, and another two elapsed before the extent of Britain's commitment to the German war was clarified in June 1758.

By July, when the ministers first turned to the issue, Frederick, in increasing desperation, made three suggestions which crystallized the divergence of objectives. Ministers quickly rejected the first two – a renewed request for a Baltic naval squadron and a plea for British troops for the army of observation – although Newcastle and Hardwicke were inclined to send troops until it was clearly too late. Holderness's letter conveying the decision, while assuring Frederick of Britain's friendship, carefully explained that Britain's priorities lay outside Europe. But Frederick's third suggestion of a diversionary raid on the French coast was accepted as compatible with the Channel fleet's tasks of defence of Britain and her trade. In fact, an expedition against Rochefort in the Bay of Biscay was decided on before Holderness's reply was sent.[17]

Pitt was fully involved in decision-making concerning Prussia, although Prussia lay outside his formal sphere of responsibility. Soon he was particularly associated with the expedition – the administration's first decisive action. While its planning throughout was a joint operation of the ministers, the king himself suggesting the commanding officers, the execution of decisions lay within Pitt's responsibilities. He pushed on preparations, drew up instructions with Sir John Ligonier, Master-General of the Ordnance, and kept in touch with the commanders when the expedition at last departed on 8 September.[18] By that time, the expedition was publicly seen as peculiarly Pitt's and, in keeping with his supposedly patriot policy, as just the sort of operation that would 'presently cure [the French] of marching the strength of their country . . . beyond the Rhine' and so allow Britain to concentrate on America.[19]

Meanwhile, however, Pitt had committed himself to substantially increased German expenditure. In supporting the army of observation in February, he had defended spending 'moderate sums' on the continent. Then in May, captivated like others by Frederick's notable victory at Prague, he had turned attention more to Frederick by suggesting that he was worth far more than 'little princes here and there'.[20] So he was able to accept, even perhaps suggest, Holderness's proposal in July that, while 'men are not to be furnished from hence; money may . . . enable his Prussian majesty to supply what is wanting on our part'.[21] After Cumberland's army of observation was defeated at Hastenbeck on 27 July, Pitt himself proposed a grant to Prussia and increased money for Hesse and Hanover, while obtaining the agreement of his supporters; 'we must depart from the rigidness of our declarations', he said.[22] He was even more annoyed than other ministers at the king's attempts to secure peace for Hanover with Austrian help, writing with typical bombast of 'the fatal consummation of the impending mischief' and 'black machinations' of Hanoverian ministers and insisting that the English ministers must 'disculpate themselves' from the moves. Newcastle thought Pitt might even resign over the threatened subordination of English to Hanoverian needs and especially the '*change of system*' suggested by 'flinging off the King of Prussia and returning to the Queen of Hungary'.[23] But the British ministers could not give advice on Hanoverian policy until given an opportunity by the king's anger at Cumberland's negotiations at Klosterseven in September, which sacrificed the electorate in order to save the army. Then Pitt was foremost in urging disavowal and active breach of the convention. At length the king was brought to this by the ministers' offer on 7 October to take the army of observation into British pay.

At one stroke this offer increased continental expend-iture sixfold and clearly recognized the German war as in Britain's interest.[24] With Pitt's full support, the disasters of Hastenbeck and Klosterseven had helped to clarify the distinction between a continental policy which was a mere 'Hanover job' and one which could, while still defending Hanover, serve British interests by supporting Prussia. The change was reflected when the army became known as 'His Britannic Majesty's Army in Germany' and acquired a new commander. When Cumberland, humiliated by the king's disapproval, resigned as Captain-General, Frederick was again asked to allow Prince Ferdinand of Brunswick, a distinguished general, to be seconded to command the army in Germany. And it soon became established that his letters passed through the northern Secretary's office, not by way of the Hanoverian authorities.[25] By the end of November Ferdin-and's army was on the move.

However, increasing commitment created political diffi-culties, especially for Pitt with his patriot pretensions – the more so because, while disorder was still rampant at home, the British theatres of war were going badly. In August and September news arrived from America of the fall of Fort William Henry in the strategically vital Hudson valley and of the abandonment of the attempt on Louisburg set in motion by the Devonshire–Pitt administration. Much more immediately embarrassing was the return of the Rochefort expedition at the end of September with very little to show for an estimated expenditure of £1 million. A public outcry ensued, one at least as serious as that Pitt had faced earlier in the year over Byng, possibly rivalling the clamour over Minorca. Anti-Hanoverian sentiment was aroused again, and the outcry was only partly defused by the eventual establish-ment of a commission of enquiry and the court-martial of Sir John Mordaunt, commander-in-chief of the land forces.[26] The black crisis of the administration's early weeks had intens-ified. Chesterfield bewailed the loss of British honour and thought the winter 'must produce a peace of some kind or other; a bad one for us, no doubt'.[27]

In these circumstances, Pitt could hardly assume that his personal supporters, let alone the Tories in parliament – where the expenditure had to be approved – or patriot opin-ion beyond, would follow him in commitment to Germany.

Not surprisingly, he remained very touchy. He even dabbled briefly with the anti-Hanoverian overtones of the popular clamour and, as the opening of parliament approached, kept his distance from administration business. And in his first major speech in December he declared that, while he 'had never been against continental measures when practicable', he 'would not now send a drop of our blood to the Elbe, to be lost in that ocean of gore' – yet another melodramatic statement that was to boomerang on him.[28]

By this time, however, two astounding Prussian victories had occurred: at Rossbach in Saxony on 5 November (an unprecedented blow to French prestige) and against the Austrians at Leuthen a month later (driving them out of Saxony). These victories began to change the fortunes of war decisively. Nevertheless, Pitt's irritability carried over into the continuing negotiations to clarify Anglo-Prussian relations. The British continued to offer a subsidy in return for agreement not to make a separate peace. But Frederick was reluctant to become a mere mercenary dependant. More important, each party still wanted reinforcements from the other, Britain for the reconstituted army fighting France in the west, while Prussia reiterated requests for British troops and a Baltic squadron.[29] This brought from Pitt a violent expostulation to Newcastle late in January against Andrew Mitchell, the greatly respected British representative in Prussia. Pitt professed to see Mitchell as 'not fit to be the instrument of the present system of administration in the vital and essential parts of the Plan of Europe' because he was one of 'the Tools of another System', 'Tools' which were 'perpetually marring every hopeful measure of the present administration'. He demanded – and temporarily secured – Mitchell's replacement. And when Frederick repeated again that he did 'not want money but men', Pitt insisted on standing over Holderness until three in the morning supervising every phrase of the dispatch detailing Britain's final terms – an experience Holderness hoped never to repeat.[30]

Tense weeks of stalemate ensued, until Frederick capitulated, scaling down his requests to two proposals: that a British battalion be sent to help secure the Prussian North Sea port of Emden, recently evacuated by the French and vital for communications with Prince Ferdinand, and that another British raid be made on the French coast. Encouraged by the striking success of Ferdinand's spring campaign, which had driven the French out of Hanover and back towards the Rhine, Pitt accepted the first proposal, provided it did not lead to more demands; he was naturally delighted by the second.[31] On 11 April 1758, a new convention with Prussia was at last signed. The simple document granted a subsidy of £670,000 and bound the two powers not to make a separate peace. An accompanying declaration stated Britain's intention to maintain an army of 50,000 in Germany and to fulfil these two recent requests.

Now the consequent expenditure needed parliamentary approval. All ministers recognized the importance of parliamentary support, but to Pitt it was especially crucial that his claim to an independent stature through command of the Tories should not be undermined.[32] Already he had assiduously courted them on a number of domestic questions. He ostentatiously supported George Townshend's act to remove difficulties in implementing the 1757 Militia Act, despite the doubts those difficulties cast on its value as a patriot shibboleth. He persuaded other ministers to reverse their opposition to George Grenville's act for the better payment of seamen, and conveniently absented himself with the gout while his supporters 'minced and managed' opposition to an untimely Tory motion for shorter parliaments. Most strikingly, he vigorously supported, at court as well as in parliament, a highly contentious habeas corpus bill intended to close gaps in the operation of the writ shown up by the seizing of men for the navy and army. Had the bill not been defeated in the Lords it would have greatly increased the difficulties of recruiting.[33]

Pitt's campaign was helped above all by Frederick the Great's rapidly rising popularity. Frederick's celebration in prints, pamphlets, newspapers and a range of artifacts, the marking of his birthday, 24 January, by '[a]ll England', with 'bonfires, illuminations and French horns playing out of windows all night', helped to unite 'all our parties in his support' and bring the Tories to declare 'they will give Mr Pitt unlimited credit for this session'.[34] So it proved when the new arrangements came before the Commons on 19 April; they passed with little difficulty. And, early in June, despite Pitt's further fears, a vote of credit to allow the necessary subsidy to Hesse-Cassel passed smoothly.[35]

Then, just two weeks later, Pitt completed the clarification of Britain's continental commitment by proposing what he had hitherto so vehemently obstructed – the sending of British troops to Germany to join Ferdinand's army. His first hint quickly grew into the immediate dispatch of nearly 9,000 men.[36] Timing was the key to this further remarkable volte-face. The suggestion was made in the context of ensuring that the second French coastal expedition – set in motion on a larger scale but by the same process as in 1757 – would be sent to sea again. Its initial success around the Channel port of St Malo had already demonstrated its value in allaying Tory anxiety.[37] More important, the proposal was first raised on the very day when the prorogation of parliament removed the most potent forum of public criticism.

There is good evidence to suggest that Pitt had long contemplated this move.[38] He probably held back first, and with good reason, out of fear of Hanoverian influence and Cumberland's role in the administration. In fact, the politics of the coalition had already altered markedly to Pitt's benefit by Cumberland's fortuitous removal the previous October. But Pitt's fears lingered – as suggested by his complaint to his cousin, John, in December that he was 'brokenhearted with the wretched interior of our condition, worse than all the foreign ills which threaten us' and his outburst to Newcastle in January against the 'lurking, diffusive poison' of 'another System'.[39] Furthermore, having been drawn into his forthright public declaration against sending troops, Pitt needed time to extricate himself.[40] He perhaps also needed the assurance of Frederick's and Ferdinand's successes, the latter's capped by a striking victory at Crefeld on 21 June. He was further reassured by being able to carry his supporters into increased financial commitment to Germany. However, he had been clearly warned that they were much more reluctant to accept the sending of troops.[41] And the ensuing public debate was indeed evidence of the powerful shock the move caused[42] – while Pitt's 'inconsistency' on this question long remained a standard charge against him.

So the framework of a continental commitment which remained until 1762 was established. Although the stable subsidy to Prussia was accompanied by a rapid escalation in the demands of Ferdinand's Westphalian army, Britain in fact deployed far fewer troops in Europe than in previous wars – never more than 18,000, compared with 30,000 in America at the war's height – and European costs remained much less than, instead of exceeding, costs elsewhere.[43] Britain's commitment was a minimal one – calculated to be just enough to defend Hanover and keep Prussia in the war against France while not detracting from British priorities elsewhere.

Pitt played a central role in shaping this commitment. He certainly helped to keep it minimal, not only by opposing the sending of troops for so long but also by vigorously resisting the suggestion of a Baltic squadron – which would probably have drawn Britain into complications.[44] But he also clearly recognized the need for a continental commitment; his differences with his colleagues on subsidies and troops were ones of timing and emphasis, not of substance. Although the king still hankered after gains for Hanover, no minister had any real interest in Prussia's problems, let alone grand continental schemes. All agreed that 'money has always been looked upon as the proper and most effective contribution that England could make to a war upon the Continent'.[45] And the process by which the solution was reached strongly suggests that Pitt's truculence was not about strategy or policy but about mollifying his supporters. It was Frederick, not Pitt, who suggested at this time that the 'way to save America is not to suffer the French to become masters of Europe'.[46]

In 1758, there was no guarantee that such a limited commitment would work. As early as July, Ferdinand's request for further reinforcements[47] suggested the frailty of Pitt's main public justification for the Prussian alliance, the claim that, unlike earlier arrangements, it would prevent Britain's being further drawn in.[48] Moreover, although Frederick was undoubtedly a brilliant soldier, he might well not be able to hold his ground against three mighty enemies. There was some justification in Frederick's complaint that Pitt thought only of France and not of Prussia's other foes.[49] It remained to be seen whether this tenuous alliance, together with the Westphalian army, would indeed provide the continental policy that struck the right balance between the spheres of war in Europe and beyond.

Very obvious from the chequered evolution of a continental policy is how rapidly Pitt had come to command respect and influence in the coalition beyond his office, despite his lack of experience. Newcastle would not move on German policy without him. His correspondence with Holderness and his conversations with Louis Michell, the Prussian representative in London – whom Pitt had courted in his earliest days as Secretary of State – and Baron Knyphausen, Frederick's special envoy, confirm his influence. Their reports brought Frederick to recognize Pitt's dominance despite considerable irritation at his opposition to requests for aid, while Joseph Yorke, Hardwicke's soldier–diplomat son, on a special mission to Prussia in April 1758, described Pitt to Frederick's ministers as the man who by then played 'the leading role in England', 'the life and soul of the whole English ministry'. By mid-1758, Frederick was urging his envoys to pay particular attention to Pitt and to explain policies 'aux ministres anglais et principalement au sieur Pitt' – a mode of expression that soon became standard in his letters – while Holderness became merely the channel for formal communications.[50] Similarly, the leading minister of Hanover, Gerlach von Munchausen, very soon regarded Pitt as the minister making the key decisions.[51] Even in the closet, Pitt, although still acknowledging his need for Newcastle's skills, could take the lead on the tricky question of a commander-in-chief to replace Cumberland, while Holderness stood silent.[52]

Such a rapid consolidation of Pitt's position suggests recognition of some intellectual power and cogency of vision. Certainly Joseph Yorke recognized 'much genius and very great talents'.[53] There is, however, more direct evidence – in his tactics over the habeas corpus bill, for example, or his harassment of Newcastle over estimates for the army in Germany[54] – that Pitt's rising influence was asserted less by persuasiveness of argument than by sheer force of personality, coupled with fear of the havoc he could wreak in parliament if not placated. And the king's hostility had not abated. In the coalition's first month he continued 'very severe upon Mr Pitt, both with regard to his abilities, and his intentions'. In 1758, over both the German war and the habeas corpus bill, the king thought of replacing Pitt. But, in Yorke's view, the king's advancing years made him prefer peace to swimming against the current – and Pitt was able to consolidate his position.[55]

. . .

THE AMERICAN WAR, 1757–60

Meanwhile, operations had been gathering momentum with far less controversy in the other major sphere of war – North America. This was certainly within Pitt's area of responsibility, and it is much more justifiable to assume that in it he took initiatives – with the help of Anson, First Lord of the Admiralty, and Sir John Ligonier, appointed Commander-in-Chief in Cumberland's place. Yet here, as for other theatres, important decisions were made jointly. Indeed, in drawing up orders for the coalition's first major campaign in America, that of 1758, Pitt anxiously sought Newcastle's help; Newcastle declined to come up from his Christmas retreat but he read the dispatches, while Pitt worked with Holderness.[56]

Pitt's anxiety was understandable. The coalition had begun, six months earlier, by sending reinforcements to the sizeable military and naval forces already in America.[57] Before they could arrive, however, the attack on Louisburg had been abandoned and Fort William Henry had fallen. Then the fleet in America with which Pitt had hoped to begin an early campaign the next year was dispersed by storm.

These reverses threw into sharp relief the problems of warfare in America, as the British commitment grew from the diffuse, defensive and ill-supported operations of 1755–56 into an offensive against Canada, shaped first under a new Commander-in-Chief in America, the Earl of Loudoun, appointed in 1756, and substantially reinforced by the Devonshire–Pitt administration in 1756–57. British troops had not before fought major campaigns there. In attacking Canada overland, they had to learn a new kind of continental warfare, opening lines of advance and supply over vast uninhabited distances and difficult terrains. Nor had the colonies ever co-operated on such a scale. They were notoriously reluctant to vote supplies, and provincial troops, while they knew the country, were often ill-trained and unreliable. The delays a cumbersome administration in Britain could impose on the arrival of reinforcements and supplies were vividly illustrated by the four months it took Loudoun's troops to get away in 1756. Then early in 1757 the problems of co-operation and communications across the Atlantic were demonstrated when Pitt altered the priorities for Loudoun's attack from Quebec to Louisburg and his tardy and imprecise dispatches deprived Loudoun of essential information. Above all, the 1757 expedition was doomed by unpredictable weather, which allowed three French fleets to slip through the western squadron's watch and congregate at Louisburg, delayed the arrival of the British reinforcements, and kept the expedition cooped up at Halifax, deprived of information by the fog that shrouded Louisburg.[58]

Failure led to the recall of Loudoun, determined chiefly by the disgrace of his patron, Cumberland, if precipitated by a characteristically impetuous outburst from Pitt in the Commons in December. Stung by criticism of army expenses by the Tory William Beckford, he dwelt on Loudoun's 'Inactivity', declaring that 'he had no hopes for this year nor could have none from the next whilst the American Affairs continued in the hands they were'.[59] Failure also meant that a totally new campaign had to be planned for 1758 – and without the benefit of Loudoun's hard-won experience.[60] Only in December – after the King's Speech had promised action in America[61] – did serious planning for the 1758 campaign begin.[62]

By this time, Pitt had received advice through a number of intermediaries.[63] However, the strategy he outlined in instructions on 30 December followed no one piece of advice. Taking up Loudoun's insistence on the need for an early start to the campaign,[64] it proposed a two-pronged attack on Canada, the capture of Louisburg once again taking priority over an advance up the Hudson valley by way of Crown Point on Lake Champlain. Instead of the long-advocated third main route of attack on Canada from Lake Ontario there was to be (to satisfy the southern colonies) a subsidiary expedition against Fort Duquesne in the Ohio valley.[65] British regulars were concentrated in the main force to attack Louisburg, comprising 14,000 soldiers and a large fleet of 23 ships of the line and additional frigates and commanded by Major-General Jeffrey Amherst and Admiral Edward Boscawen. For the Hudson valley campaign, the mainly colonial force under Major-General James Abercromby, Loudoun's deputy and now his successor as Commander-in-Chief, was to assemble by 1 May at Albany. The southern colonies were to provide troops to advance into the Ohio, to be led by John Forbes.

There was nothing innovative about the main lines of this strategy but there were features of Pitt's instructions that were to remain characteristic throughout the war. For naval operations, Boscawen's very specific additional instructions followed those of the previous year in insisting, probably at Anson's behest, on the priority of 'conjunct operations of His Majesty's Fleet and Land forces' over other objectives, such as the pursuit of the French fleet or protection of trade.[66] In military matters, in place of Loudoun's overall control of operations, the command under Abercromby was 'divided . . . effectively into three';[67] Amherst received instructions direct from London and both he and Forbes corresponded directly with Pitt. Furthermore, the instructions – for such distant and little-known areas – were notable for denying commanders any discretion over initial objectives and, particularly in connection with the attack on Louisburg, for the detail in which preparations and the main lines of action were dictated.

Much more remarkable were Pitt's moves towards more conciliatory relations with the colonies. He had evidently listened to criticisms that Loudoun preferred 'military to civil power' and had exerted 'too much authority over the people of the country, not treating the provincial troops as well as they deserved'. He was well aware of the bitter disputes between Loudoun and colonial authorities, for example with Governor Pownall of Massachusetts over quartering of soldiers.[68] Abercromby's instructions suggested more co-operative relations with colonial governors in place of the clear superiority envisaged for Loudoun.[69] Furthermore, now, in Pitt's detailed instructions to governors about the raising of provincial troops – on which the 1758 campaign relied much more than previously – the British government did not merely take responsibility for supplying, transporting and arming these troops. In order 'that no Encouragement may be wanting in this great and salutary Attempt', it also promised, from parliament, 'a proper Compensation' for other expenses incurred in raising them.[70] Such compensation was not new,[71] but the systematization of requisition and prior promise of recompense was. And it relieved Abercromby of much of the tiresome negotiation that had plagued Loudoun. The letters to governors and Abercromby's instructions also removed the grievance that hitherto all provincial officers had ranked behind all regular officers by providing that they be placed after those of equivalent rank.[72] These concessions immediately facilitated the voting of troops by colonial assemblies, for example in Massachusetts, even if they by no means removed all difficulties.[73]

In sum, Pitt's administrative changes might well be called 'almost a total revolution in America'.[74] The very high expectations of the 1758 campaign were also characteristic of him. Abercromby's 'great, and it is to be hoped decisive campaign' was to attack either Montreal or Quebec or both; after taking Louisburg, Boscawen and Amherst were to proceed against Quebec or other places in the area, or even to detach forces to attack 'Forts and Places on rivers Mobile and Mississippi' in the south.[75] The outcome was much more limited. Louisburg fell without much difficulty on 26 July, but later than hoped, and Boscawen and Amherst considered no further major action advisable. Abercromby's advance to Crown Point made a good beginning, but was decisively turned back at Ticonderoga earlier in July, at the expense of nearly 3,000 men. The only success of his campaign was a side attack, in September, along the Mohawk valley to the west, to raid Fort Frontenac at the head of the St Lawrence. By that time, Abercromby's accounts of his failure had secured his recall to England and replacement by Amherst.[76] Forbes succeeded at Fort Duquesne – and renamed it Pittsburgh – only in November. And both his and Abercromby's dispatches bear vivid witness to the difficulties of their campaigns, not least that of working with provincial soldiers.[77]

Arguably, Loudoun's plans would have had more success.[78] Pitt's over-optimistic expectations and his equally excessive 'melancholy' reaction to the failure at Ticonderoga – which Bute thought 'affects you too greatly'[79] – reflected how little he yet understood the difficulties of American continental warfare. Nevertheless, the British had won their first major victory. The news, coming simultaneously with that of the success of the second stage of the French coastal expedition in temporarily seizing Cherbourg and destroying its fortifications, at last lifted the gloomy mood at home. Now, to parallel the earlier celebration of Ferdinand's success at Crefeld, 'British' victories could be marked by displaying the guns of Cherbourg in Hyde Park and parading the standards taken at Louisburg to St Paul's.[80]

The 1758 campaign established a pattern for later American operations. Before its fortunes were fully known, Pitt had already set the colonial governors to raise '*at least as large a body of men as they did for the last campaign*'.[81] At the end of December, orders were sent for a three-pronged attack very similar in its main lines to that of 1758: an advance from Louisburg up the St Lawrence to Quebec under new commanders, General James Wolfe and Admiral Charles Saunders, another up the Hudson valley and to Lake Ontario under Amherst, and further operations to the south.[82] More clearly than ever, the planning of the campaign and the administrative effort of getting away Saunders's considerable fleet and body of transports was a collaborative effort, chiefly of Pitt, Ligonier, Anson and the Admiralty and Navy Boards. (As in 1758, the main body of regular troops was already in America.) Pitt seems to have been decisive in Abercromby's recall, Ligonier in the decision to send Amherst with the provincial troops, while he and Anson had preponderant influence in choice of officers. As before, Pitt did what he could to hasten preparations.[83]

The story of this campaign is dominated by the drama of the attack on Quebec: the long silence after the expedition left Halifax on 6 June, a month later than planned, then depressing accounts of great difficulties, followed, only two days later on 16 October, by news of the dramatic scaling of the Heights of Abraham and the battle which secured the city – at the cost of the deaths of both commanders, Wolfe and the Marquis de Montcalm, which tinged the delirious rejoicing with heroic tragedy.[84] But the margin of success was narrow. The difficulties of the following winter illustrated the tenuous British hold on the city, which was almost broken in the spring by siege from a much larger French force. Only the timely arrival of a squadron from Halifax relieved the threat.[85] And there was much less success on the inland route. Ticonderoga and Crown Point fell, and control of Lake Ontario and the lakes beyond was secured by taking Niagara. But Amherst could not advance on either Montreal or Quebec,[86] and little more came of the ambitious plans for the south than the rebuilding of Fort Dusquesne.[87]

Nevertheless, the successes were noteworthy because they came despite a diversionary threat of a French invasion at home rising from late 1758 to a peak in mid-1759. To meet

the threat, naval resources (except manpower) were reasonable but military defences were deplorably slender. For
long Pitt affected to play down the danger, to the despair
of his colleagues. However, in May, to meet the manpower
problem, he proposed that the militia regiments in various
counties should be called into active service in home defence.
When this 'embodiment' proceeded with surprising enthusiasm and success, it redounded greatly to Pitt's credit.[88] The
threatened invasion was eventually deflected by Ferdinand's
major victory at Minden in August, and especially by two
great naval triumphs, Boscawen's against the French Mediterranean fleet off Lagos in August and Hawke's over the Brest
fleet in November. The latter marked success at last for the
western squadron; both gave Britain decisive naval superiority for the rest of the war.[89]

In this context, the success of the further campaign necessary to complete control of Canada was virtually assured. This
time, Pitt's instructions – otherwise in now standard form –
allowed Amherst a discretion (only partially conceded in
1759) to direct operations 'as you shall judge proper . . .
from your knowledge of the Countries . . . and from emergent
circumstances', in both 'the vigorous attack of Montreal' and
in 'the Southern operations'.[90] Amherst's further version of
the three-pronged attack, from Quebec, Lake Champlain and
Lake Ontario, proceeded this time without a hitch once
Quebec was resecured. On 7 September, Montreal fell.

. . .

WIDENING WAR, 1758-62

Naval supremacy and success in America allowed the deployment of resources elsewhere. Indeed, already in 1758, long
before that success was assured, Pitt had initiated an expedition to the West Indies, against the important French island
of Martinique, at the expense of troop reinforcements to
America and despite Anson's concern at sending so many
ships beyond Europe. The aim here was not defensive but
'to distress [the] enemy in [a] principal branch of commerce
and cut off a considerable source of riches'.[91] By May 1759,
after a repulse from Martinique, the other major French
island, Guadeloupe, was taken. This turn to the offensive in
an area where there was little immediate French challenge

came from Pitt. And he insisted that both troops and ships should stay in the West Indies, again despite Anson's objections. However, the wider offensive had general support in the ministry. After the fall of Canada, Pitt redirected his energies to the West Indies, applying there the techniques of the American campaign in a stream of instructions which required troops from America for a large expedition against Martinique while promising transports from England. The expedition continued, again with general approval, through 1761. The eventual fall of Martinique in February 1762 capped some previous lesser successes.[92]

Even earlier, Pitt had also taken the lead in extending the war to the West African coast. In his first ministry, he had responded more warmly than other ministers to the urgings of the Quaker merchant, Thomas Cumming, to attack French stations there. Cumming's plans were taken up again 'with Vigor' in 1758, leading to the capture of Senegal in May and Gorée at the end of the year. Careful steps were taken to secure both conquests.[93]

Operations in India were a different matter. Robert Clive's victory at Plassey in June 1757, which made British influence dominant in Bengal, was certainly momentous for the Company. So too was the slower defeat of the French challenge on the Carnatic coast by victories at Wandiwash in January 1760 and Pondicherry a year later. However, both developments were, in the eyes of administration and public alike, subordinate to the main theatres of war. Moreover, for India, the issue was not one of planning and implementing expeditions, but of responding to requests for help from the East India Company – which came through the southern Secretary. In 1754 and 1755 Holderness had persuaded the administration to respond generously with ships and the first regular troops. Pitt continued this trend, even initiating contacts with the Company's Secret Committee. Further help along these lines continued to 1760 as resources permitted, while from 1757 the Company was paid an annual grant of £20,000 to help to defray its military expenses.[94]

Pitt certainly won warm gratitude for this help.[95] And in the dark days of late 1757, he seized the opportunity of Clive's success to praise him lavishly as '*that heaven-born general*'. However, Pitt did not succumb to Clive's attempt to lure the government with visions of sovereignty and rich financial rewards into direct involvement in territorial aggrandizement in India.[96] The most Clive could secure from Pitt was a projected expedition, early in 1761, to seize the French naval base on Mauritius, so important to operations in India. Although generally supported in the ministry, the plan was dropped when the situation in India improved.[97]

Forces for the abortive Mauritius expedition were to have been diverted from another French coastal attack, on the island of Belle Île. The planning for this from October 1760 well illustrates the process of decision-making at the height of the war. The initiative, once again an attempt to relieve pressure in Germany, came from Pitt. However, he had to exert a mixture of artful persuasion, high-handedness and threatening rage, both in some unusually large ministerial meetings and in the closet, to win over his reluctant colleagues whose co-operation was essential. Interrupted by the death of George II on 25 October, then by winter and the proposed Mauritius diversion, the expedition went forward in March – with the help of the new king's favourite, the Earl of Bute, by then Pitt's fellow Secretary of State. Belle Île fell in June.[98] Pitt could cajole by force of personality; but he never exercised an unquestioned dominance, nor could he manage even his spheres of the war without the co-operation of colleagues.[99]

. . .

'THAT GENIUS': THE GREAT WAR MINISTER?

As the responsible Secretary of State – by default, not choice – Pitt certainly left his mark on the war beyond Europe, if not as much as traditionally thought, and probably no more so, in America anyway, than Fox, for example, might have done. A world-wide strategy was impossible. The difficulty of communications across oceans and continents made it so, to say nothing of a cumbersome administration. Pitt did not even give an innovative thrust to American strategy – although his dispatches suggest he kept attention focused on it. To many, his dispatches seemed to breathe vigour and urgency. Forbes wrote of 'being actuated by your spirits' in capturing the fort he renamed Pittsburgh. Later, in the after-glow of victory, Americans remembered a 'new Minister' who 'by an animating Letter to each of the Provinces gave a turn to their drooping Spirits'.[100] Pitt's conciliatory attitude to the colonies certainly helped the mobilization of their resources for the immediate task; however, his colleagues recognized as well as he did the primacy of the American war and the conditions necessary for its success – as outlined by Joseph Yorke in July 1757 – and when Pitt later tried to claim that in 1756 he had found 'America unsupported by a preference for Hanover', he was, justifiably, 'contradicted flatly'.[101] The commanders in America overcame the problems on the ground – and there is something in the arguments that in this they were hindered more than helped by Pitt. The detail of his dispatches was not always appropriate and they were received relatively late in the preparations for the next campaign. The successive replacements of Loudoun and Abercromby delayed victory by removing their hard-won experience of unfamiliar conditions.[102] In London, when his health allowed, Pitt pushed vigorously for results from the creaking administrative machinery. However, he did not envisage, let alone undertake, any fundamental reform or attempt to provide the ongoing planning which might have made ambitious visions feasible. And his conciliatory attitude to the colonies aggravated long-term problems of imperial relations of which his incoming dispatches constantly reminded him,[103] not least by placing the financial burden of defence on Britain. Amherst's doubts whether ministers were 'thoroughly sensible of the vast expenses attending offensive operations' certainly applied to Pitt.[104]

Beyond his sphere, Pitt was by 1760 more obviously than ever the dominant Secretary, his correspondence with Holderness on policy matters dying away to a trickle.[105] Military commanders and diplomats, both British and foreign, regarded Pitt as the animating force in the conduct of the war.[106] Foreign ministers in London habitually made contact with him as 'the effective minister', regardless of department.[107] The German war situation and policy were discussed not only with Granby, commander of the British forces in Germany, but more notably in a long and mutually congratulatory exchange of letters with Prince Ferdinand.[108] Frederick the Great's expressions of confidence in Pitt grew steadily warmer – if not entirely without suspicion or ulterior motive. Faced with military crisis in August 1759, Frederick rested his hopes on Pitt's 'firmness and integrity'. As prospects of peace arose, his reliance on Pitt's goodwill and confidential communications to him increased. Time and again, his envoys were told to speak first to Pitt and only then, and as guided by him, to other ministers.[109] On occasion he wrote to Pitt himself, responding lavishly in kind to Pitt's public praise, assuring him, on the death of George II, of continuing faith in Pitt's 'true Roman character', of which his ministry had given such striking evidence.[110] Obviously, to Frederick, Pitt had become the mainstay of his alliance with Britain and Britain's continental war effort.

Such clear dominance shows how the opportunities offered by the Secretary's office could be exploited to stretch its constitutional limits and must modify recent refreshingly sceptical reassessments of Pitt's role.[111] However, in diplomacy, quiescent in wartime anyway, Pitt was less prominent. His first major initiative, the approach to Spain offering the return of Gibraltar, was a desperate gamble (and clearly shaped by European thinking) and fell flat, although Spain, if uncommitted, remained friendly.[112] Holderness conducted crucial negotiations with the Dutch and other northern maritime states over neutral shipping rights in 1758–59, although Pitt's skills were essential in getting through parliament the controversial Act of 1759, designed to placate these states by controlling the activities of British privateers.[113] The biggest test of skills – the negotiation of peace, yet to come – was to suggest Pitt's abilities lay more in organizing expeditions than diplomacy.

By 1760 – when Britain had won unprecedented victories giving her dominance over the French in all areas of their world-wide competition – it was evident that the two spheres of the war, in Europe and beyond, had indeed been held in productive balance. This 'true consummation'[114] of the blue-water policy had been achieved not out of any broad strategic vision, but as a result of an *ad hoc* process of adjustment to the unique circumstances of this war – a learning process in which Pitt shared as much as others. This he publicly admitted in 1759, when he declared that 'he had unlearned his juvenile errors, and thought no longer that England could do it all by herself'.[115] Although far readier to accept European commitments than this confession allows, only gradually did he, along with others, come to recognize that

German measures not only would not hinder 'the vigour to be exerted in America' but could give 'evident advantage' to operations 'both by sea and in America', and to insist on 'the totality of carrying on the war . . . in all its parts'.[116] He had no grand strategic vision; rather, the war was extended piecemeal, planned only year by year. And the coastal raids on France – Pitt's most distinctive contribution – were not successful in their strategic purpose of diverting French resources from Germany.[117]

Moreover, the 'system' by which 'America had been conquered in Germany' into which Pitt later elevated his learning process was more political than military in conception and hardly original. Twenty years before, in a different war, Hardwicke had recognized that 'America must be fought for in Europe'; Frederick the Great first made the same point in this war.[118] And Pitt's claim overlooked the very chequered fortunes of the German war, where the situation of Frederick, 'attacked and surrounded by so many considerable powers . . . concerted with such united force against him',[119] was always vulnerable. In August 1759, a victory of the Austrians and Russians at Kunersdorf virtually wiped out his army. In October 1760, he reached his lowest ebb when the Russians occupied Berlin. He was still capable of brilliant recovery, but his resources were desperately over-extended. The possibility remained ever present that Frederick might be forced to a peace requiring unwelcome sacrifices by Britain. Pitt generally supported the sending of reinforcements to Ferdinand's Rhineland army, but sometimes in 1760 the state of the war was such as to make him hesitate.[120] Certainly, at times – after the spring victories of 1758, for example, or after Minden in 1759 – Ferdinand's function could seem to be merely to protect Frederick's western flank rather than to serve any British purpose – although in 1760 the French again threatened Hanover.

Furthermore, success in all spheres of the war depended on contributions with which Pitt had little to do.[121] Anson chiefly, helped by others connected with the navy, managed the difficulties hindering its mobilization and – as Pitt was later to acknowledge[122] – found the practical solutions which allowed the western squadron to fulfil its crucial functions, at least in 1759. Ligonier's professional skill was important to the military effort, although it also owed something to other ministers – including Pitt's perhaps unduly famed opening up of Highland recruiting[123] and, more certainly, Newcastle's generally competent oversight of the commissariat. Probably the continuing contribution on policy of Granville as Lord President was important, too. Newcastle had noticed, very early in the war, that 'Mr Pitt seems better with him than anybody'. Certainly Pitt (again ready to acknowledge earlier mistakes) was later to claim that 'to his patronage, to his friendship, and instruction, I owe whatever I am'.[124]

Above all, Newcastle's skill and experience at the Treasury in activating Britain's superior fiscal system allowed the raising, often in critical circumstances, of ever-increasing financial resources. These ensured that no essential part of Britain's war effort – unlike France's – was restricted by lack of money. By contrast, Pitt was plainly irresponsible about the unprecedented costs of war – the national debt almost doubled, the annual cost more than twice that of the last war.[125] He was still 'impracticable', as contemporaries put it, 'an Inigo Jones in politics, a man of great ideas, a projector of noble and magnificent plans', but, like architects, never considering himself 'as concerned to find the means'.[126]

Even more fundamental to Britain's remarkable success were circumstances hardly attributable to any personal influence: a rising population which eased manpower problems, the greater resources of the British colonies, the neutrality of Spain for these crucial years, circumstances on the continent which, while diverting French resources,[127] were not generally seen to require major British (or Hanoverian) involvement yet gave Britain an ally willing to tolerate limited commitment and able to hold out against the odds. These circumstances were crucial in allowing the navy to be, for the only time in this century, a 'decisive instrument of power'.[128]

To a large extent, Pitt fulfilled the high expectations of him as he took office.[129] His energy, remarkably sustained despite debilitating illness and clearly evident in his papers and the comments of observers, led Newcastle to exclaim, after Pitt's resignation, that '[w]ith all his faults ... [t]here is no one so able to push an expedition as he' – although to Hardwicke the successful Havana expedition of 1762 proved he was not indispensable.[130] His spirit, to which so many responded, was typically evident in the invasion crisis – if essential measures were largely left to others. He was decisive where others would equivocate. His nerve, and a vision of British interests of greater clarity than that of his colleagues, can be seen in the determined shaping of the Prussian alliance. His courage and vision gave him a determination to press France to the limits when others might well have compromised.[131] He was 'a man who (in the political sense) *fears neither God nor Devil*'.[132] To this extent he left his imprint on the war. But no longer can it be suggested that, largely single-handedly, he shaped its strategy, directed it and determined its outcome.[133]

.   .   .

SHAPING A REPUTATION: COALITION POLITICS, 1757–61

Yet, to many contemporaries, including some close to governing circles, Pitt seemed indeed the 'directing' minister, the 'Minister as to Measures', while Newcastle was merely the disposer of 'Places', the 'Minister of Numbers'.[134] And, as the crescendo of celebration of victories by parades, services, bonfires and peals of bells rose and addresses of congratulation poured in to the king, the lustre of victory fell almost exclusively on Pitt. Even the first successes were attributed 'cheifly' to Pitt's 'Abilities and Zeal'. By 1759–60, partisan notes were muted and acknowledgement grew much more universal that Pitt was

> that great man, who had raised us from a very low state of political depression, not only in the eyes of all Europe, but in our own opinion, to make rapid progress to the highest state of national glory in which ever we had been.[135]

Thomas Percival ascribed the 'glorious success of this year . . . solely, and under God, to Mr Pitt'; Horace Walpole considered that 'it will require ten votes of the House of Commons before people will believe that it is the Duke of Newcastle that has done all this and not Mr Pitt'; and the 'Citizens of London', buoyed by prosperity unusual in war, lavished their compliments in the inscription on the foundation stone of their new 'Pitt's Bridge' at Blackfriars.[136] Undertones of criticism never entirely disappeared, yet Pitt seemed indeed to have performed the unprecedented feat of 'still uniting, the uncommon Characters of *Minister* and *Patriot*'.[137]

Some reasons for such a meteoric ascendancy are obvious. Credit for the seemingly miraculous lifting of the nation from the depths of defeat widely attributed to national degeneracy[138] accrued naturally to the most obviously new figure in the administration – especially when he began with a public image greater than any preceding minister. He was soon so clearly the dominant Secretary of State, while the most valued victories – people framed lists of them to hang on their walls[139] – came in his sphere of responsibility.

It is not often realized, however, how Pitt's ascendancy was further enhanced by artifice, not least by the way he operated in the coalition. He did not, in fact, need to bully his colleagues into submission to his views; Newcastle might often fret and fume over Pitt's 'uncertainty of . . . temper', but he now readily accepted him as a 'man of great merit, weight and consequence', consulted him carefully over patronage, and showed little sign of the old jealousy. Indeed, it is striking how quickly Pitt overcame his initial weak situation in the coalition.[140] Nevertheless, Pitt often chose to hector and harass his colleagues. Where this was not simply the effects of illness compounding an increasing arrogance, it sprang from a compulsion to distance himself, to protect that independence of Newcastle and the Old Corps he had asserted in the manoeuvres following Pelham's death.

After the frictions of 1757–58 over the German war and the habeas corpus bill, which could have broken the coalition, this compulsion might well have been eased by success. Instead, the lengths to which it took Pitt were displayed in two notable incidents at the height of the war. Early in 1759, with financial crisis threatening, Pitt was prepared, largely to oblige his City ally, William Beckford, to subvert Legge's plans for the year's supply because they included a duty on sugar. When drawn into public debate in defence of Beckford, he disingenuously paraded his detachment from Treasury business.[141] At the time, he dramatically lost the sympathy of the House. Members 'groaned as he spoke'. Tories attacked his continental measures and criticized the troubles of the West Indian expedition, while 'he hung down his head and was silent'.[142]

Later in 1759, Pitt made a prolonged and eventually successful attempt to have a vacancy in the Order of the Garter given to his ally but largely ignored colleague, Earl Temple.

Pitt set himself against the king's equal determination not to give to a man he despised this prized and personal honour, which would also recognize Pitt's status. Pitt's tactics, in this instance and the first, combined bluster and bullying of Newcastle with threats that he 'would not undertake the House of Commons' and might even retire and let the king try 'another Plan' (which Pitt 'fancied he had').[143]

These incidents also illustrate the way Pitt both asserted and abused departmental autonomy as it suited him for the same purposes of distancing himself from his colleagues. At the height of the Garter affair, Pitt took exaggerated offence at an apparent trespass on his domain when Newcastle failed to inform him of a ludicrous peace feeler made to Joseph Yorke at The Hague by an unidentified woman.[144] On questions of war financing Pitt was always ready to harry in private and abuse the Treasury 'most exceedingly' in public, while equally publicly dissociating himself from any responsibility. Similar unpredictability later provoked the comment, 'Was there ever such a whirligig as this great man?' Well might Newcastle complain that it was 'indeed amazing that a person who by his own measures has thrown the nation into an immense expense . . . shall think to lay the blame on the Treasury' and refuse any collective responsibility.[145]

Pitt did not, in fact, 'despotically' govern his colleagues, terrorizing Newcastle and dictating to other departments, as the government contractor, Sir George Colebrooke, believed; but Colebrooke's vivid account powerfully conveys the impact of Pitt's personality.[146] As time passed, Pitt was more prepared to admit the support of his colleagues, and relations eased.[147] Even the old king, it seems, was won over in his last months.[148] But Pitt's tactics ensured that the coalition never melded into a genuine alliance – and that he remained distinguished from others as successes mounted.

Even more important in shaping his reputation were Pitt's parliamentary speeches. Beyond question, he was the administration's chief spokesman in parliament, its public front, presenting the war to a wider audience. Yet he seldom acted as a conventional leader of the House, avoiding association with the pre-session circular to administration supporters and other normal ways of courting support, while readily leaving the drafting of the King's Speech to Hardwicke (although he was carefully consulted).[149] Similarly, his speeches often seemed to serve his own purposes more than those of the administration. This was most obvious in his first major speech in the critical situation of December 1757 which seemed to a foreign observer to be that of a tribune of the people rather than a Secretary of State. His characteristic impetuosity perhaps then carried him further than he intended, not only into quite unmeasured attack on Loudoun, accentuated by equally extravagant 'eastern panegyric' on Clive, but also into his initial dramatic declaration against sending British soldiers to Europe. Horace Walpole, who noted how Pitt 'warmed himself' in this speech ('admired almost beyond any of his orations'), remarked elsewhere that 'no man ever knew so little what he was going to say'.[150]

But, as Pitt's confidence grew with success, Walpole also noted the 'art' with which he seemed 'to avoid all ostentation of power, while he assumed everything to himself but the disposition of the money'. Yet Pitt insisted – while he 'provoked, called for, defied objections' – that 'heaps of millions must be raised' for the dramatic struggle he pictured in both Germany and America.[151] In November 1759, Pitt dwelt on continuing victories 'with great address, seeming to waive any merit, but stating our success in a manner that excluded all others from a share in it'. Again, he dramatized his own role and the continued effort still needed. 'He thought the stone almost rolled up to the top of the hill, but it might roll back with dreadful repercussion.' The 'least omission' in any part of the war 'might be fatal to the whole'; the country had resources to fight on for years.[152] By this time, Walpole had succumbed to Pitt's spell, writing ecstatically to him of 'the lustre you have thrown on this country', and claiming 'Mr Pitt himself had done more for Britain than any orator for Rome. Our three last campaigns had overrun more world than they conquered in a century'. Other sceptical critics likewise could not resist some admiration of Pitt's major speeches.[153]

Crucial to Pitt's swelling reputation, as to his independent power base, was the support of the Tories. His careful courting of them through the crises of 1757 and the manoeuvres of 1758, if not always successful, limited damage to his patriot reputation, so that 'British' victories, when they came, fell the more exclusively to him.[154] The courting continued, notably in 1760 with support for a Tory bill to enforce the property qualifications of members of parliament and, more consistently, over militia issues. Already Pitt had ostentatiously helped to smooth difficulties over the implementation of the 1757 Act and paraded reliance on the militia in the invasion scare of 1759. The three militia issues of 1760 he took up with varying commitment and success. A bill to establish a Scottish militia was abandoned, as was the most fundamental question, that of prolonging the term of the English Militia Act. A scheme to relieve counties of the burden of family allowances to militiamen was eventually passed only in emasculated form.[155] Over Pitt's deft manoeuvres through these difficulties, Newcastle protested (with some exaggeration) at 'a most ridiculous situation':

> Mr Pitt, by his situation and consequence, is at the head of the House of Commons, of which the Tories scarce make a sixth part; and all *extrajudicial* business, is to be agreed, and concerted with them, without any notice taken of our Friends, who compose the majority.[156]

Newcastle missed the point. Pitt wanted not to lead but to be distinguished from the majority – without endangering the administration. The disappointments of militia supporters displayed Pitt's lack of a majority in the ordinary sense. But, as his rhetoric resounded with the bells of victory, Pitt looked for political strength in other ways. His manoeuvres, while certainly not holding all Tories,[157] paraded and consolidated his independence while helping him to monopolize credit for success.

At the same time, the message was trumpeted to a wider audience by the unsolicited aid of his public advocates. The carefully tailored comment of the *Monitor*, the organ of Pitt's City-Tory ally, Beckford, provides one acute register of the movement of opinion.[158] In July 1757, it reflected the uncertainties of the popular Tory sentiment dominant in the City with its sharp warning that Pitt's coalition with Newcastle might 'induce a belief that he, who was adored for his upright professions, had veered about, deserted the cause of his country' – while soon hoping, with others, that Pitt might triumph over the 'faction', the 'old junto', which had undermined him the year before. Pitt was rescued from blame for the Rochefort fiasco by a similar argument. The next year, the *Monitor* sharply registered the shock of the sending of British troops to Germany by drawing back from growing support for more limited intervention – while using the same 'faction' argument speciously to exonerate Pitt and suggest he had been 'over-ruled' by other ministers. The first victories, which, the *Monitor* argued, reflected '*a dazzling splendor*' on Pitt's character, enabled the paper to return, by early 1759, to defend his policies against biting criticism. By 1759–60, there was no longer any need for circumspection as it reflected widely held views in claiming that the people were 'so thoroughly convinced' of Pitt's merit, 'that all the power of darkness will never be able to deprive him of their confidence and applause'. Nevertheless, the paper continued to reiterate the 'faction' argument even more vehemently (echoing Pitt's 'hot' friends in the City) as it answered continuing undercurrents of criticism and reflected fears that Pitt's policies might be undermined.[159] Pitt's manoeuvres for independence bore their fruit; he alone was distinguished as the great war minister.

Walpole described Pitt's 'greatness' as 'unfinished' or 'artificial', depending as it did not only on the 'vacancy of great men' among 'his predecessors, now his coadjutors', but also 'on his words' and his 'art'. Sceptics who saw through Pitt's 'art' were not few in number. One, Elizabeth Montagu, ruthlessly mocked his studied detachment and the 'eloquence, that did everything for you'. That eloquence inspired 'superstitious veneration' which ascribed all success to him and all failures to others and persuaded people that he 'did really work' miracles.[160] Chesterfield, who knew Pitt even better, saw him 'set out with acting the patriot', then, as a minister, managing 'with such ability' that, while he served the king's Hanoverian ends more than any before him had dared, 'He still preserved all his credit and popularity with the Publick. . . . So much easier it is to deceive than undeceive Mankind.'[161]

Such comments rightly saw the artifice in Pitt's reputation, enhanced as it was by a dominating personality, sometimes specious rhetoric and subtle propaganda. Yet to recognize this artifice is by no means to deny his real contribution. His service in the House of Commons was of the greatest value, and the solid base of his dominance. The remarkable ease with which parliament voted ever-increasing sums for the war owed much to him (if much also to Newcastle's continued management of the Old Corps[162]). Particularly important was Pitt's careful presentation of the German war. An early example of what became his standard tactics is perhaps most striking. In January 1758, when the issue was still very sensitive, he disguised a vote for the Hanoverian army with lavish praise of the King of Prussia and attacks on the Convention of Klosterseven, while insisting that all available forces were by then directed against France. Michell recognized the unprecedented unity of parliament in support of the Hanoverian army as 'the work of this minister', and Newcastle had good reason for satisfaction.[163] Pitt's defences of alliance with 'the Protestant Hero' were vital to public perceptions of it. Of the 1758–59 session, Walpole wrote that Pitt was 'absolute master, and if he can coin twenty millions, may command them'; the unanimity of 1759–60 was even more lyrically extolled.[164] By this time, Pitt's leading colleagues were convinced that without the strength given by Pitt's wider popularity the administration could neither carry on the war nor make peace.[165] To this extent, while Pitt capitalized so fruitfully on the new political strength that had come to him in 1756–57, his achievement was an important part of the process of successfully mobilizing the resources of the eighteenth-century polity for war.

More than that. As Walpole recognized, Pitt's 'passion for fame and the grandeur of his ideas' made him aspire 'to redeem the honour of his country', as 'he taught the nation to speak again as England used to speak to foreign powers'. He dramatized the struggle against France 'as if he meant . . . that his administration should decide which alone should exist as a nation, Britain or France'. Thus Pitt came to personify and articulate, with unique panache, the national mood of growing self-confidence. At this major milestone in Britain's emergence as a great power, he epitomized that competition with France which now added the new dimension of clear imperial supremacy to Britain's status. So he came to be seen as indeed 'that Genius', the great war minister.[166]

In the process, however, his already warped personality was fatally moulded. True, for once his furious energy, at least in part unleashed by the vagaries of his mental illness, was harnessed to his formidable intelligence in service to the state. But the burdens of office and physical illness weighed heavy on the private joys that nourished him. 'Business crowds upon me', he complained to Hester, urging her to kiss 'the sweet babes and talk to them of Papa'. There were mornings filled by foreign ministers 'that never left me', a day of 'Corps diplomatic, St James's, Parliament and night meeting. Dinners with the speaker, George Grenvilles' – but 'on Saturday, I trust in heaven, with my Love'.[167] Such pressures produced extremes of behaviour. The sense of melodrama that permeated his public pronouncements[168] was more evident than ever in private letters. His mood vacillated in 1758 from anxious hope for a victory so 'that this almost degenerate England may learn from the disgrace and ruin it shall have escaped' to extravagant praise of Frederick as 'the King of Kings, whose last glories transcend all the pasts'. In 1760 he swung from 'suspense, painful suspense . . . in the midst of sollicitudes and gloomy doubts' to 'joy . . . inexpressible at the [h]appy happy day' of the relief of Quebec.[169] Drama became self-delusion, as he convinced himself as well as others that he had 'all the talents he supposed in himself'.[170] His egotism and arrogance fed on public adulation, untempered by private realism. His wife joined in the adulation, while the one colleague who still wrote to him with easy familiarity, Thomas Potter, died in 1759, and even he could write of 'numberless Cabals' of 'restless Faction' hindering 'your salutary Councils'.[171] 'I will not be rid with a check rein . . . ; I cant bear a touch of command . . . ; I cannot be dictated to, prescribed to, etc.', said Pitt in 1760.[172] Not only was his reputation decisively shaped; his political conduct was affected to the end of his career.

.   .   .

PEACE, NEW REIGN AND RESIGNATION, 1759–61

By 1760 the question of ending the war was coming into prominence. How would the great war minister make peace? Initially he had no fixed ideas. The mere making of conquests did not determine their retention in the barter of eighteenth-century peace negotiations, and the conquest of Canada was first conceived to gain a bargaining counter, not an acquisition.[173] And in the first serious negotiations of 1759–60, Pitt followed similar assumptions. Already he had resisted parliamentary pressure for the retention of Louisburg. Now he did not insist on either Louisburg or Quebec, but rather places such as 'Niagara, the Lakes, Crown Point', regarded as essential to the security of the British colonies. Outside North America, he 'supposed we must have Minorca again', wanted to keep Senegal and Gorée and some West Indian islands, but seemed relatively indifferent about Guadeloupe. He made no mention of India.[174] Such terms caused no serious differences among ministers, although the king, hoping to extract more compensation for Hanover, wanted firmer terms over America. By April 1760, however – perhaps influenced by the strong tone of public discussion – Pitt favoured another campaign and was probably beginning to contemplate more far-reaching demands in America.[175]

When peace again came under serious consideration a year later, the conquest of Canada had been completed and Pitt's attitude was influenced by other circumstances. Not least of these was the death of George II on 25 October 1760. The accession of a new, youthful king naturally had an immediate effect on ministerial politics. Ostensibly, both the king and the Earl of Bute – the mentor on whom George III had come to rely – recognized the need to continue the wartime coalition. But the effective if uneasy cohabitation into which it had settled by 1760 was profoundly altered.

Pitt was most closely affected. He had unwisely allowed his former alliance with Leicester House to cool and collapse to the point where the prince, soon to be king, considered him 'the most ungrateful . . . most dishonourable of men', 'a true snake in the grass'.[176] Bitterness over Pitt's understandable but needlessly tactless failure to consult or communicate information sufficiently was intensified by his refusal to dissociate himself from the general condemnation of two Leicester House protégés, General Bligh, commander of the finally unsuccessful 1758 expedition to the French coast, and Lord George Sackville, accused of refusing to obey orders to take the British cavalry into action at the battle of Minden in 1759.[177] Indeed, in April 1760, Pitt had abruptly rejected a conciliatory overture from Bute, declaring 'I know it is impossible for me to act in a responsible ministerial office with L[ord] B[ute]'. At issue was the independence he had so successfully asserted in the coalition. Having achieved a *modus vivendi* with Newcastle which gave him an ample voice in policy, his growing arrogance precluded even a judicious show of co-operation with the political lightweight, Bute. At the king's accession, Pitt reasserted to Bute that 'he must act as an independent Minister or not at all, that his politics were like his religion which would admit of no accommodation'. The well-known hostility of the king and Bute to the German war gave Pitt good reason to defend that aspect especially of 'the system of the war' against 'the least change'.[178] And only with difficulty did he persuade the king to alter the terms of a reference to the war in an early published declaration from 'bloody and expensive' to 'expensive but just and necessary'.[179]

The determination of the king and Bute to assert their influence was immediately indicated by the king's command that Bute, though remaining Groom of the Stole, was to be present at all ministerial meetings. Devonshire noted that Bute intended to confine 'all the ministers to their separate departments'. There was no doubt that he controlled the closet. Well might Pitt soon bewail the new difficulties in transacting business now that Newcastle no longer could, if necessary, 'answer for the King's consent'.[180] He had even greater reason for concern by mid-March, when, despite his reiterated declaration that 'he would never have anything to do with Lord Bute as a minister', Bute became his fellow Secretary of State in place of the docile Holderness and with the connivance of Newcastle. Yet again, Pitt was ill, and this crucial move occurred to some extent behind his back. Walpole was undoubtedly right to see it as intended to check Pitt. But, for the present, Bute apparently agreed to 'leave Mr Pitt master of foreign affairs', unless Newcastle, Devonshire and Hardwicke 'shall think he goes too far'. And Pitt seemed to get his way as usual over the revival and planned diversion of the Belle Île expedition. For the moment, he seemed set to go on. But ministerial politics were obviously changing to his detriment.[181]

This challenge to his dominance was the more worrying because continuing anxiety about the German war seemed to incline public attitudes more towards those of the king and Bute. Growing concern about the ever-rising costs of war, increasing taxation and war profiteering was crystal-lized in November 1760 by the publication of Israel Mauduit's *Considerations on the Present German War*. Far more influential than any other wartime publication – 'the best pamphlet that has been writ a long time' – this work distilled with fresh clarity, free of partisan rancour, the arguments against involvement in Germany. It maintained bluntly that alliance with Prussia brought nothing in return for subsidies except complications with other powers. Reaction was perplexed rather than uniformly favourable, but there were parliament-ary criticisms of expense which Pitt, predictably, tried to deflect towards Newcastle.[182] Euphoria was clearly giving way to war-weariness.

In these circumstances, the question of peace again arose, and in May 1761 substantial bilateral negotiations began with France. In December 1760, Pitt had been very ready for a peace in which 'we must give up considerably, but we must retain a great deal at the same time'. He envisaged terms involving either the cession of all Canada or substan-tial gains elsewhere, together with, in both cases, an exclus-ive right to the Newfoundland fisheries, universally valued as a 'nursery' of seamen.[183] By May 1761, however, his terms had noticeably hardened, no doubt largely because suc-cess made more seem possible,[184] but also, it seems, out of annoyance at Bute's appointment.[185] He now insisted on the retention of all Canada and the exclusive right to the fisher-ies, declaring that, if he signed a treaty 'without it, he should be sorry he ever got again the use of his right hand'.[186] He was outwardly co-operative with Bute – who could hardly be treated like Holderness – but, while accepting that the substance of negotiation was a matter of collective decision, he demanded a strong line and insisted that the manner of execution of decisions was his responsibility.[187]

However, although Pitt was at one extreme of a range of attitudes among ministers, once France had offered the cession of Canada he differed relatively little from most of them on terms. They also wanted a settlement that reflected Britain's successes. Like them, he was chiefly interested in the issue on which the war had begun – security in North America – if rather more ready to keep conquests elsewhere. His peremptory manner led to some stormy ministerial meetings, meetings in which there were 'some thumps of the fist on the table' as he 'flew into a great passion' and 'would not suffer an *iota*' of a draft to be altered. His abruptness also caused offence to the principal French minister, the Duc de Choiseul (an adversary of commensurate calibre).[188] But on the two issues on which negotiations came to turn – the European terms and the extent of French exclusion from the American fisheries – the ministers were unanimous in rejecting Choiseul's backtracking on the return of Prussian territory, and Pitt had much support for firmness on the fisheries, notably from Bute, until the last stages. Then it was he who, albeit very reluctantly, went along with the others in a concession of substance on this question.[189]

Although perhaps without Pitt the concession might have been made earlier and more tactfully, the negotiations failed primarily not because of his firmness but because Choiseul's hopes had already moved from peace to the possibilities of alliance with Spain in a renewed Family Compact.[190] However, a division was emerging among ministers about the extent to which they would go to enforce their terms. Pitt, though still probably wanting peace, was set on delivering a crushing and lasting blow to France, if not by diplomacy then by renewed war. He had said, in Walpole's report, 'that some time before he should have been well contented to bring France on her knees: now he would not rest till he had laid her on her back'.[191] His colleagues were much less sure that renewed war was possible or desirable.

This difference sharpened as negotiations lapsed and attention turned to Spain. Pitt had always handled dealings with Spain carefully, recognizing the threat of a Spanish juncture with France. But relations had deteriorated from the accession of the less favourably disposed Charles IX in 1759. In response to fears of British dominance in the New World and the revival of old grievances, Pitt had continued conciliatory but increasingly firm, with the full support of his colleagues.[192] The growing threat became obvious when France formally associated herself with Spanish grievances in July 1761 (a move unanimously rejected by British ministers), and more so as news of the Family Compact arrived in early September.[193]

The prospect of a united house of Bourbon crystallized the incipient division between Pitt and his colleagues on the future of the war. Pitt was certain, despite the opinions of

Anson and Ligonier, that Britain was better prepared than Spain, and was further irked, no doubt, by recent attempts to rein him in; he came out for a swift pre-emptive blow against the annual Spanish treasure fleet from America, and war to the finish. His colleagues would not so hastily accept such a drastic extension of the war. When, this time, he could neither cajole nor browbeat them, he, with his sole supporter, Temple, took the highly unusual step of presenting a written dissenting opinion to the king, predictably to no avail. His colleagues were now prepared to contemplate with equanimity, even relief, Pitt's often threatened resignation. On 5 October it became a reality.[194] The great war minister was gone.

During these ministerial debates, Pitt went back on an initial assurance that he 'execute any resolution' that ministers came to, even if he did not agree.[195] In his last words to his colleagues he declared, in phrases that were to ring through subsequent controversy, that he 'would not continue without having the direction' and 'would be responsible for nothing but what he directed'. Granville, too, foreshadowed the controversy when he checked such claims to 'infalibility', replying that Pitt could not so 'justifye withdrawing himself from the service of his country at this crisis'. The rebuke brought Pitt to acknowledge his obligations to 'every one of the *Old Ministry*'.[196] Nevertheless, if it was not mere posturing, Pitt's emotional speech showed the degree to which he had come to believe in his constructed public image. He had never, he claimed, 'asked one single employment'; he was called to office 'by his sovereign and . . . in some degree by the voice of the people . . . when others had abdicated'; he had been obstructed in virtually all his plans; nevertheless the war and its success were imputed solely to him. And the extent to which this was also still the dominant public view was shown in the tribute of the *Annual Register*. While regretting the personal disposition that 'disabled him from acting any otherwise than alone', the tribute supported Pitt's claim to the 'voice of the people' and acknowledged the splendour and success of the war energetically waged '[u]nder him' and the 'spirit' and 'military genius' he had raised in the nation.[197]

Pitt failed either to end or to extend 'his' war as he wanted. Driven by a longstanding and intense anti-Bourbonism, his vision of what the war might achieve had grown with its progress and his arrogance until, in Walpole's words, he aspired to be 'the most illustrious man of the first country in Europe'.[198] In this sense, and certainly to most contemporaries, he was a great patriot. When the war was ended under Bute a year later, after further extraordinary successes at Havana (Cuba) and Manila in the conflict with Spain which proved unavoidable, Pitt criticized the peace terms. They were, he said, inadequate to these improved circumstances, indeed worse than those offered the previous year, dishonourable and dangerous in deserting Prussia and, above all, insecure because they 'restored the enemy to her former greatness'.[199] Pitt had some case in condemning the failure to extract more from Spain. Indeed, it is interesting to speculate whether Pitt, much as he shared the new fixation on North America, might have turned British attention back to older dreams of advantage from the El Dorado of the Spanish empire, had he remained in office. But his claims for 'his' peace negotiations were tendentious, while he failed to recognize that the time for the costly Prussian alliance had passed. And still today it is arguable whether it is wiser to conciliate or attempt permanently to repress an enemy.[200]

Pitt's criticism was driven at least as much by factiousness as by vision – or realism. It won little support, either in parliament or outside. No longer did his rhetoric resonate with the national mood or the peace need his endorsement to be acceptable.[201] What future was there now for the great war minister?

. . .

NOTES

1. T. Pownall to Pitt, 24 Jan. 1765, PRO 30/8/53, f. 170. Cf. below, p. 108.

2. Paul Langford, *A Polite and Commercial People. England 1727–1783* (Oxford, 1989), pp. 167–70.

3. Daniel Baugh, 'Great Britain's "blue-water" policy, 1689–1715', *International History Review* 10 (1988), esp. pp. 37–41; John Brewer, *The Sinews of Power. War, Money and the English State 1688–1783* (1989), ch. 6.

4. Much of the excellent recent work variously assessing naval power is reviewed in Hamish Scott, 'The second "Hundred Years War", 1689–1815', *Historical Journal* 35 (1992), pp. 452–64. The work of Daniel Baugh and Richard Middleton is

especially relevant here. Geoffrey Holmes and Daniel Szechi, *The Age of Oligarchy. Pre-industrial Britain 1722–1783* (1993), pp. 255–7, provides one overview.

5.   Richard Middleton, 'British naval strategy, 1755–1762. The western squadron', *Mariner's Mirror* 75 (1989), pp. 349–55; idem, *The Bells of Victory* (Cambridge, 1985), pp. 24–5, 34–5, 39–40; for a longer-term view, Michael Duffy, 'The establishment of the western squadron as the linchpin of British naval strategy', in idem (ed.), *Parameters of British Naval Power 1650–1800* (Exeter, 1992), esp. pp. 68–72, 74–6, 77, 78.

6.   In fact, despite Frederick the Great's insistence, British ministers were surprisingly unconcerned, probably because France launched no offensive there.

7.   *Memoirs George II*, II, pp. 187, 189.

8.   Middleton, *Bells*, pp. 9, 25.

9.   Marie Peters, 'The myth of William Pitt, Earl of Chatham, great imperialist. Part I', *Journal of Commonwealth and Imperial History* 21 (1993), pp. 41–2; Middleton, *Bells*, pp. 7–8, 12, 17, 52n.

10.   For recent assessments, see Middleton, *Bells*, esp. pp. 19–21, 28, 49–50, 69–70, and E.J.S. Fraser, 'The Pitt–Newcastle coalition and the conduct of the Seven Years' War 1757–1760', D. Phil. thesis, University of Oxford, 1976, esp. ch. 2.

11.   Newcastle to Hardwicke, 23 Oct. 1757, in Philip C. Yorke, *The Life and Correspondence of Philip Yorke Earl of Hardwicke* 3 vols (Cambridge, 1913), III, p. 193.

12.   For this process in the coalition's early days, see e.g. Yorke, *Hardwicke*, III, pp. 173, 192–3, and Stanley Pargellis (ed.), *Military Affairs in North America 1748–1765* (New York, 1936), pp. 380–1.

13.   Pitt to Bute, 28 June 1757, in Romney Sedgwick (ed.), 'Letters from William Pitt to Lord Bute; 1755–1758', in Richard Pares and A.J.P. Taylor (eds), *Essays presented to Sir Lewis Namier* (1956), p. 124; Pitt to Hardwicke, 22 June 1757, in Yorke, *Hardwicke*, II, p. 407.

14.   Peter D. Brown and Karl W. Schweizer (eds), *The Devonshire Diary . . . Memoranda on State of Affairs 1759–1762* (1982), p. 88 (6 March 1761); Jeremy Black, *Pitt the Elder* (Cambridge, 1992), pp. 198–9. Pitt's energy is suggested by his office records, notably the summaries of correspondence he required; see PRO, SP109/68–71, and several more specific abstracts in the Chatham Papers.

15.   Pitt to Keene, 23 Aug. 1757, *Chatham Correspondence*, I, pp. 247–56.

16. Karl W. Schweizer, *Frederick the Great, William Pitt, and Lord Bute. The Anglo-Prussian Alliance, 1756–1763* (New York, 1991), pp. 43–4, 53–4.

17. Ibid., p. 55; Newcastle to Hardwicke, 25 July, 3 Aug. 1757, Newcastle Papers, Add. MSS 32872, f. 320, Yorke, *Hardwicke*, III, pp. 161–2; Holderness to Mitchell, 17 July 1757, in Andrew Bisset, *Memoirs and Letters of Sir Andrew Mitchell, K.B.* 2 vols (1850), I, pp. 254–65; Middleton, *Bells*, pp. 26–7.

18. Middleton, *Bells*, pp. 26–7, 28–9, 30; Mordaunt, Hawke to Pitt, 30 Sept., 21 Oct. 1757, PRO 30/8/78, ff. 112–17, 186–91.

19. *Monitor*, 20 Aug., cf. 3 Sept. 1757; *Memoirs George II*, II, pp. 272–5; Marie Peters, *Pitt and Popularity. The Patriot Minister and London Opinion during the Seven Years' War* (Oxford, 1980), pp. 92–3.

20. Black, *Pitt the Elder*, p. 135 (quotation); *Memoirs George II*, II, pp. 255, 257–8.

21. Bisset, *Mitchell*, I, p. 263.

22. Peters, *Pitt*, p. 92.

23. Middleton, *Bells*, p. 35; Pitt to Holderness, [10 Sept. 1757], British Library, Leeds Papers, Eg.3432, f. 164; Newcastle to Hardwicke, 10 Sept. 1757, in Yorke, *Hardwicke*, II, pp. 173, 174–5.

24. Peters, *Pitt*, pp. 93–4; Middleton, *Bells*, pp. 37–8.

25. Schweizer, *Frederick the Great*, pp. 60–1.

26. Peters, *Pitt*, pp. 94–101; Middleton, *Bells*, pp. 40–3.

27. Chesterfield to his son, 4 Nov. 1757, in Bonamy Dobrée (ed.), *The Letters of Philip Dormer Stanhope, fourth Earl of Chesterfield* 6 vols (New York, 1932), V, pp. 2255–9.

28. Peters, *Pitt*, pp. 96–7, 103–4; Middleton, *Bells*, pp. 41–2, 47–8; *Memoirs George II*, III, p. 3; cf. below, p. 93.

29. Middleton, *Bells*, pp. 57–63; Schweizer, *Frederick the Great*, ch. 3.

30. Pitt to Newcastle, 28 Jan., Holderness to Newcastle, [25 Feb.] 1758, Add. MSS 32877, ff. 256–7, 32878, f. 33; Calcraft to Home, 26 Feb. 1758, Calcraft Papers, Add. MSS 17493, ff. 147–8; Middleton, *Bells*, p. 60. Newcastle still favoured sending troops: Newcastle to Hardwicke, 29 Jan. 1758, in Yorke, *Hardwicke*, III, pp. 197–8.

31. See e.g. account of Pitt–Holderness conversation, 27 March 1758, Eg.3432, ff. 176–81.

32. E.g. ibid.

33. Peters, *Pitt*, pp. 104, 106–9.

34. Walpole to Mann, 9 Feb. 1758, *Correspondence*, XXI, p. 171; Chesterfield to his son, 8 Jan. 1758, in Dobrée (ed.), *Letters*,

V, p. 2285; Suzanne Cookson, 'The patriot king: the English reputation of Frederick the Great during the Seven Years' War', M.A. thesis, University of Canterbury, 1994.

35. Peters, *Pitt*, pp. 109–11.

36. Middleton, *Bells*, pp. 73–4.

37. Ibid., pp. 64–73; Peters, *Pitt*, pp. 105–6.

38. Peters, *Pitt*, p. 116; Fraser, 'Coalition', pp. 148–51.

39. Pitt to John Pitt, 27 Dec. 1757, in Georgiana, Lady Chatterton (ed.), *Memorials . . . of Admiral Lord Gambier* 2 vols (1861), I, p. 81; see above, n. 30.

40. Calcraft to Home, Add. MSS 17493, f. 148; cf. D'Abreu's speculations to Wall, 3 March, *Chatham Correspondence*, I, pp. 294–8, and Joseph Yorke's explanation to Frederick's ministers, April 1758, in J.G. Droysen *et al.* (eds), *Politische Correspondenz Friedrichs des Grossen* 39 vols (Berlin, 1879–1935), XVI, p. 364.

41. Peters, *Pitt*, pp. 110, 116–17.

42. Ibid., pp. 118–22.

43. H.M. Scott, *British Foreign Policy in the Age of the American Revolution* (Oxford, 1990), pp. 42, 45–6; Carl William Eldon, *England's Subsidy Policy towards the Continent during the Seven Years' War* (Philadelphia, PA, 1938), pp. 162–3; John Shy, *Towards Lexington* (Princeton, NJ, 1965), p. 35, cf. Middleton, *Bells*, who gives 45,000 regular and provincial troops in 1759.

44. E.g. account of Pitt–Holderness conversation, 27 March 1758, Eg.3432, ff. 176–7.

45. Newcastle to Holderness, 26 Feb. 1758, quoted in Middleton, *Bells*, p. 60.

46. Middleton, *Bells*, p. 58.

47. Ibid., pp. 77–8.

48. Made in the Commons, 19 April 1758, see Peters, *Pitt*, p. 110; cf. May 1757, as above, p. 89.

49. Frederick to Knyphausen, 21 July 1758, in Droysen *et al.* (eds), *Correspondenz*, XVII, p. 126.

50. Eg.3432, ff. 164–95, esp. 174–5, 176–81, 184–9; Newcastle to Hardwicke, 4 Jan. 1757, Add. MSS, 32870, f. 23; Finckenstein to Frederick, 4 April 1758, in Droysen *et al.* (eds), *Correspondenz*, XVI, p. 364 (quotations translated from the French). Frederick's changing attitude to Pitt can be charted in his correspondence: see e.g. letters of 18, 21 Feb., 12 April, 21 May, 8 June, 8 Oct., 1 Dec. 1758, XVI, pp. 253, 256, 375, XVII, pp. 23–6, 55 (quotation), 293, 409.

51. Uriel Dann, *Hanover and Great Britain 1740–1760* (Leicester, 1991), pp. 110–11.

52. Newcastle to Hardwicke, 23 Oct. 1757, in Yorke, *Hardwicke*, III, p. 192 – a vivid vignette of the functioning of the coalition at this stage.

53. Finckenstein to Frederick, 4 April 1758, in Droysen *et al.* (eds), *Correspondenz*, XVI, p. 364.

54. Middleton, *Bells*, p. 61.

55. Newcastle to Hardwicke, 25 July 1757, memorandum for the king, 14 March, Newcastle to Hardwicke, 16 May 1758, Add. MSS 32872, ff. 320–1, 32878, ff. 210–11, Yorke, *Hardwicke*, III, p. 46; Finckenstein to Frederick, 4 April 1758, in Droysen *et al.* (eds), *Correspondenz*, XVI, p. 364.

56. Middleton, *Bells*, pp. 54–5.

57. Stanley McCrory Pargellis, *Lord Loudoun in America* (Princeton, NJ, 1933), p. 238; Richard Middleton, 'A reinforcement for North America, Summer 1757', *Bulletin of the Institute of Historical Research* 41 (1968), pp. 58–72.

58. Middleton, *Bells*, pp. 9–10, 11–12, 39–40; Pargellis, *Loudoun*, pp. 35–44, chs 2, 9; idem (ed.), *Military Affairs*, pp. xiv–xix; Middleton, 'Naval strategy', pp. 355–6.

59. Calcraft to Loudoun, 16 Dec. 1757, HL, Loudoun Papers, LO5025 (quotation); Pargellis, *Loudoun*, pp. 337–48; Middleton, *Bells*, p. 51.

60. Pargellis (ed.), *Military Affairs*, p. xviii.

61. *Parl. Hist.*, XV, col. 829.

62. For Middleton's account see *Bells*, pp. 49–57.

63. E.g. John Bradstreet to Sir Richard Lyttelton, 15 Aug., 5 Sept. 1757, Sir Charles Hardy to Pitt, 14 Dec. 1757, PRO 30/8/95, ff. 304–5, 308–19, 356–61. Although Loudoun did not send official advice, his views became known to Pitt: ibid., vol. 96, ff. 27–41, Pargellis, *Loudoun*, pp. 252, 345, 356.

64. E.g. Loudoun to Holderness and Pitt, 16 Aug./17 Oct. 1757, HL, LO4239.

65. Pitt to the governors of the northern and southern colonies and to Abercromby, 30 Dec. 1757, in Gertrude Selwyn Kimball (ed.), *Correspondence of William Pitt when Secretary of State with Colonial Governors and Military and Naval Commissioners in America* 2 vols (New York, 1906), pp. 136–51.

66. Pitt to Holburne, 18 July 1757, HL, LO3967 (quotation); Boscawen instructions, 27 Jan. 1758, SP109/69, p. 104.

67. Middleton, *Bells*, p. 53.

68. Calcraft to Loudoun, 29 Dec. 1757, HL, LO5140 (quotation); copies and précis of Loudoun–Pownall letters, PRO 30/8/95, ff. 337–55, 362–8, 371–4, vol. 96, ff. 1–6.

69. Abercromby's instructions, 30 Dec. 1757, SP109/69, p. 101; Pargellis, *Loudoun*, pp. 57–9, 351.

70. Kimball (ed.), *Correspondence*, I, pp. 138–9.
71. See e.g. Robinson to New England governors, 11 Nov. 1755, Fox to all governors, 13 March 1756, HL, LO678, LO924.
72. Kimball (ed.), *Correspondence*, I, p. 139; SP109/69, p. 101; cf. Middleton, *Bells*, p. 55.
73. Pownall to Pitt, 14, 23 March 1758, in Kimball (ed.), *Correspondence*, I, pp. 203–4, 213–14.
74. Calcraft to Loudoun, 29 Dec. 1757, HL, LO5140.
75. Pitt to Abercromby, 30 Dec. 1757, in Kimball (ed.), *Correspondence*, I, p. 144, 10 June 1758, HL, Abercromby Papers, AB343 (quotation); Boscawen's instructions, 27 Jan. 1758, SP109/69, p. 104.
76. Middleton, *Bells*, pp. 79–80, 99–100; Boscawen and Amherst to Pitt, 8 Aug. 1758, PRO 30/8/20, ff. 152–3; Kimball (ed.), *Correspondence*, I, p. 146n.; Abercromby to Pitt, 10 Sept., Pitt to Abercromby, 18 Sept. 1758, HL, AB675, 676.
77. Forbes to Pitt, 27 Nov. and e.g. 17 June, 6 Sept., Abercromby to Pitt, 22 May, 12 July 1758, in Kimball (ed.), *Correspondence*, I, pp. 406–9, 278–81, 338–43, 248–50, 297–302; Pargellis, *Loudoun*, p. 355.
78. Pargellis, *Loudoun*, pp. 356–8.
79. Grenville to Pitt, 23 Aug., Bute to Pitt, [20 Aug.] 1758, *Chatham Correspondence*, I, pp. 338, 335.
80. Peters, *Pitt*, pp. 124–5.
81. Pitt to the governors and Amherst, 9 Dec. 1758, in Kimball (ed.), *Correspondence*, I, pp. 414–24.
82. Pitt to Amherst, 29 Dec. 1758, 10 Feb., to Forbes, 23 Jan. 1759, in ibid., pp. 432–42, II, pp. 37–8, 16–18; Middleton, *Bells*, pp. 100–2.
83. Middleton, *Bells*, pp. 99, 100–7.
84. *Memoirs George II*, III, pp. 74–6.
85. Kimball (ed.), *Correspondence*, I, pp. lv, lxi–xii.
86. Ibid., pp. lv–vii; Middleton, *Bells*, pp. 132–3, 138.
87. Kimball (ed.), *Correspondence*, I, pp. lviii–ix.
88. Middleton, *Bells*, pp. 94, 107–12, 118, 125; Peters, *Pitt*, pp. 143–5.
89. Middleton, *Bells*, pp. 132, 119, 120–5, 142–5, cf. idem, 'Naval strategy', pp. 360–5; Scott, 'The second "Hundred Years War"', pp. 463–4.
90. Pitt to the governors and Amherst, 9 Jan. 1760, in Kimball (ed.), *Correspondence*, II, pp. 232–43, cf. 29 Dec. 1758, I, pp. 438–9.
91. Instructions to Hopson, 16 Oct. 1758, SP109/70, p. 76.
92. Kimball (ed.), *Correspondence*, I, pp. xlvi–l, lxiv–vi, and table of contents, both vols; Middleton, *Bells*, pp. 80, 85–7, 103, 120, 176, 189, 207.

93. Cumming to Pitt, 28 Jan., 1 Feb. 1757, memorial, 20 Feb. 1759, PRO 30/8/30, ff. 64–70, Pitt to Cumming, 9 Feb. 1757, *Chatham Correspondence*, I, pp. 221–2; SP109/68, pp. 114–15, vol. 70, pp. 86–7, 170–1; Bedford to Pitt, 29 Aug. 1759, PRO 30/8/19, f. 157 (quotation); Kate Hotblack, *Chatham's Colonial Policy* (1917), pp. 32–41.

94. See above, p. 68; Secret Committee to Pitt, 12 Jan. 1757, 16 Aug. 1759, progress of ships to India 1757–58, Pitt to Admiral Stevens, 30 Dec. 1760, PRO 30/8/99, ff. 332–5, 324–5, vol. 78, f. 171, vol. 79, f. 234; SP109/68–71; *Commons Journal* 28, pp. 153, 552, 892, 1077, vol. 29, pp. 270, 560; Middleton, *Bells*, pp. 12, 46, 49, 98, 112.

95. E.g. George Pigot to [Pitt], 7 March 1759, Laurence Sulivan to Pitt, 8 April 1760, PRO 30/8/99, f. 317, vol. 60, f. 107; but cf. Peters, 'Myth', n. 133.

96. *Memoirs George II*, III, p. 4 (quotation); Peters, 'Myth', pp. 45–6.

97. Middleton, *Bells*, pp. 176–7, 180; PRO 30/8/100, ff. 245–66.

98. Middleton, *Bells*, pp. 166–9, 173, 181, 186.

99. Cf. ibid, p. 159, on army matters, and Hardwicke to Pitt, 15 Jan., 20 Nov. 1760, Add. MSS 35423, f. 201, PRO 30/8/39, f. 228 (giving advice on diplomatic and military instructions).

100. Forbes to Pitt, 27 Nov. 1758, in Kimball (ed.), *Correspondence*, I, p. 409; De Berdt to Dartmouth, [July 1765], in Albert Matthews (ed.), 'Letters of Dennys De Berdt, 1757–1770', *Publications of the Colonial Society of Massachusetts* 13 (1910–11), p. 431; cf. Burgoyne to Chatham, 4 Dec. 1766, PRO 30/8/24, f. 241.

101. Newcastle to Devonshire, 9 Dec. 1761, Add. MSS 32932, f. 81; Yorke to Newcastle, 15 July 1757, in Yorke, *Hardwicke*, III, p. 157.

102. Middleton, *Bells*, p. 164; Pargellis (ed.), *Military Affairs*, pp. xvii–xx.

103. Peters, 'Myth', p. 48.

104. Amherst to Stanwix, 5 April 1759, PRO 30/8/96, f. 212.

105. Eg.3432, ff. 196–228; Newcastle, 'Business' notes, 18 Feb. 1760 (copy), Dropmore Papers, Series II, Add. MSS 69093, f. 18; Middleton, *Bells*, pp. 145–6.

106. For some of many examples, see Black, *Pitt the Elder*, pp. 181, 207–8, 210, and the later compliments of Sir William Draper and Admiral Sir Charles Saunders: *Chatham Correspondence*, III, pp. 325–9, IV, pp. 231–2, PRO 30/8/10, f. 8, vol. 31, f. 177.

107. *Memoirs George III*, I, p. 44.

108. Granby to Pitt, 1759–62, PRO 30/8/33, ff. 119–36; Prince Ferdinand and Pitt, 1759–61, ibid., vol. 90, ff. 11–93, cf. vol. 89 on the army in Germany.

109. For some of many examples, see Frederick to Knyphausen and Michell, 25 Dec. 1758, to Knyphausen, 5 Jan., 14 March, 17 May, to Finckenstein, 20 Aug., to Knyphausen, 1 Sept., to Finckenstein, 10 Oct., 17 Nov. 1758, to Knyphausen, 23, 24 Jan., 5 Feb., 10 April 1760, all in Droysen *et al.* (eds), *Correspondenz*, XVII, p. 436, XVIII, pp. 8, 112–13, 232, 494 (translated quotation), 512, 588, 646, XIX, pp. 38–40, 43, 63, 228.

110. E.g. Frederick to Pitt, 7 Nov. 1760, in ibid., XX, p. 63; *Chatham Correspondence*, I, pp. 385–6, 393–4, II, pp. 77–8; Newcastle to Hardwicke, 3 Dec. 1760, in Yorke, *Hardwicke*, III, p. 313.

111. Chiefly Middleton's (see above, n. 10). Fraser (also n. 10) rightly argues that Pitt achieved a personal dominance, but tends to exaggerate that dominance.

112. See above, p. 87; cabinet minute, 18 Aug. 1757, PRO 30/8/92, f. 245; Keene to Pitt, 26 Sept. 1757, *Chatham Correspondence*, I, pp. 236–77; Middleton, *Bells*, p. 44.

113. Middleton, *Bells*, pp. 92–6; Peters, *Pitt*, pp. 146–8.

114. Brewer, *Sinews*, p. 174.

115. *Memoirs George II*, III, p. 78 (13 Nov. 1759); cf. *Annual Register* 4 (1761), p. 48.

116. West's accounts, 20 Jan. 1758, 13 Nov. 1759, Add. MSS 32877, f. 183, 32898, f. 223, *Parl. Hist.*, XV, col. 930 (King's Speech, 23 Nov. 1758); cf. Peters, 'Myth', pp. 44–5, Middleton, *Bells*, pp. 198, 211.

117. Middleton, *Bells*, pp. 84–5.

118. Peters, 'Myth', pp. 44–5; Hardwicke to Newcastle, 17 Aug. 1741, in Yorke, *Hardwicke*, I, p. 263; Middleton, *Bells*, p. 58.

119. *Memoirs George III*, I, p. 78 (13 Nov. 1761); King's Speech, 13 Nov. 1759, *Parl. Hist.*, XV, col. 949.

120. Peters, *Pitt*, p. 170; Black, *Pitt the Elder*, pp. 196–7.

121. For what follows, cf. Middleton, *Bells*, pp. 213–18, 231 and passim.

122. *Parl. Hist.*, XVI, col. 1102 (22 Nov. 1770).

123. Middleton, *Bells*, pp. 10, 125–6.

124. Newcastle to Hardwicke, 4 Jan. 1757, Add. MSS 32870, f. 24, cf. 22 Aug. 1755, in Yorke, *Hardwicke*, II, pp. 234–5; *Parl. Hist.*, XVI, col. 1097 (22 Nov. 1770).

125. Peters, *Pitt*, p. 197; Langford, *A Polite and Commercial People*, p. 346.

126. Cf. above, p. 73; James Harris, Parliamentary Memorials, 12 May 1762, Hampshire Record Office, Malmesbury Collection, 9M73/G709, p. 54, cf. *Memoirs George II*, III, p. 52.

127. For qualification of this usual view, see N.A.M. Rodger, 'The Continental commitment in the eighteenth century', in Lawrence Freedman *et al.* (eds), *War, Strategy and International Politics* (Oxford, 1992), pp. 39–55.

128. Scott, 'The second "Hundred Years War"', p. 454; cf. idem, *British Foreign Policy*, p. 29, citing the analysis of Venetian ambassadors.

129. See above, pp. 67, 71.

130. Middleton, *Bells*, pp. 197, 212–13.

131. Peters, 'Myth', p. 52 and n. 189.

132. Lyttelton to Elizabeth Montagu, 5 Oct. 1761, HL, Montagu Papers, MO1295.

133. Holmes and Szechi, *The Age of Oligarchy*, pp. 259–64, still credit Pitt with too much.

134. Calcraft to Home, 26 Feb. 1758, Add. MSS 17493, f. 147; Temple to Wilkes, 16 Oct. 1761, in William James Smith (ed.), *The Grenville Papers* 4 vols (1852), I, p. 405; cf. Walpole to Mann, 27 Nov. 1758, *Correspondence*, XXI, p. 257; *Memoirs George II*, III, p. 41.

135. W. Mure to Pitt, 10 Oct. 1758, PRO 30/9/50, f. 149; J.H. Burton (ed.), *Autobiography of the Rev. Dr Alexander Carlyle* (Edinburgh, 1860), p. 383; Peters, *Pitt*, pp. 125, 126–7, 149–52.

136. Percival to [anon.], 16 Nov. 1759, HMC, *Fourteenth Report*, pt. 4, p. 496; Walpole to Montagu, 21 Oct., cf. to Mann, 16 Nov. 1759, *Correspondence*, IX, p. 250, XXI, p. 347; *Gentleman's Magazine* 30 (1760), p. 538.

137. [John Douglas], *A letter addressed to two great men* (1760), p. 50; cf. Walpole to Mann, 4 March 1759, *Correspondence*, XXI, p. 277.

138. Cf. John Brown's influential *Estimate of the manners and principles of the times* (1757) with Robert J. Phillimore (ed.), *Memoirs and Correspondence of George, Lord Lyttelton* 2 vols (1845), II, p. 512, quoting Burke, and Brown's *An explanatory defence of the Estimate* (1758).

139. Janssen to Pitt, 1 Dec. 1762, PRO 30/8/46, f. 216.

140. Newcastle to Granby, 27 Nov. 1759, Add. MSS 32899, f. 141; Middleton, *Bells*, p. 139; cf. above, pp. 94–5.

141. *Memoirs George II*, III, pp. 53–4; West's account, 9 March 1759, Add. MSS 32888, ff. 428–9.

142. Charles to George Townshend, 13 March 1759, Bodleian Library, MS Eng Hist, D211, ff. 5–6 (which also analyses the depth of the financial crisis).

143. 'Heads of Mr Pitt's Conversation', 17 Oct. 1759, Add. MSS 32897, ff. 173–5; cf. Yorke, *Hardwicke*, III, pp. 23–6, 57–91.

144. Yorke, *Hardwicke*, III, pp. 22–3, 68–73.

145. Calcraft to Draper, 21 March 1759, PRO 30/8/86, f. 328; Elizabeth to Edward Montagu, [Dec. 1760/Jan. 1761], HL, MO2424; Middleton, *Bells*, p. 116 (third quotation), cf. Newcastle to Pitt, 5 April 1758, *Chatham Correspondence*, I, pp. 307–8. Walpole (*Memoirs George II*, III, p. 52) reflects on this 'artful, new, and grand' tactic of Pitt's.

146. Sir George Colebrooke, *Retrospection: or Reminiscences* Part I (1898), pp. 34–7, partly quoted in Sir Lewis Namier and John Brooke, *The House of Commons 1754–1790* 3 vols (1964), III, p. 294; Newcastle to Hardwicke, 27 Sept. 1759, in Yorke, *Hardwicke*, III, p. 62.

147. E.g. *Memoirs George II*, III, p. 78 (13 Nov. 1759), Pitt's conversation with Viry, Aug. 1760, quoted in Sir Lewis Namier, *England in the Age of the American Revolution* 2nd edn (1966), p. 108; cf. Middleton, *Bells*, pp. 146, 147, 148, and below, p. 147.

148. Lord Edmond Fitzmaurice (ed.), *Life of William Earl of Shelburne* 3 vols (1875–6), I, p. 91; James Harris, memoranda, 13 May 1767 (conversation with Robert Wood, formerly Pitt's Under-Secretary), Hampshire County Council, Malmesbury Collection, 9M73/G745.

149. Peters, *Pitt*, p. 103; *Memoirs George II*, III, pp. 41–2 (also pointing out that Pitt on occasion sent circulars to his Tory supporters); Pitt to Hardwicke, 10 Nov. 1760, Add. MSS 35423, ff. 212, 214; *Correspondence*, XXI, pp. 344–5n.; Middleton, *Bells*, pp. 47–8, 97.

150. Prince Czartoriski to his father, 20 Dec. 1757, in Arnold Schaefer, *Geschichte des siebenjahrigen Kriegs* 2 vols (Berlin, 1867–74), I, p. 666; *Memoirs George II*, III, pp. 3–4, 79. Walpole, never an impartial observer and initially unsympathetic to Pitt, is, for this very reason, an acute indicator of Pitt's tactics and their effect. The story that Pitt's anger at being publicly rebuked that morning while giving evidence at Mordaunt's court-martial provoked his attack on Loudoun rings true: Calcraft to Loudoun, 25 Dec. 1757, HL, LO5092.

151. *Memoirs George II*, III, pp. 37–8; Walpole to Mann, 27 Nov. 1758, *Correspondence*, XXI, pp. 256–7; West's account, 23 Nov. 1758, Add. MSS 32885, ff. 524–5. Cf. Elizabeth to Edward Montagu, 28 Nov. 1758, HL, MO2357.

152. *Memoirs George II*, III pp. 77–8, West's account, 13 Nov. 1759, Add. MSS 32898, ff. 223–4.

153. Walpole to Pitt, 19 Nov. 1759, *Chatham Correspondence*, I, p. 456; *Memoirs George II*, III, p. 80, cf. Walpole to Montagu, 22 March 1762, *Correspondence*, X, p. 22; Elizabeth to Edward Montagu, 28 Nov., 19 Dec. 1758, [Jan. 1759], HL, MO2357,

2365, 2377. Her developing warm friendship with Pitt was cut short in 1755–56 by Pitt's opposition manoeuvres.

154. See above, p. 92, and Peters, *Pitt*, pp. 266–7; *Memoirs George II*, III, p. 42 comments on Pitt's 'artful' courting.

155. See above, pp. 92, 101; Peters, *Pitt*, pp. 159–62, 89, 106–7, 144–5; Middleton, *Bells*, pp. 156, 157.

156. To Hardwicke, 15 March 1760, Add. MSS 32903, f. 297.

157. See e.g. Peters, *Pitt*, pp. 138–40, 156, 173–4, 268–9.

158. Ibid., p. 269.

159. *Monitor*, 2 July, 13 Aug 1757, 15 (cf. 29) July 1758, 10 March, 14 July 1759; memorandum for the king, 20 March 1759, Add. MSS 32889, f. 155; Peters, *Pitt*, pp. 85–7, 101, 118–19, 122, 127, 130, 134–8, 150–2, 158. Cf. Austin Gee, 'English Provincial Newspapers and the Politics of the Seven Years' War, 1756–1763', M.A. thesis, University of Canterbury, 1985, chs 5, 6.

160. *Memoirs George II*, III, pp. 1–2, 51; 'Simon or Simeon Stylites & and Mr Secretary [Pitt]', [1760?], HL, MO2997. She was to make the same point after Pitt's death (to Pepys, 23 May 1778: ibid., MO4036).

161. 'A Character of Mr Pitt' (1762) in Colin Franklin, *Lord Chesterfield. His Character and* Characters (Aldershot, 1993), pp. 127, 40.

162. Richard Middleton, 'The Duke of Newcastle and the conduct of patronage during the Seven Years' War, 1757–1762', *British Journal of Eighteenth-Century Studies* 12 (1989), esp. pp. 184–5.

163. Michell's report, 24 Jan. 1758, in Schaefer, *Geschichte* II, part 1, p. 530; West's report, 20 Jan. (quotations), Newcastle to Hardwicke, 21 Jan. 1758, Add. MSS 32877, ff. 183, 194.

164. Walpole to Mann, 27 Nov. 1758, *Correspondence*, XXI, p. 257; *Memoirs George II*, III, pp. 47, 92.

165. Hardwicke to Newcastle, 23 Sept., Newcastle to Hardwicke, 25 Oct. 1759, in Yorke, *Hardwicke*, III, pp. 60, 73; Brown and Schweizer (eds), *Devonshire Diary*, pp. 27, 37, 52, 54 (11 Nov. 1759, 30 Jan., 2, 5 Oct. 1760).

166. *Memoirs George II*, III, pp. 2, 1, 51–2; cf. the comment of the French peace negotiator, François de Bussy, quoted in Black, *Pitt the Elder*, p. 215, and above, p. 83.

167. Pitt to Lady Hester, [1759?], PRO 30/8/5, ff. 157, 177, 175.

168. Even official letters, e.g. to Amherst, 9 Jan. 1758, in Kimball (ed.), *Correspondence*, II, p. 424.

169. Pitt to Lady Hester, 1 July 1758, [June 1760], [n.d. 1760?], *Chatham Correspondence*, I, p. 322, II, p. 45, PRO 30/8/2, f. 5; Pitt to Ann Pitt, 12 Sept. 1758, Add. MSS 69289, no. 45.

170. *Memoirs George II*, III, p. 1.

171. Potter to Pitt, 20 Aug. 1758, PRO 30/8/53, f. 69.

172. Gilbert Elliot's account, quoted in Namier, *American Revolution*, p. 106. Pitt's 1760–61 conversations with Elliot (see below, n. 178, p. 161, nn. 52) are probably the most self-revelatory of which records remain.

173. E.g. Loudoun to Cumberland, 22 Nov.–26 Dec. 1756, in Pargellis (ed.), *Military Affairs*, pp. 279–80.

174. *Memoirs George II*, III, p. 38; Peters, *Pitt*, p. 163, cf. idem, 'Myth', p. 49; Brown and Schweizer (eds), *Devonshire Diary*, p. 26 (26 Oct. 1759 – quotations).

175. Peters, *Pitt*, pp. 164–9; Newcastle to Hardwicke, 9 April, Hardwicke to Newcastle, 10 April 1760, in Yorke, *Hardwicke*, III, pp. 244–5.

176. Romney Sedgwick (ed.), *Letters from George III to Lord Bute* (1939), pp. 45 (4 May), 47 (?5 Oct. 1760); cf. James Harris, memoranda, 13 May 1767, 9M73/G745, on deteriorating relations with Bute.

177. Peters, *Pitt*, pp. 142, 172.

178. Gilbert Elliot's accounts in Namier, *American Revolution*, pp. 106, 121.

179. Newcastle to Hardwicke, 26 Oct. 1760, in Yorke, *Hardwicke*, III, pp. 304–5, cf. p. 262.

180. Brown and Schweizer (eds), *Devonshire Diary*, p. 43 (27 Oct.); Newcastle to Hardwicke, 3 Dec., in Yorke, *Hardwicke*, III, p. 315; cf. Hardwicke to Newcastle, 29 Oct. 1760, Add. MSS 32913, f. 426.

181. Brown and Schweizer (eds), *Devonshire Diary*, pp. 90, 91, 93 (13, 15 March, 9 April 1760); cf. pp. 72–90 for Devonshire's acute account of the long background to this manoeuvre, which vividly demonstrates the complex tensions now unsettling politics; Walpole to Mann, 17 March 1761, *Correspondence*, XXI, pp. 487–8; Middleton, *Bells*, pp. 171–2. Frederick the Great was soon referring his envoys to both Pitt and Bute.

182. Edward to Elizabeth Montagu, 19 Nov. 1760, HL, MO1293; Peters, *Pitt*, pp. 182–9.

183. Brown and Schweizer (eds), *Devonshire Diary*, p. 61 (26 Nov. 1760); Newcastle to Hardwicke, 3 Dec. 1760, in Yorke, *Hardwicke*, III, p. 314, cf. p. 269.

184. Note his increasing emphasis on fortifying and defending American conquests; cf. Pitt to Amherst, 7 Jan., 24 Oct. 1760, 7 Jan 1761, in Kimball (ed.), *Correspondence*, II, pp. 241–2, 345–6, 386.

185. Middleton, *Bells*, p. 184; cf. Brown and Schweizer (eds), *Devonshire Diary*, p. 93 (15 March 1761); Hardwicke to Newcastle, 18 April 1761, in Yorke, *Hardwicke*, III, p. 317.

186. Memorandum, 10 April, Newcastle to Hardwicke, 16, 17 April, Add. MSS 32921, ff. 381–2, 32922, ff. 5–6, Yorke, *Hardwicke*, III, pp. 315–16 (quotation); Brown and Schweizer (eds), *Devonshire Diary*, pp. 92–3 (9 April 1761).

187. E.g. Brown and Schweizer (eds), *Devonshire Diary*, pp. 94–5, 97, 111–12, cf. 68 (22, 27 April, 15 Aug. 1761, 9 Dec. 1760); Karl W. Schweizer, 'Lord Bute, William Pitt, and the peace negotiation with France, April–September 1761', in idem (ed.), *Lord Bute. Essays in Re-interpretation* (Leicester, 1988), pp. 41–55, esp. n. 67. For other accounts of varying emphasis, see Middleton, *Bells*, pp. 174, 184–92; Peters, 'Myth', pp. 49–50; Black, *Pitt the Elder*, pp. 209–18 (valuable for its French perspectives).

188. Hardwicke to Royston, 15 Aug. 1761, in Yorke, *Hardwicke*, III, p. 320; Brown and Schweizer (eds), *Devonshire Diary*, p. 111 (15 [14] Aug. 1761); Black, *Pitt the Elder*, pp. 213, 215, 216.

189. Hardwicke to Royston, 22 Aug., Hardwicke's notes, 24 Aug. 1761, in Yorke, *Hardwicke*, III, pp. 321, 273; Schweizer, *Frederick the Great*, p. 128 and ch. 5 passim.

190. Peters, *Pitt*, pp. 200–1; Schweizer, 'Lord Bute', pp. 44, 47–8.

191. Pitt to Temple, 10 [Aug.] 1761, in Smith (ed.), *Grenville Papers*, I, p. 386; Bedford to Gower, 27 June 1761, PRO 30/29/1/14; *Memoirs George II*, III, p. 84 (more certainly true of 1761 than 1759).

192. SP109/68–71; PRO 30/8/92, ff. 248–69, 294–306, vol. 93 passim and, e.g., vol. 6, ff. 8–9; Middleton, *Bells*, pp. 160–3.

193. Middleton, *Bells*, pp. 189–90; Peters, *Pitt*, pp. 200–1.

194. Brown and Schweizer (eds), *Devonshire Diary*, pp. 126–40; Yorke, *Hardwicke*, III, pp. 274–80, 322–8; Peters, *Pitt*, pp. 201–2; Middleton, *Bells*, pp. 193–8.

195. Brown and Schweizer (eds), *Devonshire Diary*, pp. 133, 135.

196. Ibid., p. 139 (2 Oct.); Newcastle's minutes, 2 Oct., reproduced in full in William Hunt, 'Pitt's retirement from office, 5 Oct. 1761', *English Historical Review* 21 (1906), pp. 131–2. Devonshire's version (quoted), and *Annual Register* 4 (1761), p. 44, both make Granville's rebuke more sweeping than Newcastle's does.

197. *Annual Register* 4 (1761), pp. 47–8, extensively quoted in Peters, *Pitt*, p. 265, Middleton, *Bells*, p. 199; cf. the City thanks to Pitt, 22 Oct., *London Evening Post*, 24–27 Oct. 1761.

198. Peters, 'Myth', pp. 52–4; *Memoirs George II*, III, p. 2.

199. *Parl. Hist.*, XV, col. 1270. On versions of Pitt's speech, see Peters, 'Myth', n. 178.

200. Middleton, *Bells*, pp. 210–11; Peters, 'Myth', pp. 50–2; and, the best full assessments, Paul Langford, *The Eighteenth Century 1688–1815* (1976), pp. 145–52, and idem, *A Polite and Commercial People*, pp. 350–2.
201. See above, p. 114; Peters, *Pitt*, pp. 256–9, 162–3; Brown and Schweizer (eds), *Devonshire Diary*, p. 52 (2 Nov. 1760).

Chapter 4

PITT, WILKES AND EMPIRE, 1761–66

When he resigned in October 1761, and despite the constraints of the new reign, Pitt was incontestably the most outstanding figure in British politics, not only in popular reputation but in achievement in office. Yet never again was he to exercise the power he had come to wield in the wartime coalition. Indeed, he was to be active in office again only for a few months in 1766–67. The rest of his career was increasingly shaped by the interaction of his ill health with his personality. The periods of partial or complete withdrawal punctuated by bursts of intense activity pose an enigma of ineffectualness.

There is much to suggest that Pitt intended his resignation to lead to retirement from active politics. Disillusionment with changed circumstances, compounding the burdens of office and ill health, had seemed for some while to point that way, as did statements at the time.[1] Although the favours Pitt finally accepted after resignation – a pension of £3,000 a year for himself and a barony for his wife – left him in the Commons, more than once he had said he would attend only if attacked and otherwise 'should be ready to support government'.[2] However, the detached role of elder statesman did not come easily to one of his temperament. The role became even harder to sustain as developments in war and peace negotiations made earlier policies contentious. And they were the more contentious because they interacted with the change naturally consequent on the accession of a new king and with already excited public politics to create a new volatility.

NEW REIGN, NEW POLITICS

The new reign began auspiciously. The young George III, who could claim that, '[b]orn and educated in this country, I glory in the name of Briton',[3] inspired an effusion of loyalty quite unparalleled at the accessions, or indeed during the reigns, of previous Hanoverian monarchs. He seemed the epitome of the patriot king long promised by Leicester House. Yet euphoria was short-lived. Pitt's resignation renewed public contention over the role of the king in politics. This grew to levels unprecedented in Hanoverian political debate when Bute became First Lord of the Treasury following Newcastle's resignation in May 1762 over the refusal to continue the German war. Public turmoil was hardly assuaged when Bute abruptly resigned less than a year later, yet seemed set to remain the king's confidant. Indeed, public politics – encouraged over many years by the development of the press, more recently excited by the successes of war and the celebration of Pitt, only to be agitated by war-weariness and the issues of peacemaking – were to be inflamed by political change to new levels of sustained intensity.[4] Postwar social and economic dislocation added further disturbances, while the political effects of long-term economic and social change – notably commercial development, urbanization and the growth of a middle class – although less obvious, were increasingly apparent. And already before Bute's fall, the pen of the most skilful demagogue of the eighteenth century, John Wilkes, had entered the conflict. In the course of the decade, his provocation to governments not only helped to keep public politics more continuously agitated and more influential in high politics, while more independent of parliamentary politicians, than hitherto in the Hanoverian period. New social groups – artisans in London, the urban middle class all over the country – were also aroused to more consistent involvement, while new, 'radical' modes of organization and demands were stimulated.[5]

Politicians were even more directly affected by upheaval in the new reign. As the war drew to its close, the collapse of the coalition was to be expected; its unusual breadth and tenuous stability were the products of the same extraordinary circumstances that allowed Pitt to shape his dominance.

However, the advent of a naïve young king, at 22 barely out of a prolonged adolescence enforced by his hitherto cloistered life, accentuated the political change he was not well equipped to manage. Certainly, he had no intention of refurbishing the powers of the Crown in novel ways (as used to be believed). But, equally certainly, he despised Pitt and Newcastle and idealistically wanted to inaugurate more virtuous politics. (In personal morality, at least, he was a lifelong contrast to his grandfather.) Moreover, he was devoted to his favourite who, while meeting the young man's desperate need for friendship, was 'a man of learning without wisdom',[6] quite lacking in knowledge of the world, yet ambitious to make his mark in politics. Even when his effrontery turned to craven resignation under the barrage of largely undeserved criticism his ministry provoked,[7] he still intended to guide from behind the scenes.

The activism of George III and Bute was in marked contrast to the resigned acceptance of the ways of British politics into which the old king had grown by the end of his reign. The attitudes politicians encountered at court increased their bewilderment and suspicion as changes in office gathered speed. A marked reluctance to work with Bute became widespread. Those Whigs long used to a monopoly of office were particularly affected. For many Bute became, with some justification, the sinister *éminence grise* of politics, with whom they would not work. For some, their views of politics were to be permanently reshaped. In unaccustomed opposition, they came to see themselves in magnified 'country' terms as virtuous defenders of the constitution against a courtly conspiracy of 'secret influence'.

The sense of disorientation was compounded by the confusion of Whig/Tory party distinctions, for so long major landmarks of politics. In fact, they had long been mitigated by the normally careful management of both Walpole and Pelham in the interests of stability and blurred by 'patriot' oppositions. Party distinctions were further attenuated by the political manoeuvring of the mid-1750s and even more by the emphasis of much wartime propaganda on unanimity in success 'under an administration, that disdains the aid of party'.[8] Now the 'patriotism' of the young 'British' king, determined to be ruler for all his people, drew Tories to kiss hands at a Hanoverian court as never before, while some were rewarded with honours and lesser office. Pitt had actively encouraged these developments. Always nonchalant about party ties, he had swung abruptly from blatant appeals to the Whigs in the 1754–55 parliamentary session to courting the Tories a year later, and then to projecting himself as a war leader above party, as the strains of war divided City from country Tories. In the new reign he actively encouraged Tory appointments to office, while rejoicing 'at the extinction of parties' and acknowledging his contribution to it.[9]

The clear end to long proscription from court and office further weakened the Tories' sense of identity. In a parallel process, the Old Corps of the Whigs was also deprived of cohesiveness, first by the very breadth of the wartime coalition, and then by the ending of its monopoly of power, brutally signalled in 1761–63 over the winding down of the war. The process which saw the loss first of Pitt and then of Newcastle culminated in the dismissal of those of Newcastle's recognized followers still in office who opposed the peace – the so-called 'slaughter of the Pelhamite innocents'. In parliament during the 1760s, as they adapted to new circumstances, Whigs and Tories alike gradually dispersed in various directions, leaving political competition to be structured by personal parties – groups adhering, more on personal than ideological terms, to leading politicians like Pitt, Newcastle and his successor the Marquess of Rockingham, Bedford, Grenville. In the same process, rapid ministerial changes made more evident a group that came to be called 'King's Friends' – those sympathetic to the court or more interested in office than politics.

Party labels did not, however, completely disappear. Newly defined and only tenuously relating to political realities, they continued to be bandied about in public, as some opposition groups sought to appropriate the Whig label and denigrate their courtly opponents – often equally Whig in lineage and policy – as newly revived 'prerogative' Tories.[10] In such fractured and agitated politics, the task of securing a competent ministry with the confidence of both king and Commons was greatly complicated: the decade saw six administrations fall. As the mould of Walpole–Pelhamite politics was decisively broken, the very stability of the Hanoverian constitution sometimes seemed at risk. Certainly the tackling of major problems of the financial burden of war and the administration

of vastly increased overseas possessions was gravely compromised. So the euphoria of victory and a new reign quickly gave
way to deep-seated anxiety and disenchantment.[11]

Pitt's resignation was the first clear sign of political change;
its aftermath made incipient political turmoil obvious; and
Pitt was inevitably drawn in. He came to be inextricably associated with the turmoil, helping to fuel it and deeply marked
by its force. Debates over his actions, especially in 1761–62
and 1766, were integral parts of the public contentions, while,
as the decade ended, he returned to politics after a prolonged
withdrawal seemingly determined to provoke controversy.
His unpredictability and arrogant unco-operativeness – to
say nothing of his ill health – greatly accentuated the volatility of ministerial politics, not least in his own administration of 1766. He, too, reshaped his party affiliations and
ideology under the decade's pressures.

. . .

PITT: PATRIOT OR MAVERICK? 1761–63

To many of the public, Pitt's resignation 'seemed equal to
a revolution in the state'.[12] For three months, public debate
raged in what became, with the help of paid publicists, the
most sustained attack of all the war years on his policies and
popularity.[13] In ways that are often not recognized, it merged
into and helped to shape later and greater controversies.

By far the most damaging criticisms were the personal ones.
The favours granted Pitt were alleged to cap past 'inconsistencies' and broken promises and to show him up more clearly
than ever as an arrogant, presumptuous 'patriot unmasked'
– and, moreover, one who had deserted his post to avoid
difficulties in a crisis.[14] Even Walpole ironically mocked himself as 'an old fool' for having fallen 'a dupe to virtue and
patriotism'.[15] Closely connected were considerations of Pitt's
policies. The broken promises and allegedly questionable
benefits of the German war were still by far the most contentious questions. The great costs of war were seen as tar-
nishing the successes, usually, but not always, credited to Pitt.
When the declaration of a further 'ruinous' Spanish war
seemed briefly to revive Pitt's reputation, he was accused
either of not recognizing the Spanish threat early enough
or of provoking an unnecessary war. In large part, the

debate merely summed up, more forcefully than before, the undertones of criticism that had regularly punctuated the war years.[16] Running through it, however, were subordinate but significant new arguments about the constitutional propriety of Pitt's wartime dominance.[17] A case, based partly on 'the peoples voice', for allowing Pitt to be 'to sight at least and in the general estimation, a Prime Minister', with responsibility beyond his department,[18] was set against an equally assertive case, limiting ministerial responsibility and allowing a large role to the king, which gradually prevailed. The new features of both cases – overtly 'populist' and 'royalist' respectively – are potent signs of a fundamental change in political circumstances, soon to be even more evident.[19]

The force and significance of these 'violent conflicts' deserve emphasis. In them, the *Annual Register* noted, 'the popular cause was worse sustained, and the ministerial better ... than is usual in such discussions'. The 'torrent of popular rage' on Pitt's behalf was 'beaten back' and returned only 'weakened, divided, and ineffective'.[20] This time, in contrast to the thirteen gold boxes granted Pitt in 1757, the outspoken City vote of thanks to Pitt was followed by only eight other places – a disappointing tribute after four years of glorious success.[21] The lustre of the patriot minister – now competing with a patriot king – had undoubtedly been dimmed.

In the first session of the newly elected parliament, however – the much more important test – the shock of Pitt's resignation was considerably less. Issues about Pitt's wartime status were far less prominent,[22] and only the venom of a new member, Colonel Isaac Barré, amazed members, by bringing the scurrility of the press into the House.[23] However, the resignation inevitably intensified debate over past and future policy prompted by changing circumstances. Complaints against the German war which 'would have been reckoned as indecent insults upon the Sovereign in the late reign'[24] were increasingly vociferous. And, despite his recent declarations, Pitt was present and soon drawn to justify himself in the forum where he enjoyed such sway.

In a series of now well-reported speeches, often substantive and cogent, Pitt comprehensively defended the coalition's German policy. He claimed that he had turned an inherited policy to Britain's advantage, at the same time making the German war a continuing burden 'heavy on the neck of France'.[25] On the peace negotiations, when taxed by Beckford, he regretted that he had been 'overborne by numbers' in making concessions over French exclusion from the fisheries.[26] On relations with Spain, he justified at length his call for vigorous measures. He denied that he had courted war, yet assumed credit when war came. And when, in May, the question of aid to Portugal arose, he warmly supported the measure while deploring any suggestion of withdrawal from Germany. Britain could afford to borrow, he argued, to continue the continental measures 'practised by all our great princes' from Queen Elizabeth to King William.[27]

Many observers agreed in seeing in these speeches 'great dignity and temper', which, in the words of the *Annual Register*, 'set a seal upon his character'.[28] The Prussian ambassador attributed to Pitt's speech the approval without division in December of continued subsidies for foreign troops.[29] And there was indeed consistency, unmodified by concession to royal or public war-weariness, in his insistence that the war should be pushed on in all directions, regardless of expense. He 'did not stoop to . . . opposing whatever was the measure of the adversary. He had stood forth for general war, and for the reduction of the House of Bourbon. To advise still larger war was constancy to the same plan.'[30]

Other commentators, however, saw in Pitt's justification of the German war only 'the old trite argument of being connected essentially with the conquests in all parts of the globe', and Barrington rightly challenged 'Mr. Pitt's assertion, that America had been neglected for Hanover in 1756'. Walpole, while often admiring, saw Pitt's first speech as 'artful and inflammatory'. Several observers noted his theatricality.[31] With the statesmanlike moderation and affected reluctance to be drawn into debate went well-tried devices of calling for information which could embarrass, hinting he knew more than he could divulge, seeming to praise in order to highlight disarray and affecting modesty while drawing credit to himself.[32] He said he 'hoped never to be a public man again. He would never come into place again'. But in defending his policies he could not avoid being a 'public man'.[33]

Through the summer and autumn, as Newcastle resigned, further successes in war rivalled those of 1759–60, and peace negotiations were at last successfully concluded, Pitt remained quiet. He denied reports that he approved the peace terms and would not attend parliament. On the other hand, Temple wrote of Pitt's 'resolution of retirement', and by the end of November, as parliament opened, Pitt was once again seriously ill.[34]

When at last, on 9 December, he appeared for the peace debate deferred to enable him to attend, he came accompanied by acclamations of the crowd outside, dramatically borne as an invalid, swathed in flannel, in the arms of his servants. By all accounts his speech of three and a half hours was ineffective, 'very tedious, unconvincing, heavy, and immethodical', and he left before the division, which approved the terms by 319 votes to 65. He seemed 'to bid adieu to politics, and to despair of his own health'.[35] Nevertheless, there was much in Pitt's speech that still spoke of active opposition and the cultivation of his own image, not least his tendentious claim to have stood firm alone in 'his' peace negotiations and his new projection of himself as defender of *this lovely Constitution* against a 'new cobbler', and of 'revolution principles' of opposition to France against a new system of policy.[36] For the rest of the session, Pitt's behaviour remained enigmatic. He swung between inactivity and warm support for the administration's decision to maintain a large peacetime army in North America, which paralysed any opposition to the measure. Yet he intervened against the budget and belatedly opposed the new cider tax.[37]

Thus, as the war was finally ended, Pitt's intentions remained as uncertain as his future in the new politics of the 1760s. He remained detached, striking an elder statesman pose with some conviction. Yet he was obviously concerned with backward-looking self-justification and defence of his reputation – despite his affected disdain for 'party-papers'[38] – in a way which did not suggest retirement from active politics. But so far he had only tentatively moved – by opposing the cider tax on grounds of personal liberty from intrusive excise officers – to the fresh issues his dimmed patriot reputation needed to sustain itself in peacetime. Despite his longstanding preoccupation with foreign policy, he showed no awareness of new postwar European or imperial issues.

What was clear was the support Pitt had lost, not only out-of-doors but also inside the House. In the 1761–62 post-resignation debates, while he could still attract crowds and hold the attention of the House, few supported him with speeches and only Beckford attempted to defend him against Barré. By December, the king could rightly remark, 'I suppose his party consist of that Lord [Strange], Mr Beck[ford], Mr Cooke, and perhaps a very few more who are of the same hot headed stamp'. 'Mr Pitt may still have his partizans in the City,' remarked another, 'but at present, it does not appear he has many at Westminster.'[39] He had shown himself disdainful of the Tories, whose support had formerly helped to maintain his prized independence of 'connection'; it was now largely lost.[40] Where now would he find 'forces to follow him', to realize his potential to 'be very considerable in Parliament'?[41]

Furthermore, his own 'personal party' had been weakened rather than strengthened by his time in office. Beckford, although now a warm friend and, as Lord Mayor, holding the City loyal, was no substitute for Potter as colleague or ally in the House.[42] Barrington, a follower from the 1740s with whom as Secretary at War Pitt had co-operated easily, was now a typical officeholder turned King's Friend. Warm relations with Legge had turned to open breach by 1759.[43]

Even the Grenville family support was now bitterly divided. The as yet faithful Temple and the amiable James had resigned with Pitt, but George – the ablest and a valuable lieutenant in the House – was now totally alienated. Dissatisfaction with lack of advancement coupled with growing discomfort over an expensive war had brought him closer to Leicester House in the late 1750s, as Pitt's contact there was broken. Resentment grew as Pitt 'threshed' him in the House over taxes in 1761 and put them on opposite sides when Grenville became leader of the House after Pitt's resignation (although he then refused Pitt's seals); Grenville spoke out against war costs, among other things suggesting (foreshadowing modern debates[44]) that 'want of seamen', rather than the German war, had crippled France in America. Pitt's heartless humiliation of Grenville as the 'Gentle Shepherd' in the cider tax debates was the most bruising of several later exchanges. For Hester, now Lady Chatham, the cost of her husband's political differences was, not for the last time, personal: an enforced and painful rift within her family.[45]

Weakened though he was, however, Pitt not only continued to reject approaches from Bute in late 1762 and early 1763, on the grounds that 'he would never abet the transcendancy of power his Lordship was arrived at'. He also oscillated quite unpredictably in attitude to Newcastle and his remaining supporters, as they moved surprisingly quickly towards unaccustomed opposition – ironically, under the tutelage of the very Duke of Cumberland whose supposed pretensions they had previously so feared and who now re-emerged to bring his considerable skills and nerve to bear again on politics.[46] Pitt came to the peace debates proclaiming himself 'unconnected', following 'no party'. Then the cider tax brought warm, if brief, co-operation with Newcastle's group.[47] For Pitt, such nonchalance about connection and party ties could well mean political ineffectiveness.

As ministerial politics became clearly unsettled with Bute's resignation in April 1763, Pitt's role remained enigmatic – if not without some developing inner logic. In the light of George Grenville's recent politics, it was no bolt from the blue when he allowed himself to be persuaded by Bute to succeed him as First Lord of the Treasury. But the king accepted him with great reluctance and, as the administration struggled to establish its credibility as more than a façade for Bute's continuing influence, its relations with the king were further compromised.[48] By July and August, the king was putting out piecemeal feelers to Hardwicke and Newcastle and even indirectly to Pitt – but all refused to come in as individuals.[49]

Then suddenly, late in August, a 'great political storm' broke which brought Pitt right into the limelight and to the verge of office again – under the sponsorship of Bute and with Beckford as intermediary. The storm was precipitated by the death of the Earl of Egremont, a leading member of the administration. On Bute's urging, the king saw Pitt for three hours on 27 August, when Pitt

went through the infirmities of the peace; the things necessary . . . to improve and preserve it; the present state of the nation, both foreign and domestic; the great Whig families and persons which had been driven from His Majesty's Council and service, which it would be for his interest to restore.

144

Convinced he had persuaded the king into this major change of men and measures, Pitt then spent hours in negotiation with Newcastle and his group. But, when he returned to the king two days later, to Pitt's repeated insistence on the 'great families' the king replied, 'Well, Mr Pitt, I see . . . this won't do. My honour is concerned, and I must support it.' Bute, it seems, had taken fright in the interlude at the extent of change demanded. The negotiation was over – and the king was forced into a humiliating reconciliation with Grenville and acceptance of Bute's complete retirement from politics.[50]

'Never, in any history, was there so curious a scene', said contemporaries of this episode.[51] Pitt's behaviour does indeed seem incredible in the light of his recent declarations and attitude towards Bute and Newcastle. Observers wondered at his high-handed negotiating style, which was drawn to public attention for the first time in a bout of spirited controversy which illustrated how contentious was the suggestion that Pitt had sought to impose an 'imperious plan' on the young 'amiable, but unhappy' sovereign.[52] There is no doubt that Pitt's arrogance led him to misjudge the desperation and sensitivities of the young king and his favourite. As Lyttelton put it,

My old friend was once a skilful courtier; but since he himself has attained a kind of *royalty*, he seems more attentive to support his own majesty than to pay the necessary regards to that of his sovereign.[53]

However, those in closest contact with Pitt obviously believed that he negotiated in good faith. There were, after all, significant new circumstances about the opportunities now so suddenly offered. Bute's aspirations to office were clearly destroyed, and Pitt was never to share the exaggerated fears, now developing, of Bute's secret influence 'behind the curtain'.[54] Pitt – who had declared unwillingness to hold office against the king's goodwill[55] – was now negotiating directly with the king in circumstances which gave him the upper hand over his proposed allies.[56] The episode was, in fact, a formative experience in shaping his attitudes to ministerial negotiations in the 1760s. Its outcome suggested that a 'party' approach was not the way either to secure his dominance or to regain the confidence of the king. Nor would he again accept the offices of any influential intermediary.[57]

Immediately, all Pitt gained were three new adherents, to be of considerable importance later. John Calcraft, for many years in minor but lucrative office, transferred his 'man of business' services from Fox (now Baron Holland) to Pitt; with him came the Earl of Shelburne, who resigned the Board of Trade, disillusioned with his lack of advancement under Grenville, and Shelburne's protégé, that same Colonel Barré who had so recently savagely attacked Pitt.[58] To Pitt, Calcraft brought industry and a web of valuable lesser contacts. Shelburne had an acute if untrained intelligence and had demonstrated ability and diligence in gathering information at the Board of Trade. But already, as a young peer of some rank who had switched allegiance from Fox to Bute and now to Pitt, he was gaining an unenviable reputation for duplicity which was to win the sobriquet, 'the Jesuit of Berkeley Square' (his London home). Barré brought welcome debating weight. All were prepared to give admiring and unquestioning service.

. . .

WILKES – AND WITHDRAWAL, 1763–65

The greatest ferment of 1763, however, arose not from ministerial instability but from public politics. Agitation continued over the cider tax and a much more widespread wave of addresses approving the peace, which embarrassed both Newcastle as Chancellor of Cambridge University and Pitt as MP for Bath, when both refused to present their constituents' addresses.[59] But the major ferment had deeper roots in that quickening tempo of press controversy through 1762 generated by the anxieties raised by Pitt's resignation and the frustration of his supporters at the force of attack on him.

In defence of Pitt in debate over Spanish policy early in 1762 John Wilkes – to become the most notorious political publicist of the century – made his début. On 22 May, just as Bute was taking over from Newcastle, Wilkes wrote a daring article on favourites in the *Monitor*, still Pitt's most consistent and effective advocate. Soon, Wilkes's more provocative energies were diverted to a new essay paper, the *North Briton*.

As Bute founded his own papers, the *Briton* and *Auditor*, a renewed battle of the weeklies was joined. Within a month, Walpole wrote: 'My father was not more abused after twenty years than Lord Bute is in twenty days', and the *North Briton* became the centrepiece of the campaign of unprecedented virulence that was to rage over the next eleven months. Personal abuse of Bute as Scotsman, royal favourite and, by implication, lover of the king's mother gave the campaign its cutting edge, but it also clearly contrasted the policies, successes and constitutional position of Bute and Pitt as ministers. From September, peacemaking provided further grounds for forceful discussion, which continued through the parliamentary session.[60]

In April 1763, just after Bute's surprise resignation, this vehement controversy was given entirely new importance by the government's response to the soon infamous *North Briton* no. 45. This issue was not notably more forceful than some preceding ones; but it did accuse the ministers of putting lies into the king's mouth when, in closing the parliamentary session, he praised the peace, and could plausibly be represented as stirring the people to sedition. Grenville's administration decided to act. Those concerned with publishing no. 45 were arrested on a general warrant (one which did not name individuals), and Wilkes was then charged with seditious libel. Ministers had reckoned without Wilkes's flair for publicity. He successfully challenged his arrest on grounds of privilege as an MP and proceeded to win damages against the ministers for the 'theft' of his seized papers. As he publicized his every move as defences of the rights of Englishmen, enthusiastic crowds responded with the first cries of 'Wilkes and Liberty'. No one had challenged action against the press like this before. In retaliation, the humiliated administration decided to bring the issues before parliament in November. Opposition politicians were offered the possibility of harnessing unprecedented public excitement to their cause.

The opportunities seemed greatest for Pitt. Wilkes had been a supporter from the time he entered parliament in 1757 and visited Pitt late in 1762.[61] Temple was Wilkes's intimate friend and patron – not least as more-or-less approving backer of the *North Briton* – and openly took up his cause in the furore over no. 45.[62] Yet this was a dangerous game,

certain to offend the king and – as support for the government in the 1763–64 session was to show – many MPs. Pitt,
like other opposition leaders, was more cautious.[63]

Thus, as the Wilkes affair became the chief question of
the session, Pitt consistently and increasingly seized on the
broad issues of principle involved while distinguishing them
carefully from the person and publications of Wilkes.[64] In
early debates he condemned no. 45 as 'a scandalous, licen-
tious paper, and false', and the whole *North Briton* series
as 'illiberal, unmanly, and detestable', especially abhorrent
for its 'national [anti-Scots] reflections'. Wilkes was 'the blas-
phemer of his God, and libeller of his King', with whom Pitt
vehemently denied not only his own connection but (remarkably) any knowledge of Temple's, while equally warmly
acknowledging his own alliance with Temple.[65] But at the
same time, against the government's first move, to have the
House condemn no. 45 as a seditious libel, he objected that
libels were properly tried in the courts. Next, when a resolution was sought that privilege did not extend to seditious
libel, Pitt 'vehemently reprobated the facility with which
parliament was surrendering its own privileges', which would
put the House 'at the mercy of the crown'.[66] Most strikingly,
in debates in the new year, he stood out strongly for tackling as broadly as possible the legality of the arrests and
seizure of papers under a general warrant. In the main debate
on an opposition motion condemning general warrants,
having admitted and defended his own issuing of them in
wartime emergencies, he sought to raise the argument above
its long, dry, legal exchanges. '*General warrants are always
wrong*', he had earlier asserted. Now, in a final clarion call,
he asked, 'What will our constituents say if we do not ascer-
tain their liberties?' If the House defeated the motion they
would be, he said, 'the disgrace of the present age, and the
reproach of posterity'.[67]

Pitt's were major contributions to these exciting post-
Christmas debates, the first – when, in the early hours of the
morning, he 'poured forth one of his finest rhapsodies on
liberty' – the longest sitting of the century, the other attract-
ing one of the largest attendances. Now, in marked contrast
to the earlier divisions, government majorities of merely
ten and fourteen were virtual defeats.[68] Now, too, Pitt had
certainly begun to define new issues. For more than a year,

in accord with contemporary trends, he had been representing himself again as a Whig on Revolution principles who 'would stand upon no other ground'; Tories might be taken into a Whig administration (as in the wartime coalition), but he would 'never come into' one whose 'bottom and groundwork' was Tory.[69] The Wilkes affair gave this stand some new ideological content. His 'own first wish', Pitt now said, 'had been to crush foreign enemies; now it was to crush domestic. When that was done he should die willingly'.[70]

At the same time, however, his careful distancing of himself from Wilkes's provocative person divided him from his long-term supporters in the City, and to Newcastle he 'spoke with much less respect for the City and regard for popular applause than I have ever heard him before'.[71] It is perhaps significant that, while in April Pitt and Temple were reportedly the '*constant public-toasts*' of Exeter, a later squib omitted Pitt's name from 'The Worthys of England in the year 1763' but included Temple and Wilkes.[72] Pitt's attitude was politically wise, no doubt. But it cut him off from his popular base just when Wilkes was raising excitement to unprecedented levels. It also accentuated the growing rift between parliamentary and public politics which left Wilkes's followers leaderless after his flight to France early in 1764.[73]

While ideologically Pitt redefined himself as Whig, in practice he quickly drew back from the party stance he had briefly adopted in August alongside those he himself recognized as the 'great Whig Lords . . . the Duke of Newcastle's friends'.[74] The Wilkes affair complicated relations by accentuating the legal rivalry between Charles Yorke, who as Attorney-General had approved the general warrant, and Pitt's supporter, Charles Pratt, who as Chief Justice of Common Pleas had pronounced for Wilkes.[75] By October, Pitt had slipped back into detached elusiveness.[76] At the opening of parliament, he startled a supporter by proclaiming that 'he stood single' and paying 'candid' compliments to ministers and king.[77] He offered no more than minimal co-operation in opposition on general warrants questions and did nothing to help on other issues. So Grenville's careful strategy against Wilkes was embarrassed but not halted. With Wilkes both expelled and deprived of privilege, the seditious libel charge could now proceed, and when Wilkes failed to appear he was outlawed.

Moreover, throughout the session Pitt had been hampered by illness.[78] His February appearances were to be the last for nearly two years, despite a wealth of issues in the 1764–65 session that might have been expected to attract him. 'Mr Pitt . . . we begin to know only by tradition', was Walpole's comment.[79]

By this time, Pitt had clearly established principles of political behaviour to which he had instinctively been moving since 1761. These principles, not simply illness, arrogance or old fears of Newcastle, shaped Pitt's continuing aloofness and 'determined inactivity'.[80] It might remain 'the unanimous opinion of all [Newcastle's] friends, young and old, that nothing can be done without Mr Pitt at the head of us to some degree'.[81] Pitt, on the other hand, in marked contrast to his pre-war behaviour, was now convinced that 'the subversion of the administration was not to be brought about by parliament', that 'all opposition was to no purpose'. He 'would never come in by force; or, without the King's good will; and that of the person who has the great weight with His Majesty'.[82] So he would attend parliament only 'upon any national or constitutional points' or matters 'of the first magnitude'; he would not 'mix [in opposition] . . . in any bargains or stipulations whatever', but rather would 'oppose or . . . promote . . . independent of the sentiments of others'. '[M]easures, and not men', the Prussian envoy Michell told Newcastle, 'were his point'.[83]

Such a stance was much more congenial than party co-operation to Pitt's personality, especially as moulded by his wartime experience. It was also driven by a deep, backward-looking resentment. To his complaints in 1762 that, after his resignation, he had been 'out-Toried by Lord Bute and out-Whigged by the Duke of Newcastle', and left with 'nobody to converse with but the clerk of the House of Commons', were now added bitter and repeated recriminations 'that his [war and peace] measures had been unsupported' in the budget debate of March 1764, 'that he did not know who would join with him, or act upon his plan, and principles, if there was to be a change of administration'.[84] Pitt's mood was undoubtedly intensified by illness. There was, however, nothing about his attitudes that suggested his withdrawal was a retirement. Rather, he was caught again at one extreme of the oscillations between ambition and ill health that patterned so much of his life.

In 1765, Pitt's tenets of political behaviour were again to be tested as once again he came almost to the point of taking office. Meanwhile, however, Grenville's administration continued to show its parliamentary and administrative strength, not least in its 'programme' for America. This was a comprehensive series of measures, the evolution of which had begun under Bute, to settle a range of urgent issues highlighted by the war. The greatly increased national debt made economy the chief concern of most British opinion – hence the attraction of the proposals, first outlined in Grenville's budget in March 1764, to make existing customs duties effective and raise an internal stamp duty in America.[85]

Pitt was no more prescient than others about the consequences either of these measures or of the earlier declared intention to make the colonists pay for the army to be stationed in America. His chief concern was that the peace was 'hollow and insecure', 'an armed truce only'.[86] True, to Newcastle in August 1763 he mentioned his disposition against 'measures of power, or force' in 'the settlement of our colonies, upon a proper foot, with regard to themselves, and their mother country', but this was incidental to his concern about an 'inadequate' peace.[87] By March 1764, Pitt was reliably reported to be 'against *all* taxation' of America. But not until after the passage of the Stamp Act early in 1765 did he add to his growing litany of complaint about the Newcastle group 'the American Tax being not sufficiently objected to *this* year' and warmly praise Barré's vigorous opposition to it.[88] He did nothing himself; he was later to claim that illness prevented him,[89] although he was certainly well enough at times to come to London. Still his overriding concern, when it was not backward-looking self-justification,[90] was France.

The ministerial crisis that cut short Grenville's promise of being another Walpole or Pelham was precipitated by his abysmal relations with the king. His punctilious, overbearing personality, which made him incapable of imagining the young monarch's feelings, had prevented any improvement. By May 1765, king and minister were brought to such a point by mutual misunderstanding over the Regency Act proposed by the king after his recent illness that he could stand Grenville no longer.[91] He commissioned his uncle, the Duke of Cumberland, to approach Pitt and the Newcastle group to form a new ministry. The latter were willing, but when Cumberland himself went to Pitt's country house at Hayes in Kent, Pitt declined to co-operate. Forced into a further bitterly humiliating capitulation to Grenville, within a month the king was driven to another breaking point. This time, Pitt again had two audiences with the king. After the second, on 22 June, all seemed set for success. Then Temple declined to serve as Pitt wished, as First Lord of the Treasury, and to everyone's amazement Pitt refused to come in without him. Cumberland, following the terms of this second commission, went ahead to negotiate an administration without him, nominally headed by one of Newcastle's 'young friends', the Marquess of Rockingham, but in effect led by Cumberland. It took office on 10 July.

It is easy to explain Pitt's refusal in May. His stipulations, eventually reduced to three – that army officers and others dismissed for opposition in parliament be restored, that the illegality of general warrants be established, and that an anti-Bourbon alliance be formed, preferably with Prussia – were accepted, after some demur over the third.[92] But this time Pitt was not in control. The mediation of Cumberland, whom he had long disliked, 'nettled' him. More than that, Pitt knew there was little chance of 'settling an Administration upon his own plans'. The 1763 negotiations had taught him wariness of Bute, and he may also have wondered about the implications of Grenville's fate.[93] Temple, on the point of reconciliation with Grenville, was already much cooler about negotiations than Pitt, to whom the reconciliation was 'merely private family satisfaction'.[94]

Cumberland was still involved in June, to Pitt's annoyance, but it was Temple, not Pitt, who now condemned the planned arrangements as 'Butal-Ducal'.[95] This time Pitt negotiated directly with the king, who readily accepted his terms. Pitt considered circumstances promising and his appeals to Temple confirm that he was set to take office until Temple refused. His bewailing of 'the most difficult and painful' crisis of his life further bears out his seriousness.[96] It seems, therefore, that his own explanation of his obduracy to all pleadings after Temple's refusal should carry weight. Temple's refusal seems suddenly to have made him aware of the 'difficulties that threatened from different quarters' – in closet, cabinet and parliament.[97] Without his one longstanding ally and in his present state of health, he feared, as always, for that independence which would allow him to be 'guiding everything'.[98] His attitude, both now and in May, confirms the principles towards which he had been instinctively moving since 1761. His audiences with the king were reassuring and they parted on apparently cordial terms.[99] But Pitt was still neither free of intermediaries nor sure that he could dominate the administration he was called to. Ill health probably exacerbated his fears; certainly it contributed to the obscurantism, the 'Fustian', with which he clothed his pronouncements.[100]

It was a sad sign of the changing generations that, in default of Pitt, the remnants of the Old Corps Whigs still with Newcastle could provide no one with significant experience of any political office to take the major departments of state. Instead, Rockingham, at 35, was First Lord, the even younger Duke of Grafton, with little inclination for business, one of the Secretaries of State, the other, Henry Seymour Conway, rather older but happier as a soldier, also expected to lead in the Commons – where the ministry depended for debating weight on friends of Bute reluctantly left in lesser office. 'An Administration *of Boys*', the king came to call it.[101] Newcastle, increasingly isolated by age and the loss of experienced friends,[102] held only subordinate (although honourable) office. Rockingham had immense influence in Yorkshire; office, together with his integrity and genuinely conciliatory disposition – to say nothing of the support of his astute wife and the outstanding abilities of his new secretary, the Irishborn Edmund Burke – was in due course to make him a leader; but hitherto he had been more at home in his Bedchamber post than in the House of Lords, where his extreme reticence was always to make him almost incapable of speaking. The leading members of 'his' administration were bound more by their common interest in horse-racing – shared with Cumberland – than by more overtly political ties. Their 'policy' amounted to an extreme fastidiousness about any accommodation with those they had hitherto opposed, an equally extreme suspicion (matching Grenville's) of Bute's supposed 'influence' – and an initial subservience to Pitt.

So the Rockingham ministry was widely regarded, and at first largely regarded itself, as a stop-gap for Pitt. In time it was to evolve a strong group identity shaped almost as much by Pitt's attitudes to it as by its growing conviction of a malign 'secret influence' at court; Pitt would show to the group to the end of his life a similar ambivalence to that he had developed about Newcastle. For the present, the negotiations had confirmed a marked deterioration in Pitt's relations with them.[103] Hopes of Pitt's support were quickly 'brushed . . . off', and Pitt required his close supporters 'to declare' that he had 'not the smallest share in the advising or the directing of measures'.[104] Soon he was playing the part of 'a Somersetshire by-stander' in his new estate at Burton Pynsent.[105] Clumsy indirect approaches to him at Bath, after the death of Cumberland on 31 October, brought no change of attitude.[106] In December, overtures to his supporters were repulsed with his approval. To two direct approaches the next month, Pitt replied that Newcastle would have to go and the present ministry be dissolved if he was to come in; he would negotiate only on the king's express command and for an 'ample and full' change. When asked whether Temple's inclusion was still essential, he replied with obfuscating bombast.[107]

With Pitt's insistent coolness went a shrill crescendo of venom against Newcastle, from whom, he said, he could expect no 'solid system for the public good'. Complaints of having had his 'principles, and system of measures . . . so often sacrificed' by Newcastle and resolutions 'never to be in confidence or concert again' with him were of recent origin. Accusations that 'that Duke was of so irksome, and meddling a nature that He would marr, and cramp all Councils' looked much further back, to pre-war wounds.[108] Newcastle himself saw the irony of these complaints in the context of his much declined influence.[109] Pitt's complaints, especially when mixed with obscure castigations of 'faction' and 'corruption',[110] seem at best an obsession induced by illness, more probably a vent for his rampant but frustrated ambition. Pitt had claimed early in these approaches that he moved 'in the sphere only of measures'; it seemed, however, that his 'Pride' overruled his 'Patriotism', whatever the 'Service of his Country' might require.[111]

. . .

AMERICA AND THE POLITICS OF POWER, 1766

Then, however, without warning, in January 1766, Pitt emerged again into the public eye after two years' absence.

He suddenly resolved to 'crawl, or be carried' to the House, to deliver his 'mind and heart'[112] on the major issue then facing the Rockingham administration: a crisis of unprecedented proportions in relations with the American colonies.

The crisis brought to a head the gravest issues of the postwar 1760s. Among Grenville's range of measures for America, the Stamp Act – imposing for the first time internal stamp duties, similar to those in Britain, on newspapers, legal documents and other printed matter – had provoked resistance throughout the colonies. Protests culminated in a congress of colonial representatives in October 1765 to co-ordinate a boycott of British trade. Deciding an appropriate British response was not easy. Resources were quite inadequate to enforce the duty; modification of the Act – much discussed and attractive to the king – was unlikely to satisfy the colonists; yet repeal looked like an abrogation of authority. Cumberland's death and an economic recession in Britain shifted the balance within the ministry towards conciliation. Yet the king and – as early debates were to show – many in parliament were dubious.[113] Only over Christmas did the administration evolve an ingenious package proposing a declaratory act asserting parliament's authority over the colonies, to be followed by repeal of the Stamp Act. Not until February were specific proposals put to parliament. Meanwhile, a further firm King's Speech on 14 January initiated two months when American debates dominated proceedings.

For once with little exaggeration, Pitt claimed this issue to be the most important to arise in parliament since the Glorious Revolution. Having taken it up, his interest was strong and sustained. And, from his first speech on 14 January when, after so long a silence, his 'torrent of eloquence flowed like a spring-tide', his views made a considerable impact.[114]

Enough was known of his views[115] for few to be surprised when Pitt called unequivocally for repeal of the Stamp Act. What startled his hearers were his grounds for doing so. They were not those of expediency, as earlier put, apparently with Pitt's approval, by Shelburne, now recognized as one of his followers.[116] Rather, Pitt roundly declared the principle of no taxation without representation: that '*the House of Commons did not represent North America*'; it therefore

155

had '*no right to lay an internal tax upon America*'.[117] It was, he claimed, 'a nonsensical absurdity' to argue that the Americans were 'virtually' represented in the Commons like Englishmen who had no vote. Thus he crystallized, far more clearly than any other leading politician was prepared to do, the issue of right on which Grenville had invited challenge when he first proposed the stamp duty. He went on in later debates to claim, in 'old Whig' language untempered by the responsibilities of office, that Britain had broken '*the original compact*' by taxing America. True, in response to accusations of sounding 'the trumpet to rebellion' and in face of obvious loss of support,[118] he quickly modified his stand and went on to justify the repeal of the Stamp Act more on grounds of expediency and the needs of British manufacturers than of right. Nevertheless, he firmly maintained his stand on rights in debates on the Declaratory Act, trying unsuccessfully to remove the clause asserting authority 'in all cases whatsoever'.[119]

As Horace Walpole saw it, the major impact of Pitt's views came from 'the novelty and boldness of his doctrines, the offence he gave by them at home, and the delirium which they excited in America'.[120] The exaggerated gratitude of many Americans unjustly neglected the Rockinghams' contribution – while undoubtedly enhancing Pitt's penchant for self-dramatization. That said, however, it is clear that Pitt's stand – despite the reaction against him – did help to maintain the momentum towards repeal of the Stamp Act. Moreover, his unequivocal support for the principle of representation added a new dimension to his recent defences of 'liberty' on issues raised by Wilkes. It possibly led him to contemplate American representation in the imperial parliament.[121] When he praised the representation of the counties and 'great cities' of Britain and predicted that the 'rotten' boroughs would be 'amputated . . . in less than a century', he became the first politician of his standing to foreshadow parliamentary reform. Certainly, he helped to stimulate the debate on the fundamentals of representation that the Stamp Act crisis precipitated.[122]

Nevertheless, from the beginning, with Pitt's pronouncements on American rights ran an emphasis on the 'high rights and privileges' of parliament over the colonies – an emphasis much more generally shared. It was at least as important to him as American rights and was increasingly insisted upon. Even over the Stamp Act, he made it clear that he was not countenancing resistance to an act of parliament. 'An act *de facto* if not *de jure* must be submitted to', he said.[123] In everything but taxation, he was increasingly ready to see authority forcefully exerted if necessary, especially in 'confining and regulating [colonial] trade and manufactures' in the interests of the mother country. When the needs of British manufacturers were concerned, he would, he said, 'be an Englishman first and then an American'. This theme – much less remarked on, especially by Americans, because quite unoriginal – was informed by a growing but equally unoriginal appreciation of the economic benefits of empire.[124]

Pitt attempted to solve the dilemma created by his combination of American rights with British authority by an abstruse distinction between parliament's right to levy internal taxation and the right to lay external duties, which he still allowed. The concept of parliamentary sovereignty, increasingly prominent in British constitutional thinking, made this distinction a nonsense to most of his Westminster audience. Certainly, he never clearly explained it, despite an amalgam of appeals to an '*original compact*', to Locke and 'the penetralia of Common Law', and to history.[125] There is no doubt of Pitt's sympathy with the Americans, or of his instinct for conciliation. Neither was new; now he asked of those determined to enforce the Stamp Act, 'will you sheathe your sword in the bowels of your brothers, the Americans?'[126] However, his complex position was more an instinctive stand on general principles of liberty – made with the characteristically exaggerated claim that he was more proud to be in the majority over repeal than of his part in the last war[127] – than a carefully thought out response to specific problems of imperial relations. The overriding impression is that his stand was adopted on the spur of the moment, to attract attention and with little regard for his earlier views.[128] Certainly, he did not go on to develop the hopes he expressed that 'something like a system may be set up which may secure and bind the union between these two countries', or that the 'commercial system' governing imperial trade might be modified.[129] And when, somewhat later, the ministry proposed its own carefully calculated variations, Pitt mounted what was rightly seen to be a 'peevish and perverse opposition' to them.[130]

Much more immediately important, in fact, than the intricacies of Pitt's views was the drama of his resurrection, with the renewed energy and ambition that it demonstrated. Cumberland's death had reopened opportunities. Now, the intensity of the American crisis drew Pitt to make a political claim – a claim to stand distinguished from the Rockingham administration's attempts to co-opt his support. His first speech advertised yet again that he stood 'unconcerted and unconnected', as he publicized his well-known antipathy to Grenville's measures while at the same time probing the divisions in the administration.[131] The feelers put out by Rockingham in late January and again a month later[132] allowed the devious game for power on Pitt's terms to be advanced in private as well as public. In March, it came into the open again.[133] It rose to a climax in the House in mid-April, as Pitt 'suddenly turned his artillery against the ministry' on a number of measures.[134]

Pitt's behaviour convinced 'everybody' that he 'wished to be in office', 'with full power of modelling the administration as he pleases'.[135] In seconding a bill to repeal the cider tax, he continued his stand for liberty with an impassioned plea for 'every man's house, his castle', the poor man's 'mud' and 'thatch' as much as any; a little later, he paraded his patriotism with a pointed reminder of his support for the militia.[136] Above all, his pronouncements were punctuated with indirect messages to the king. From his first speech, he detached himself from hostility to Bute simply as a Scotsman. In March, he 'praised my Lord Bute and said though he did not wish to see him minister yet it was shameful to proscribe his relations and his friends'. He continued to show himself 'independent of any personal connections whatever' and desirous 'that all our factions might cease; that there might be a ministry fixed, such as the King should appoint, and the public approve'.[137]

The Rockingham administration reeled under these blows from Pitt. Already, the unexpected strength shown by the passage of its major American legislation in the face of many problems had been frittered away. Its exaggerated fears of Bute's influence led it to refuse rapprochement with the 'King's Friends' and bedevilled relations with the king. At the same time, while Rockingham was now convinced of the futility of approaches to Pitt, others continued the courting of him which diminished the administration in many eyes besides the king's.[138] At the end of April, the Duke of Grafton told the king that he wished to resign as Secretary of State because Rockingham refused to make another approach to Pitt.[139] When it proved very difficult to replace him, the king lost all confidence in the ministers' ability to strengthen their base.

With no experienced advisors to turn to, the young monarch was now desperate for the stable and acceptable administration that had eluded him for over three years. When a last, plaintive plea to Bute brought no response, the king welcomed contacts with Pitt through Lord Chancellor Northington, a king's man in the administration, and Pitt's old lawyer friend, Charles Pratt, recently made Baron Camden on the advice of the Rockinghams in their efforts to please Pitt. These contacts reinforced Pitt's public messages that he would this time form an administration 'of the best of all party's and an exclusion to no descriptions'. But no immediate call came. The king had good reason for wariness of Pitt; anyway, he had now learnt to prepare carefully for change.[140] It took two more months of unwitting ministerial maladroitness before the king was ready. Meanwhile, Walpole thought Pitt had overplayed his hand and Pitt was left bewailing that 'all the Lethe of Somersetshire' could not 'obliterate' thoughts of 'a public world, infatuated, bewitched . . . unintelligible'.[141]

Then on 7 July Pitt was at last summoned to town.[142] This time negotiations went relatively smoothly. Having displayed his moderation to Northington, Pitt saw the king. He now answered questions complaisantly and without obfuscation: he 'ardently wish'd' to have Temple at the Treasury, but would if necessary go on without him; he was ready to see some of Bute's friends in office again; while wishing 'to dissolve all factions' and take in 'the best of all party's', he proposed 'the Subsisting administration' – who had now amply displayed their subservience to him – as the basis of a new ministry.[143] Newcastle and Rockingham were proscribed on the further political tenet Pitt was henceforth to adhere to, which was never to contemplate a ministry containing former 'prime' ministers.

Only Pitt could have seriously expected Temple to accept the offer then made to him. Differences between them had been growing, and now Temple's proposed officeholders were abruptly rejected.[144] After a long interview in which Pitt saw only 'kind and affectionate behaviour', Temple later vented to his sister, Hester, his not unjustified indignation at 'being stuck into a ministry as a great cipher ... surrounded with other ciphers, all named by Mr. Pitt'. He would not, he said, *go in like a child, to come out like a fool*'.[145] This time his acrimony spilled over into a vitriolic pamphlet dispute.[146]

Very few of the Rockinghams were deterred by Pitt's dictatorial style from continuing in office, encouraged as they were by Newcastle and Rockingham despite their own proscription. The faithful but young and inexperienced Grafton was at first reluctant to take the head of the Treasury designated for him. There was a typical display of irresolution from Charles Townshend, a long-term lesser officeholder whose undoubted brilliance was already long compromised by a well-established reputation for fickleness and who was now proposed by Pitt as Chancellor of the Exchequer, an office he had already refused under Rockingham. Pitt himself now had only two followers to reward with major office, Camden as Lord Chancellor and Shelburne as Secretary of State.[147]

Pitt's choice of office for himself was shaped by his health. From the beginning he had maintained that his health prevented his taking 'an active Office'.[148] The strain on his health of a rapid journey and difficult interviews was the main cause of delay in finalizing the new administration.[149] When he saw the king again on 23 July it was decided that he should take the Privy Seal and go to the Lords as Earl of Chatham, leaving Henry Seymour Conway to continue as Secretary of State and leader in the Commons. The announcements and the formal exchange of offices took place on 29–30 July.

The king's relief at the prospect, at last, of an 'able and dignified' ministry[150] that would not compromise his 'honour' breathes through all his communications. To many people, even those unsympathetic to Pitt, his coming to office had for some time seemed the only answer to growing problems.[151] Some had high expectations that his 'great abilities and honesty added to the confidence of the people' would enable him 'to complete the great works and after restoring reputation to our arms and safety to our possessions abroad' he would now 'by infusing spirited measures into several departments of government' restore financial stability and commercial prosperity.[152] In the press, even before the king summoned Pitt, favourable comment had noticeably revived. Soon all other politicians were eclipsed by praise of Pitt's anti-party stance, his supposed disinterestedness and public spirit.[153]

Over the previous three years and more, Pitt had done something to refurbish his patriot reputation on important new issues – although there were good reasons to think his popularity not as great as it once was.[154] Not only his earlier achievements but also his new stand against 'connection' had been thrown into high relief by the disintegration of ministries. Now he was taking power on his own terms, with the unqualified support of the king. Could the patriot minister, the great war minister, again surmount the burden of ill health, stabilize and revitalize the politics of the 1760s and work the miracles once more expected of him?

. . .

NOTES

1. Cf. e.g. George F.S. Elliot, *The Border Elliots and the Family of Minto* (Edinburgh, 1897), pp. 363–4 [May 1760], Pitt to Newcastle, 8 Feb., to Bute, 7 Oct. 1761, Newcastle Papers, Add. MSS 32918, f. 358, *Chatham Correspondence*, II, p. 150 (refusing honorific office); Marie Peters, *Pitt and Popularity. The Patriot Minister and London Opinion during the Seven Years' War* (Oxford, 1980), pp. 193–4, 203–4.

2. Peter D. Brown and Karl W. Schweizer (eds), *The Devonshire Diary . . . Memoranda on State of Affairs 1759–1762* (1982), p. 140 (5 Oct.), 119 (11 Sept. 1761); Sir Robert Wilmot to Devonshire, 13 Oct. 1761, Devonshire Papers, HP; Elliot, *The Border Elliots*, p. 367; but cf. Hardwicke to Newcastle, 13 Oct. 1761, Add. MSS 32929, ff. 227–8, suggesting a more active defensive role.

3. *Parl. Hist.*, XV, col. 982.

4. Cf. Kathleen Wilson, 'Inventing revolution: 1688 and eighteenth-century popular politics', *Journal of British Studies* 28 (1989), pp. 375–6, and, more extensively, John Brewer, *Party Ideology and Popular Politics at the Accession of George III* (Cambridge, 1976), esp. chs 1, 8, 11, 12.

5. See below, pp. 146–9, 184–5, 194–5; H.T. Dickinson, *The Politics of the People in Eighteenth-Century Britain* (1994), esp. ch. 7, summarizes the new circumstances, as does P.D.G.

Thomas, *John Wilkes. A Friend to Liberty* (Oxford, 1996), pp. 12–16. Thomas (see esp. ch. 13) provides a welcome, reliable biography and excellent context. Brewer, *Party Ideology*, ch. 9, and George Rudé, *Wilkes and Liberty* (Oxford, 1962), are still the best accounts of Wilkes's impact.

6. John Brooke, *King George III* (1972), p. 47.

7. See below, pp. 146–7.

8. *Monitor*, 10 March 1759.

9. See above, pp. 24, 38, 61, 71, 92–3, 111–12; Peters, *Pitt*, pp. 138–40; Brown and Schweizer (eds), *Devonshire Diary*, pp. 63, 65, 67–8, 69; West's account, 12 May 1762, Add. MSS 32938, f. 188 (quotation), cf. *Memoirs George III*, I, p. 130.

10. Brewer, *Party Ideology*, ch. 3, esp. pp. 48–54; Marie Peters, ' "Names and cant": party labels in English political propaganda c.1755–1765', *Parliamentary History* 3 (1984), esp. pp. 116–22.

11. Cf. Linda Colley, *Britons. Forging the Nation 1707–1837* (New Haven, CT, 1992), pp. 101–5.

12. *Annual Register* 4 (1761), p. 44.

13. For this and the following description, see Peters, *Pitt*, pp. 205–29. Karl W. Schweizer, 'Lord Bute and William Pitt's resignation in 1761', *Canadian Journal of History* 8 (1973), pp. 111–25, 'Lord Bute and the press; the origins of the press war of 1762 reconsidered', in idem (ed.), *Lord Bute: Essays in Reinterpretation* (Leicester, 1988), pp. 83–98, quite convincingly exonerates Bute from an initial attempt to discredit Pitt, but other ministers are not thereby exculpated (cf. Peters, *Pitt*, pp. 206–7), and Bute's publicists were certainly active later.

14. Pitt moderated the effects of early versions of this criticism, at least in the City, by a letter to Beckford: see Peters, *Pitt*, pp. 208–10. Cf. his reported defence that the rewards were deserved, Bedfordshire Record Office, Wrest Park-Lucas Papers, L31/108, pp. 3–4.

15. Walpole to Mann, 10 Oct. 1761, *Correspondence*, XXI, p. 541.

16. Peters, *Pitt*, chs 3–6.

17. Marie Peters, 'Pitt as a foil to Bute: the public debate over ministerial responsibility and the powers of the Crown', in Schweizer (ed.), *Lord Bute*, pp. 99–115.

18. *The conduct of a rt. honourable gentleman . . . justified . . . By a Member of Parliament*, [Nov.] 1761, pp. 4, 33, 54; *London Chronicle*, 24–26 Nov. 1761.

19. For these, see Brewer, *Party Ideology*, ch. 7.

20. *Annual Register* 4 (1761), pp. 44, 45; the *Monitor's* 'faction' argument, rising to new heights, could no longer effectively defend Pitt: Peters, *Pitt*, pp. 217–28, 222–4.

21. Newcastle to Bedford, 20 Oct. 1761, Add. MSS 32929, f. 403; Peters, *Pitt*, pp. 208–9, 212–13.
22. But see Peters, 'Foil', p. 110 and n. 65.
23. *Memoirs George III*, I, pp. 86–7, 94–6.
24. Sackville to Irwin, 16 Nov. 1761, HMC, *Stopford-Sackville*, I, p. 86.
25. Karl Schweizer, 'An unpublished parliamentary speech by the Elder Pitt, 9 December 1761', *Historical Research* 64 (1991), pp. 98–105 (quotation p. 102); cf. above, p. 121, and Marie Peters, 'The myth of William Pitt, great imperialist: Part I', *Journal of Imperial and Commonwealth History* 21 (1993), n. 125, on the significance of this speech.
26. *Memoirs George III*, I, p. 77.
27. Ibid., pp. 74, 76 (13 Nov.), 92–4 (11 Dec. 1761), 104–6 (19 Jan.), 128–9, 130 (12 May 1762); James Harris, Parliamentary Memorials, 12 May 1762, Hampshire Record Office, Malmesbury Collection, 9M73/G709 (quotation). For fuller accounts, see Peters, *Pitt*, pp. 232–4, 238, and Jeremy Black, *Pitt the Elder* (Cambridge, 1992), pp. 229–34.
28. Harris, Parliamentary Memorials, 13 Nov. 1761, 1 March 1762, 9M73/708, 709; *Annual Register* 4 (1761), p. 48.
29. Report, 11 Dec. 1761, in Arnold Schaefer, *Geschichte des siebenjährigen Kriegs* 2 vols (Berlin, 1867–74), II, part 2, p. 744.
30. *Memoirs George III*, I, p. 128, cf. pp. 75–6 (13 Nov. 1761).
31. Sackville to Irwin, 16 Nov., HMC, *Stopford-Sackville*, I, pp. 87, 86; Simmons and Thomas, I, p. 373 (Newcastle's account, 9 Dec. 1761); *Memoirs George III*, I, p. 77 (but cf. p. 131 for a sympathetic use of 'artful').
32. Cf. Peters, *Pitt*, pp. 234–5.
33. *Memoirs George III*, I, p. 75 (quotation), cf. Harris, Parliamentary Memorials, 13 Nov. 1761, 9M73/G708. Pitt's agitation over the militia outside the House scarcely suggested retirement: see Peters, *Pitt*, pp. 235, 237.
34. 'Conversation between Mr Pitt and Mr Nuthall', 5 Nov., Philip C. Yorke, *The Life and Correspondence of Philip Yorke Earl of Hardwicke* 3 vols (Cambridge, 1913), III, p. 430; 'Minutes taken at Hayes, [Nov.] 1762', Wilkes Papers, Add. MSS 30867, f. 200; Temple to Pitt, 14 Nov. 1762, PRO 30/8/61, f. 82; Temple to Wilkes, 25 Nov. 1762, in William James Smith (ed.), *The Grenville Papers* 4 vols (1852–3), II, p. 7.
35. *Memoirs George III*, I, pp. 176–7, 181; Burke to O'Hara, 12 Dec. 1762, in Thomas W. Copeland (ed.), *The Correspondence of Edmund Burke* 9 vols (Cambridge, 1958–70), I, p. 160.
36. *Memoirs George III*, I, pp. 179, 181 (Fox, guiding the peace through the House, was the 'cobbler'); Peters, 'Myth', p. 51.
37. Simmons and Thomas, I, pp. 440–1 (4 March); Rigby to Bedford, 10 March, in Lord John Russell (ed.), *Correspondence*

of John, Fourth Duke of Bedford 3 vols (1842–6), III, pp. 218–20; *Parl. Hist.*, XV, cols 1307 (27 March), 1314–15.

38. *Memoirs George III*, I, pp. 74–5, cf. p. 105; Thomas, *Wilkes*, p. 20.
39. Symmer to Mitchell, 11 Dec., *Chatham Correspondence*, II, p. 169n.; *Memoirs George III*, I, p. 77; George III to Bute, 11 Dec., in Romney Sedgwick (ed.), *Letters from George III to Lord Bute 1756–1766* (1939), p. 73; Ellison to Grafton, 14 Dec. 1761, Suffolk Record Office, Grafton Papers, 423/718; cf. Peters, *Pitt*, pp. 236–7, 239.
40. Rigby to Bedford, 10 March 1763, in Russell (ed.), *Bedford Correspondence*, III, p. 219; Peters, *Pitt*, pp. 212–13, 236, 253–4.
41. Granville to Egremont, 31 May 1[7]62, Egremont Papers, PRO 30/47/29.
42. See above, pp. 59, 115; 'Heads of Mr Pitt's conversation', 17 Oct. 1759, Add. MSS 32897, f. 173; Peters, *Pitt*, pp. 12–13, idem, 'Myth', p. 47.
43. Peters, *Pitt*, p. 172.
44. E.g. N.A.M. Rodger, 'The Continental commitment in the eighteenth century', in Lawrence Freedman *et al.* (eds), *War Strategy and International Politics* (Oxford, 1992), pp. 47–8.
45. Philip Lawson, *George Grenville. A Political Life* (Oxford, 1984), pp. 106–7, 109–28, 148–9; Elizabeth to Edward Montagu, [n.d. 1761], HL, MO2424; *Memoirs George III*, I, pp. 81 (9 Dec. 1761 – cf. above, pp. 140–1), 198 (March 1763); Rigby to Bedford, 10 March 1763, in Russell (ed.), *Bedford Correspondence*, III, pp. 218–19.
46. E.g. Pitt–Nuthall conversation, 5 Nov., T. Walpole–Pitt conversation, 13 Nov. 1762, in Yorke, *Hardwicke*, III, pp. 430–1.
47. *Memoirs George III*, I, p. 181; Newcastle to Devonshire, 31 Jan., 5 Feb., Devonshire to Newcastle, 6 Feb., Chatsworth, Devonshire Papers, 182.317, 182.320, 260.400; Rigby to Bedford, 10 March, in Russell (ed.), *Bedford Correspondence*, III, pp. 219–20; Newcastle to Rockingham, 27 March, Sheffield Central Library, Wentworth Woodhouse Muniments, Rockingham Papers, R1–370; Hardwicke to Newcastle, Rockingham to Newcastle, 1 April 1763, Add. MSS 32948, ff. 1–4.
48. Lawson, *George Grenville*, pp. 149–58.
49. Frank O'Gorman, *The Rise of Party in England. The Rockingham Whigs 1760–82* (1975), p. 74; Brooke, *King George III*, p. 104; Bute to Bedford, 2 April, Rigby to Bedford, 15 Aug. 1763, in Russell (ed.), *Bedford Correspondence*, III, pp. 22, 236–7; Harris, memoranda, 14 Aug. 1766 (conversation with Lyttelton), 9M73/G746.
50. Quotations from Hardwicke to Royston, 4 Sept. 1763, in Yorke, *Hardwicke*, III, pp. 525–9, which is arguably the most reliable of many accounts, none directly from the two chief

participants; Grenville's account can be accepted on why Bute changed his mind (Smith [ed.], *Grenville Papers*, II, p. 197); Lawson, *George Grenville*, pp. 163–4.

51. David Hume to Mure, 1 Sept. 1763, in W. Mure (ed.), *Selections From The Family Papers Preserved At Caldwell*, 2 parts, 3 vols (Glasgow, 1854), part 2, I, p. 191, cf. Hardwicke to Royston, 4 Sept., in Yorke, *Hardwicke*, III, p. 525, Royston to Hardwicke, 5 Sept. 1763, Hardwicke Papers, Add. MSS 35352, f. 426.

52. Charles Townshend to Chase Price, 10 Sept. 1763, Nottingham University, Portland Papers, PwF7910; cf. Wray, Birch to Royston, 17 Sept. 1763, Add MSS 35401, f. 279, 35400, f. 126.

53. To Royston, 19 Sept. 1763, Add MSS 35607, f. 72; cf. Royston to Lyttelton, 13 Sept. 1763, Hagley Hall, Lyttelton Papers, V, f. 174.

54. As Cumberland soon realized; Newcastle's account, 20 Sept. 1763, Add. MSS 32951, ff. 103–5.

55. Thomas Walpole's account, 13 Nov. 1762, in Yorke, *Hardwicke*, III, p. 431.

56. He had already moved towards them as opportunities for office arose, and clearly foreshadowed his present tactics; see e.g. Newcastle to Devonshire, 11 Aug., Add. MSS 32950, ff. 66–8, 79, Rigby to Bedford, 15 Aug. 1763, in Russell (ed.), *Bedford Correspondence*, III, p. 236.

57. Pitt's only direct comment attributes failure to some 'master-spring in the interior of the court . . . foul play . . . somewhere' (to Lincoln, [30 Aug. 1763], Nottingham University, Newcastle–Clumber Papers, NeC4006).

58. See above, p. 140.

59. *Memoirs George III*, I, pp. 198, 222–3.

60. Walpole to Mann, 20 June 1762, *Correspondence*, XXII, p. 42; Peters, *Pitt*, pp. 240–7, 258–60; Thomas, *Wilkes*, pp. 16–26; and on the debate's wider significance, Brewer, *Party Ideology*, pp. 116–21, idem, 'The misfortunes of Lord Bute: a case study in eighteenth-century political argument and public opinion', *Historical Journal* 16 (1973), pp. 3–43, and Colley, *Britons*, pp. 105–15.

61. See above, n. 34; Thomas, *Wilkes*, pp. 9–11, 17–18, 22–3.

62. Rudé, *Wilkes and Liberty*, pp. 18–22; Thomas, *Wilkes*, pp. 29–30.

63. E.g. Newcastle to Hardwicke, 2 June 1763, in Yorke, *Hardwicke*, III, p. 498; Thomas, *Wilkes*, p. 20.

64. His correspondence and papers, printed and unpublished (e.g. PRO 30/8/83, ff. 135–9), vouch for his interest. Thomas, *Wilkes*, pp. 41–5, 48–54, gives a characteristically lucid account of the debates.

65. *Memoirs George III*, I, p. 251 (15 Nov.); *Parl. Hist.*, XV, cols 1363–4 (24 Nov. 1763). The government had placed before the Lords Wilkes's privately circulated, obscene and blasphemous 'Essay on Woman', which Pitt and Potter had relished together when it was first written (Thomas, *Wilkes*, pp. 229–30, n. 23). Wilkes was justifiably incensed with Pitt's hypocrisy over their connection (ibid., n. 23, pp. 229–30, p. 44 and n. 98, cf. pp. 27, 33).

66. *Parl. Hist.*, XV, cols 1363–4, cf. col. 1402 (17 Feb. 1764).

67. *Memoirs George III*, I, pp. 286, 290–1 (13–14 Feb.), 293–4 (quotation), 297, 301–2 (17–18 Feb. – quotation); *Parl. Hist.*, XV, cols 1395–6n., 1401–3 (17–18 Feb. 1763 – quotation 1403).

68. *Memoirs George III*, I, p. 290; Walpole to Mann, 20 Feb, to Hertford, 15 Feb. 1764, *Correspondence*, XXII, pp. 206–8 and nn., XXXVIII, pp. 315–16.

69. E.g. Thomas Walpole's conversation with Pitt, 13 Nov. 1762, in Yorke, *Hardwicke*, III, p. 431; Hardwicke to Newcastle, 8 June, Newcastle to Devonshire, 11 Aug. 1763, Add. MSS 32949, f. 61 (quotations), 32950, ff. 67–8, 73.

70. *Memoirs George III*, I, p. 286.

71. Hardwicke to Newcastle, 8 June, Newcastle's account of conversation, 28 Sept. 1763, Add. MSS 32949, f. 57, 32951, f. 195; Peters, *Pitt*, pp. 262–3.

72. W. Collins to Pitt, 30 April 1763, PRO 30/8/27, f. 68; verse in Harris's hand, memoranda, Oct.–Nov. 1763, 9M73/G730.

73. Cf. Wilson, 'Inventing revolution', pp. 375–6.

74. Hardwicke to Newcastle, 8 June 1763, Add. MSS 32949, f. 61.

75. See esp. Newcastle to Devonshire, 11 Aug., Add. MSS 32950, ff. 73–8, partially in Yorke, *Hardwicke*, III, pp. 516–19; Hardwicke to Newcastle, 15 Oct. 1763, in ibid., pp. 535–6.

76. E.g. Newcastle's account of conversation, 28 Sept., Hardwicke to Newcastle, 15 Oct. 1763, Newcastle to Devonshire, 19 Oct, Add. MSS 32951, ff. 201–2, 430, 32952, f. 40.

77. Countess to Earl Temple, 20 Nov. 1763, in Smith (ed.), *Grenville Papers*, II, p. 164.

78. E.g. *Correspondence*, XXII, pp. 186, 208 and nn., XXXVIII, pp. 240, 326.

79. O'Gorman, *Rise of Party*, pp. 90–1; Walpole to Mann, 11 Feb. 1765, *Correspondence*, XXII, p. 284.

80. Rockingham to Newcastle, 23 March 1765, Add. MSS 32966, f. 91.

81. Newcastle to Devonshire, 31 Jan. 1763, Devonshire Papers, 182.317. This view was often reiterated, although by late 1764 some were more sceptical and even Newcastle was irritated; see e.g. Albemarle to Newcastle, 24, 31 Oct., Rockingham

to Newcastle, 15 Sept., 23 Nov., Newcastle to Legge, 20 July 1764, Add. MSS 32963, ff. 19, 122, 113, 32964, f. 93, 32960, f. 332.

82. Newcastle's account of conversation, 28 Sept. 1763, Add. MSS 32951, ff. 201–2; Newcastle to White, 19 June 1764, Devonshire Papers, 182.382; conversation with Michell 'yesterday', 12 Aug. 1764, Add. MSS 32961, f. 187.

83. Devonshire to Newcastle, [17 Feb. 1763], Hardwicke to Newcastle, 15 Oct. 1763, conversation with Michell 'yesterday', 12 Aug. 1764, Add. MSS 32947, f. 21, 32951, f. 430, 32961, f. 187; Pitt to Newcastle, [19] Oct. 1764, *Chatham Correspondence*, II, p. 297.

84. Newcastle to White, 19 June 1762, Devonshire Papers 182.382; Pitt to Newcastle, [19] Oct. 1764, *Chatham Correspondence*, II, p. 297; cf. *Memoirs George III*, I, p. 309.

85. P.D.G. Thomas, *British Politics and the Stamp Act Crisis* (Oxford, 1975), chs 3–7, provides the best account.

86. Simmons and Thomas, I, pp. 140–1 (4 March 1763); *Memoirs George III*, I, p. 195.

87. Newcastle to Devonshire, 11 Aug. 1763, Add. MSS 32950, ff. 71, 70, cf. f. 83 where Newcastle suggested that a rumoured plan to reorder colonial government 'would call forth Mr Pitt'.

88. Charles Townshend to Newcastle, 23 March 1764, Onslow to Newcastle, 19 March 1765, Add. MSS 32957, ff. 239–40, 32966, f. 69; Calcraft to Shelburne, 15 April 1765, in Lord Edmond Fitzmaurice (ed.), *Life of William Earl of Shelburne, afterwards First Marquess of Lansdowne* 3 vols (1875–6), I, p. 323.

89. Simmons and Thomas, II, p. 85 (16 Jan. 1766).

90. E.g. Harris, Parliamentary Memorials, 14, 17 Feb. 1764, 9M73/G713.

91. Brooke, *King George III*, pp. 106–13.

92. Cumberland's account, in Earl of Albemarle (ed.), *Memoirs of the Marquess of Rockingham and his Contemporaries* 2 vols (1852), I, pp. 193, 203; Mary Bateson (ed.), *A Narrative of the Changes in the Ministry 1765–1767* (1898), p. 14.

93. Calcraft to Shelburne, [28] May 1765, in Fitzmaurice (ed.), *Shelburne*, I, pp. 329–30; Lord Charles Fitzroy to Grafton, 19, 29 May 1765, in Sir William R. Anson (ed.), *Autobiography and Political Correspondence of Augustus Henry Third Duke of Grafton* (1898), pp. 79, 51; Lord Frederick Cavendish to Rockingham, 21 May 1765, Wentworth Woodhouse Muniments, R1–449.

94. Anson (ed.), *Grafton*, pp. 45, 49; Fitzroy to Grafton, 19 May 1765, in ibid., p. 79.

95. Grenville's account, 26 June, Temple to Grenville, 2 July 1765, in Smith (ed.), *Grenville Papers*, III, pp. 202, 64.

96. Lyttelton to W.H. Lyttelton, 28 July, Hagley Hall, Lyttelton Papers, VI, f. 235; Pitt to Temple, [22 June], in Smith (ed.), *Grenville Papers*, II, pp. 60–1, cf. Basil Williams, *The Life of William Pitt Earl of Chatham* 2 vols (1913), II, pp. 175–6; Cumberland to Albemarle, 26 June, in Albemarle (ed.), *Rockingham*, I, pp. 213–14; Harris, memoranda, 2 July, 9M73/ G741 (and all well-informed accounts); Pitt to Lyttelton, 1 July 1765, *Chatham Correspondence*, II, p. 316.

97. Shelburne to Barré, 2 July, in Fitzmaurice (ed.), *Shelburne*, I, p. 331, cf. Lyttelton to W.H. Lyttelton, 28 July 1765, Lyttelton Papers, VI, f. 234; Bateson (ed.), *A Narrative*, p. 24; Paul Langford, *The First Rockingham Administration 1765–1766* (1973), pp. 67–8.

98. Edward to Elizabeth Montagu, 11 July 1765, HL, MO1982.

99. Sir John Fortescue (ed.), *The Correspondence of King George the Third from 1760 to December 1783* 6 vols (1927–8), I, pp. 121, 123–5.

100. Anson (ed.), *Grafton*, pp. 46, 51; Burke to Flood, 18 May [1765], in Copeland (ed.), *Burke Correspondence*, I, p. 194; cf. *Memoirs George III*, II, p. 131.

101. Quoted in Langford, *Rockingham Administration*, p. 236.

102. Hardwicke, Legge and Devonshire all died in 1764.

103. Burke to C. Townshend, 25 June, in Copeland (ed.), *Burke Correspondence*, I, p. 205; Rigby to Sandwich, [23 June 1765], Sandwich Papers, HP.

104. Sackville to Irwin, 29 July, HMC, *Stopford-Sackville*, I, p. 101.

105. Ibid.; Pitt to Grafton, 24 Aug. 1765, *Chatham Correspondence*, II, pp. 321–3; on Burton Pynsent, see below, ch. 6.

106. Langford, *Rockingham Administration*, p. 105.

107. Pitt to Shelburne, [26] Dec. 1765, *Chatham Correspondence*, II, pp. 359–60; N[uthall] to Rockingham, 28 Feb. 1766, PRO 30/8/51, f. 278; Langford, *Rockingham Administration*, pp. 136–9, 143–5, 222; Brooke, *King George III*, pp. 126–7, 128.

108. Pitt to Grafton, 24 Aug., to Cooke, 7 Dec. 1765, *Chatham Correspondence*, II, pp. 322, 342–3; Langford, *Rockingham Administration*, pp. 144–5.

109. Thomas, *Stamp Act*, p. 168n.

110. Pitt to Shelburne, [26] Dec. 1765, *Chatham Correspondence*, II, p. 359.

111. Pitt to Thomas Walpole, 5 Nov. 1765, *Chatham Correspondence*, II, p. 329; Burke to Flood, 18 May [1765], in Copeland (ed.), *Burke Correspondence*, I, p. 194.

112. Pitt to Nuthall, 9 Jan. 1766, *Chatham Correspondence*, II, p. 362.

113. Simmons and Thomas, II, pp. 54–60 (17 Dec. 1765).

114. Ibid., p. 80. Pitt spoke in seven debates, making at least four major speeches, over the next two months. For fuller

NOTES

references to them, see Marie Peters, 'The myth of William Pitt, great imperialist. Part II', *Journal of Imperial and Commonwealth History* 22 (1994), pp. 395–7.

115. See above, p. 151.
116. Shelburne to Pitt, 21 Dec., Pitt to Shelburne, 21 [Dec.] 1765, *Chatham Correspondence*, II, pp. 354–5, 358–9.
117. Simmons and Thomas, II, p. 82.
118. Ibid., pp. 91, 86 (14 Jan.), 111 (27 Jan. 1766), cf. I, p. 489 (Grenville, 9 March 1764); Langford, *Rockingham Administration*, pp. 154–5.
119. E.g. Simmons and Thomas, II, pp. 288 (21 Feb.), 150 (3 Feb. 1766).
120. Ibid., p. 81.
121. Basil Williams, 'Chatham and the representation of the colonies in the imperial parliament', *English Historical Review* 22 (1907), pp. 756–8.
122. Simmons and Thomas, II, p. 86 (14 Jan. 1766); Brewer, *Party Ideology*, ch. 10.
123. Simmons and Thomas, II, p. 161 (5 Feb. 1766).
124. Ibid., p. 288 (21 Feb.); cf. pp. 150, 284–5, 286–7; Rouet to Mure, 22 Feb. 1766, in Mure (ed.), *Caldwell Papers*, part 2, II, p. 74 (first quotation); cf. Peters, 'Myth, Part II', nn. 19, 20.
125. Sackville to Irwin, 17 Jan., HMC, *Stopford-Sackville*, I, p. 104; Elizabeth Montagu to Elizabeth Vesey, 1 Feb. 1766, HL, MO6386; Simmons and Thomas, II, pp. 111, 150 (27 Jan., 3 Feb. 1766).
126. See above, p. 151; Simmons and Thomas, II, p. 83; Peters, 'Myth, Part II', pp. 395–6.
127. Simmons and Thomas, II, p. 315 (4 March); cf. letters exchanged with Lady Chatham [4, 6 Feb. – misdated in source], 22 Feb. 1766, *Chatham Correspondence*, II, pp. 363–70, 375–6, 391–3.
128. Peters, 'Myth, Part II', p. 396.
129. Simmons and Thomas, II, pp. 285 (21 Feb.), 89–90 (14 Jan. 1766).
130. Burke to O'Hara, 23, 24 April 1766, *Correspondence, XXII*, p. 413, in Copeland (ed.), *Burke Correspondence*, I, pp. 251–2; Peters, 'Myth, Part II', pp. 396–7.
131. Simmons and Thomas, II, pp. 81, 82.
132. See above, p. 154.
133. Simmons and Thomas, II, pp. 313–16 (4 March 1766).
134. Walpole to Mann, 20 April 1766. The measures were a minor one concerning the militia, the proposal for a free port at Dominica, the administration's moves to declare general warrants illegal; for details see Black, *Pitt the Elder*, pp. 257–8,

Peters, 'Myth, Part II', p. 396, Langford, *Rockingham Administration*, pp. 215–16, Thomas, *Wilkes*, pp. 55–6.

135. Sackville to Irwin, 11 March, HMC, *Stopford-Sackville*, I, p. 109; David Hume to [Hertford], 8 May 1766, HL, HM7203.

136. Harris, Parliamentary Memorials, 7 [March], 14 April 1766, 9M73/G716.

137. Simmons and Thomas, II, pp. 91–2 (14 Jan.); Sackville to Irwin, 11 March, HMC, *Stopford-Sackville*, I, p. 109; Rigby to Bedford, 24 April 1766, in Russell (ed.), *Bedford Correspondence*, III, p. 333.

138. Very obvious in Harris, Parliamentary Memorials, 14 April 1766, 9M73/G716, on the militia.

139. Langford, *Rockingham Administration*, pp. 221–4; for what follows, see ibid., ch. 7, Brooke, *King George III*, pp. 132–4, and idem, *The Chatham Administration* (1956), pp. 1–4.

140. George III to Bute, [12 July 1766], in Sedgwick (ed.), *Letters from George III to Lord Bute*, pp. 251–2, 253; George III to Pitt, 7 July 1766, *Chatham Correspondence*, II, p. 436.

141. Walpole to Mann, 22 May, 9 June, *Correspondence*, XXII, pp. 419, 425–6; Pitt to Lady Stanhope, 20 June 1766, PRO 30/8/86, f. 320.

142. *Chatham Correspondence*, II, pp. 434–8.

143. Northington to the king, [11 July], memorandum by the king, [corrected date, July 1766], in Fortescue (ed.), *Correspondence of George the Third*, I, pp. 371, 175–6.

144. Newcastle to Devonshire, 11 Aug. 1763, Add. MSS 32950, f. 78; Rockingham to the king, 15 Jan., in Albemarle (ed.), *Rockingham*, I, pp. 270–1; Temple to Lady Chatham, 20, 24 Jan. 1766, PRO 30/8/62, ff. 111, 113; Temple to Grenville, 18 July 1766, in Smith (ed.), *Grenville Papers*, III, p. 267.

145. Pitt, Temple to Lady Chatham, 17, 27 July, *Chatham Correspondence*, II, pp. 448, 468–9; cf. the king to Northington, 17 July 1766, in Fortescue (ed.), *Correspondence of George the Third*, I, p. 377.

146. *Memoirs George III*, II, p. 245n.

147. For this paragraph and what follows, see Brooke, *Chatham Administration*, pp. 5–19, but cf. Thomas, *Stamp Act*, pp. 283–5, Langford, *Rockingham Administration*, pp. 258–63.

148. Northington to the king, [11 July 1766], in Fortescue (ed.), *Correspondence of George the Third*, I, p. 371.

149. Pitt to Lady Chatham, 15 July 1766, *Chatham Correspondence*, II, pp. 444–5.

150. George III to Pitt, 7 July, cf. 29 July 1766, ibid., p. 436, III, p. 21.

151. E.g. Elizabeth to Edward Montagu, 9 July, 16 Nov., Edward to Elizabeth, 11 July 1765, Hume to [Hertford], 8 May 1766,

HL, MO2569, 2590, 1982, HM7203; Sir Joseph Yorke to Mitchell, 29 Aug. 1766, *Chatham Correspondence*, III, p. 42n.

152. George Prescott (a City lawyer) to Pitt, 16 July; cf. T. Walpole to Pitt, 15 July (reporting general London opinion), PRO 30/8/53, f. 177, vol. 66, f. 82, H. Walpole to Mann, 18 July and 21 March 1766 (reporting French dread of Pitt's return to office), *Correspondence*, XXII, pp. 436, 410.

153. *London Evening Post*, 19–21 June; cf. e.g. 28 June–1 July, 9–12, 12–15 July, *London Chronicle*, 10–12 July 1766.

154. Whately to Grenville, 19 July 1766, in Smith (ed.), *Grenville Papers*, III, p. 271.

Chapter 5

THE EARL OF CHATHAM, EMPIRE AND WILKES, 1766–71

. . .

CHATHAM'S MINISTRY: BLIGHTED EXPECTATIONS AND COLLAPSE, 1766–68

In fact, as Walpole foresaw,[1] the great war minister was very quickly proved no minister for times of peace. Within days, the fragility of Chatham's revived popularity was very clear. By the end of 1766, confusion threatened both the policies and the cohesion of the ministry. In March 1767, Chatham withdrew from politics again, this time a mental wreck. Instead of being alleviated, ministerial instability was aggravated. No more than any other postwar minister had he ameliorated Britain's problems of foreign policy, his overriding long-term concern.

Such bitter disappointment of high hopes was not inevitable at the outset. True, the illness so apparent in the weeks of negotiations continued virtually unabated. But the apparent damage of the peerage was, as Burke saw, not 'so fatal . . . as is commonly imagined', because Chatham now stood, not on the strengths of the Commons and popularity, but 'on the Closet Ground'.[2] The ministry had much potential strength. Only when Chatham failed to mobilize that strength did disintegration set in.

There is no doubt that Pitt's emergence as Earl of Chatham provoked more intense public indignation than any other episode in his career.[3] The official announcement on 4 August produced universal astonishment.[4] The City of London had already reacted to earlier rumours. 'Lord Cheattem' was only the first of the 'opprobrious nicknames' bandied around in the rage of opinion there, the illuminations planned to celebrate Pitt's return to office were cancelled by none other than a former stalwart ally, and there were even threats not 'to lend Lord Chatham's Administration sixpence'.[5] This time there was no respite. A month later, the City was reported to 'consider him as dead'; two months later, they were 'as inveterate as ever'.[6] And the 'country', too, was said to be 'as much out of humour'. There was wide agreement that 'the ebb of his popularity is as sudden and great as the flow was'.[7]

Three themes dominated in newspaper and pamphlet comment, the latter continuing to December. Again Chatham was alleged to be a false patriot, like Pulteney, whose apostasy proved 'That Patriotism's a Jest'.[8] He was now the '*late Great Commoner*', his 'passing' genuinely mourned,[9] but his achievements as war minister almost entirely overlooked. Most damaging of all was the soon dominant new theme that Pitt had been seduced into connection with Bute.[10] Undoubtedly, Temple's 'long foot' was instrumental in kicking up '[t]his dust',[11] and Chatham did not lack defenders. However, the strength of hostile feeling was patent and defenders could do little better than plead (as in 1757):

> But he is the Man,
> To help, or none can,
> But grant him for that, TIME and SEASON.[12]

The peerage brought other, more substantial disadvantages than this severe blow to Chatham's popular reputation. To his great French antagonist, Choiseul, Chatham out of the Commons was like Samson after his hair was cut. He was taken from that 'great scene of business' which was 'the proper sphere of his eloquence and democratic power', into a more intimate forum, less susceptible to his rhetoric.[13] The ministry was likely to feel his absence; it might have been wise to delay the move, however pressing the demands of his health for respite from the hurly-burly of the Commons.

Nevertheless, Chatham had advantages which more than outweighed these considerations. He now revelled in the absolute and unchallenged confidence of the king. There was no rival for the loyalty of his colleagues. For the first time in his life, Chatham as minister was, as he well knew, incontestably dominant.[14] Nor was the ministry without coherence or talent. The result of Chatham's declared intention 'to pick and cull from all quarters and break all parties' was hardly 'the best of all party's',[15] but to a solid Rockinghamite core Chatham's small contingent brought some infusion of talent. Shelburne might be distrusted for his changes of allegiance, but he was clever and conscientious. Even after mass Rockinghamite resignations were provoked in November by Chatham's deliberate disregard for party scruples in the award of office, most of the party's more ambitious and talented MPs stayed with the administration.[16] Three attempts between August and early December to bring in the Bedford group failed; Chatham wanted them but, persisting in *his great point . . . to destroy faction*', refused to offer enough to win them.[17] However, the December appointments replacing the Rockinghamites saw more of Bute's friends restored to office. They, with the remaining Rockinghamite 'men of business', provided a stable 'court and treasury' foundation after the disruptions of recent years. As the parliamentary session got under way, the administration had much going for it, while the opposition, despite a battery of good speakers, was divided.[18]

However, the ministry still needed management, which only Chatham could give – and skills in the management of men he had never had. Rather, his was a politics of command, expecting implicit obedience. Together with the king, he would command away the 'connections' that so disillusioned him with Hanoverian politics and achieve once again a miraculous renewal of national greatness. 'Unions . . . give me no terrors', he wrote to Grafton: 'I know my ground: *faction will not shake the Closet, nor gain the publick.*'[19]

So, instead of cementing the administration whose members so deferred to him, Chatham was concerned only 'to shew, that he had the absolute sole power, both in the closet, and in the administration'. So confident was he that he could contemplate six weeks in Bath 'for his health'.[20] His absence through October compounded the problem. He would not mollify Conway, unhappy about his thwarted army career and slights to his friends, nor placate the pretensions of the able but volatile Charles Townshend. He airily dismissed Grafton's suggestions for helping Conway in the vital task of managing the Commons by lessening the risk of 'a strong phalanx of able personages' in opposition.[21] By

December, because 'Lord C[hatha]m is very absolute and [has] very little communication with the best of them', there was a serious risk 'of the ministers disagreeing among themselves'.[22] And once again Chatham left for Bath.

Chatham's priority was policy, not management – and first and foremost foreign policy. In imperial matters, he very soon signified an interest in East India affairs, while other ministers were left to grapple with manifold American issues.

In all negotiations for office, Chatham had made known his concern about infractions of the peace and the need to relieve Britain's isolation in Europe. His views were forcefully if briefly expressed in debate in January 1766. And from his summer retirement in Somerset he declared: 'France is still the object of my mind, whenever a thought calls me back to a public world.'[23] His concerns were widely shared. Britain's isolation in face of the continuing alliance of France with Austria and Spain contributed powerfully to widespread postwar pessimism. Against a background of ongoing disputes with France and Spain about fulfilment of the peace terms, previous ministers had sought to strengthen Britain's position, whether by restoring relations with old allies like Russia or even Austria, or by renewing damaged relations with Prussia. By mid-1766, these efforts had achieved nothing but a commercial treaty with Russia and the restoration of ambassadorial relations with Prussia with the dispatch of the experienced and newly knighted Sir Andrew Mitchell. Very real difficulties had emerged to hinder further advance: Frederick the Great had no interest in further conflict with France, while, in return for an alliance, Russia demanded unacceptable concessions – a promise of aid against Turkey and, possibly, subsidies to Sweden and Denmark to resist French influence.

Nevertheless, Chatham hoped that his name and reputation would override such obstacles. His vision was a grand one: not just the improvement of relations but the fixing of the '*great cloud of power*' he saw in the north into a 'firm and solid system for the maintenance of the public tranquillity'. At its heart was to be a triple alliance with Russia and Prussia, to which Denmark, Sweden, the Dutch, and other German states could adhere in due course. And a 'new form' was to be given to the stalled negotiations with Russia by sending

Hans Stanley, Pitt's envoy in the abortive peace negotiations of 1761, as 'ambassador extraordinary' to St Petersburg, with accreditation also to Berlin.[24]

Even before the administration was sworn in, Chatham began preparations with an obviously reluctant Stanley to implement the 'system'. Chatham heeded his concerns and those of Conway, the responsible Secretary of State, to the extent of agreeing that Mitchell should be approached to test Berlin's attitude before Stanley departed. But more fundamental objections concerning relations with Russia and recent approaches to Austria were ignored, and Stanley's appointment was publicly announced before either Mitchell or Sir George Macartney, Britain's very competent ambassador to Russia, could be informed.[25] Chatham simply overrode his own Secretary in a way he would never have tolerated while Secretary himself.

Mitchell's first reactions were pessimistic. When at last, in mid-September, he was able to report Frederick's response, it was decidely averse to 'new and stricter connections with England' in which he could see no value.[26] Chatham, however, was quite unmoved, and the remarkable language of Conway's instructions to Mitchell to renew the approach echoed Chatham's voice: Frederick should understand that England was not 'asking a boon'; how could he fail to recognize the threat of 'the most formidable combination ever formed'? He 'ought to be told' that Prussia's possession of Silesia (seized from Austria in 1740) was most likely to rekindle war; no concessions could be offered until Frederick showed readiness to treat; a 'continuance of hesitation' would 'be looked on as refusal' which he would 'probably repent, ere long'.[27] When this extraordinary language of command achieved no better results Chatham lost interest, and Stanley's mission was aborted.[28]

Chatham took no further initiatives in foreign policy. Although he gave some attention to ongoing disputes with France and Spain in the early months of the administration, his papers suggest no particular contribution on the growing dispute with Spain over the Falkland Islands in the South Atlantic, vital though they were seen to be for British rights of navigation in the Atlantic and Pacific. Undoubtedly he discussed the issue with Shelburne, the responsible Secretary; he was present at a cabinet meeting which reached a crucial decision; he could strike attitudes with foreign ambassadors. But action was left to others.[29] He showed no greater official concern than other ministers at this time over possible French designs on Corsica, despite the urgings of correspondents.[30] Indeed, he seems not to have shown sustained interest in the detail of relations with France. Consulted in Bath about the instructions for the new ambassador, Lord Rochford, he doubted whether 'any lights of mine . . . at this distance' could be useful, although he did write to Rochford.[31] No better than any others did he understand France's change of priorities towards a 'blue-water' policy in seeking revenge against Britain after the Seven Years War.[32] He took some interest in the navy but provided no detectable impetus for its expansion, and while it is true that he appointed admirals – first Sir Charles Saunders, then Sir Edward Hawke – to head the Admiralty, his first choice, in pursuit of the Bedfords, was the utterly inexperienced Earl Gower.[33]

Britain's international situation had long been Chatham's chief concern. Yet, after six months, British diplomacy was weakened, not strengthened. His scheme for a grand northern alliance was based not on clear analysis of current circumstances but on outdated solutions. It took no account of the diminution of Britain's shared interests with Prussia – minimal enough during the last war – and Russia by the shift of their focus towards the east, to Poland and Turkey, and their alliance in 1764. Indeed, relations with Russia were worsened by Chatham's efforts.[34] Nor was it clear how the grand alliance would help Britain when France was no longer threatening Hanover. Chatham's views were at this stage shallow and rigid; he was at best a front man for striking attitudes; the brilliance of mind in surveying 'the actual situation and interests of the various powers in Europe' which so struck Charles Townshend at his first cabinet meeting[35] gave rise to no new concepts, no alternative policies.[36]

Chatham made another issue his own in the early weeks of the administration: the confident hopes of huge profits from the East India Company's now greatly extended territorial influence in India.[37] These hopes were brought to a head by the news, received in April, that Robert Clive – '*that heaven-born general*' of expansion,[38] sent back by the Company to manage the consequent problems – had accepted the *diwani* (or right to collect land revenue) in Bengal. This news set off speculation in Company stock and attempts to manipulate its dividend which focused attention on it. Within a month of Chatham's taking office the Company had been informed that its affairs would probably be brought before parliament in the coming session.[39]

This was clearly Chatham's initiative. The matter was, he declared, 'the greatest of all objects, according to my sense of great'. He it was who insisted that the 'object' be dealt with by parliamentary enquiry, rather than by negotiation with the Company.[40] His motives were never clearly stated. But, despite his wartime experience, he had shown no long-term interest in India and the manifold problems of the Company in its new situation.[41] Rather, like virtually every-one else, he simply wanted 'a kind of gift from heaven' for the Treasury coffers from the profits of India. This would provide for 'the *redemption*' of the nation from the burden of debt 'his' war had doubled and allow hopes of further glory.[42] It was to come from a parliamentary decision that the territorial rights in India belonged, not to the Com-pany, but to the Crown. This would be followed by an agree-ment with the Company that it should administer the rights in return for a share of the revenues.

However, because Chatham 'never did open' to his col-leagues 'what was his real and fixed plan', he failed to mobilize support against those in the ministry – Conway and Townshend (key speakers in the Commons) – who favoured immediate negotiation with the Company over the revenues. Rather, 'I will have this done' was his way of proceeding; 'no reply, not one iota shall be altered'.[43] Furthermore, Chatham chose, not one of the ministers, but his City friend, William Beckford, a known enemy of the Company and not a re-spected speaker in the House, to introduce the issue into parliament. Nevertheless, despite a wavering cabinet and opposition in parliament, by the Christmas recess Chatham's enquiry was firmly on course.[44]

The King's Speech opening the session in November dwelt on an issue of much greater public interest: a severe shortage of grain, the consequent unrest and the govern-ment's earlier embargo on the export of grain. This move, warmly approved by Chatham, was widely welcomed.[45] Nev-ertheless, Grenville seized the opportunity to attack the embargo as an exercise of the king's suspending power without parliamentary approval and hence illegal. The administration quickly extricated itself from embarrassing opposition by an indemnity bill,[46] but not before Chatham, in the first of only two speeches while in office, apparently revelled in the role of 'Great Prerogative Minister', quoting Locke to justify the embargo 'as an act of *power, justifiable . . .* on the ground of necessity; . . . not strictly speaking *legal,* yet . . . *right'.*[47] The supposed defender of the constitution was decisively outclassed by the Earl of Mansfield, his old Commons rival of the 1740s and 1750s, now a distinguished judge and the best debater in the Lords. More intelligently used, the affair might have been a springboard for reviving Chatham's popularity, but he showed no interest in longer-term solutions, much discussed in the press, to the problem of grain supply.

Of more far-reaching importance were the American issues which claimed the attention of ministers but not parliament in the administration's early months. At the outset, Chatham ignored the need for more coherent oversight of American affairs by refusing renewed proposals for a third Secretary of State for this purpose.[48] Grafton and Shelburne were soon busy on possible solutions to fundamental American problems – including ways of raising revenue other than by internal taxation – but no proposals came to the cabinet. Although Chatham must have known of this work – and had reportedly seen America, with India, as one of the 'two great objects' for parliament[49] – no comment from him has survived. On the immediate problem of New York's refusal to implement fully the provisions of Grenville's Mutiny Act, the cabinet quickly decided to demand compliance.[50] This authoritarian emphasis was reiterated when, in Chatham's negotiations with the Bedfords, he promised to secure 'the proper subordination of America', although disavowing 'any violent measures . . . unless absolutely necessary'.[51]

No doubt, Chatham's constant struggle with ill health – the reason for his taking a non-executive office – prevented steady application to foreign or imperial problems[52] and sharpened his arrogance towards the people he dealt with. When, in early December, he departed for his second sojourn in Bath since taking office, he left a ministry strained by his widely observed autocratic style of management but still functioning effectively in parliament. However, when he was unable to return in January, his absence brought 'all business' to 'a stop'; 'the business of Great Britain and the affairs of all Europe' awaited his recovery.[53]

Not least among this business were East India affairs. The Company had offered to negotiate and, early in January, Townshend put to Chatham a thoughtful and realistic case for taking up the offer. In reply, Chatham merely reiterated his general line on 'this transcendant object, India'. On the other hand, Beckford was floundering for lack of guidance on the parliamentary enquiry.[54] In fact, both negotiations and enquiry proceeded in uneasy tandem. Soon ministerial disagreements were open knowledge. On 20 February, Townshend and Beckford had a remarkable public altercation in the Commons.[55] Still Chatham refused advice on substantive issues, still 'referring the whole determination to the wisdom of' parliament. However, he did provide guidance on how the matter could be kept in the hands of parliament, culminating in early March in detailed proposals for the procedure of the enquiry.[56]

This was not enough to resolve the confusion. Although the idea of a declaration of right came very close to success – and Chatham's presence might have made the difference – eventually the Company's contribution to the Treasury coffers was agreed on by negotiation. The enquiry revealed much about Company affairs and, with legislation eventually arising from it, established the principle of parliamentary intervention. For this, perhaps, Chatham deserves some credit. But neither this nor Chatham's intended declaration of right tackled the fundamental problems of the Company.[57]

Meanwhile, the situation in the Commons careered out of control. 'Mr Grenville and Mr Burke daily trim Lord Chatham, no one defends him', it was reported.[58] On 27 February, the government was delivered an 'unprecedented' defeat on an opposition motion reducing the land tax, which Walpole attributed to 'the absence of Lord Chatham'.[59] In this undisciplined situation, and quite unplanned by the ministers, American questions now came before parliament. On 26 January, Townshend was provoked by an intervention from Grenville into an unauthorized promise to raise a revenue from America towards the costs of the army there. He also made a much-noticed declaration that the distinction – adopted by Chatham

– between internal taxation and external revenue was '*perfect nonsense*'.[60]

Chatham soon knew of Townshend's flouting of his known views.[61] This time there was no magisterial rebuke such as Townshend had been given in December.[62] He did, however, advise the cabinet to lay other American matters fully before parliament. These included continuing defiance from New York, not only of the Mutiny Act, but also (in a recently arrived merchants' petition) of regulation of trade. New Jersey, too, was defying the Mutiny Act. To Chatham, this 'gloomy prospect' showed a 'spirit of infatuation', and eventually he came down firmly for the strong line already agreed on by the cabinet against New York.[63]

Not only was Chatham's increasing authoritarianism thus confirmed; his insistence that parliament should decide these issues was remarkably consistent with his approach to East Indian problems and suggests no mere paralysis of his powers of decision but a genuine belief in the collective wisdom of the representative body.[64] But again, his attitudes scarcely advanced constructive solutions. In due course, Townshend's fateful scheme to raise revenue by external duties, which was to provoke new heights of protest in America, went ahead without any comment from Chatham. Indeed, given the recent trend of his views, he might not have objected.[65] The hopes of him as 'the only man who can either bring the Americans to submit peacably by his authority; or subdue them by his vigour' were cruelly disappointed; even American enthusiasm for him began to wane.[66]

By March, the full extent of Chatham's incapacity was becoming obvious. At least a much-interrupted journey brought him back to London on 2 March. He made an attempt to reimpose his will by offering Townshend's post to Lord North, an able Lord of the Treasury and speaker in the Commons. But North refused,[67] and Townshend continued defiant.[68] With this, Chatham's role in his administration was virtually over. He remained immured in a friend's house at North End, Hampstead, ignoring fellow ministers, answering the king's letters with mere fulsome phrases. On 12 March he saw the king for the last time.[69]

As Chatham returned to London, Horace Walpole had 'no doubt of his still being triumphant'; three weeks later, the collapse of control in the Commons, together with his loss of popularity, convinced another observer that 'Lord Chatham's power is very near its end'; by mid-April it seemed that, unless he could exert himself, 'those expectations raised from his taking the lead will fall altogether with the author of them'.[70] The king's unswerving support might still have saved him.[71] But when, at last, in early June, he yielded to the king's insistence that he see Grafton if not the king himself, his *utter disability* to offer more than expressions of confidence to save his tottering administration had to be accepted. At least these were sufficient to encourage his supporters to continue, in hope of his eventual return.[72]

For weeks it had been clear that something more than physical illness ailed him; indeed, he could appear quite well until 'a word of business' brought 'tears and trembling'.[73] In June, Grafton found him much worse than expected, 'his great mind bowed down', 'his nerves and spirits . . . affected to a dreadful degree'.[74] Soon his condition deteriorated further to 'the lowest dejection and debility that mind or body can be in'. He sat 'all the day, leaning on his hands', mostly alone, hardly speaking, unable to tolerate any company except Lady Chatham's, flying 'into a raging fit of passion' when offered 'a letter of business'. '[C]riminal to ask how he does', went one report, 'servants turned off for enquiring'. In August, Lady Chatham was given power of attorney for his affairs.[75]

The king, sorrowing to see 'A Man that had appeared in so very great a light fall into such a situation', continued sympathetic. In January 1768, he still hoped for Chatham's return, assuring him that 'your name has been sufficient to enable my administration to proceed'. When, in October 1768, Chatham finally wished to go, the king insisted he should stay to assist 'in resisting the torrent of Factions this country so much labours under'.[76] But Chatham, stung not by issues of policy but by slights to supporters, was adamant. Ostensibly, he went on the grounds of health. Only Shelburne – increasingly isolated in a changing administration – and Barré went with him.[77]

Chatham's abysmal disappointment of all the hopes rested on him was the gravest blow yet to his reputation. The king, who had so fully supported him, was so disillusioned by

Chatham's refusal of his command that never again did he contemplate office for Chatham. As for politicians, Burke was right to ask who would 'engage under a person who is incapable of Forming any rational plan, and is above communicating even his reveries to those who are able to realize and put them in execution'. Northington commented bitterly in like vein on the 'ridiculous farce of a ministry' in which he was Lord President.[78] Any hope of a revival of popularity seemed gone. By December 1766, newspaper comment suggested that the earlier sharp disillusionment had been blunted, and some positive expectations continued into February and March.[79] Then came contradictory reports of illness and seclusion, and finally silence.[80] The little attention given to Chatham's eventual resignation was matter-of-fact, overshadowed by the rising star of John Wilkes.[81]

Chatham's illness was the crucial precipitating cause of the weakness of his administration. But the failure went deeper than that. The ministry could certainly have survived his elevation to the Lords and the wave of unpopularity, even his contempt for connection and lack of well-conceived policies. It could not survive without the management which, even when not seriously ill, Chatham seemed incapable of giving. Grafton sadly commented, 'Lord Chatham, with his superior talents, did not possess that of conciliating mankind'.[82] His autocratic manner, which had so marred relations in opposition, his politics of command, constrained rather than enabled the talents of others – Townshend, Shelburne – talents which might have compensated for his own inadequacies. His administration fractured.

Chatham's conviction of superiority, heightened by the earldom, now began to show itself in ridiculous ostentation – a 'profusion and extravagance', a 'wild wantonness and prodigality', 'a pomp of equipage and retinue quite unequalled in this age' – in a way of life he could ill afford and which contrasted markedly with his frugal manner in the war years.[83] More than ever, these traits seem signs of a deeply flawed personality, intimately connected with persistent illness, and now brought to breakdown by a sense of the overwhelming difficulties that personality had aggravated.

The great war minister – now part tragic, part ridiculous – was indeed no minister for years of peace.

. . .

'COMING FORTH AGAIN' ON A CHANGED SCENE, 1769

Lifting the threat of the burdens of office seems to have had an immediate beneficial effect on Chatham's mental state, especially when soon coupled with a reconciliation with Temple. Temple found him 'in bed, rather weak, . . . but his mind and apprehension perfectly clear'. Other reports suggest he was still vulnerable to 'low spirits' and 'nervous' fits of weeping. Not until March 1769 was he said to be 'coming forth again'.[84]

The political world into which Chatham was 'coming forth' was changing rapidly. Grafton, it is true, propelled so unexpectedly to high office by the vagaries of the 1760s, had survived in administration without Chatham. Assistance had come from the accession of the Bedfords in December 1767 and the elevation of Lord North to the Exchequer on Townshend's sudden death three months earlier. The continuing disunion of the Rockingham and Grenville groups and the handful of Chatham supporters in opposition had also helped. However, the administration soon faced another crisis in America, where Townshend's external duties were no more acceptable than the Stamp Act. It proved incapable of a strong stand against France's annexation of Corsica in 1768. Above all, there was serious domestic unrest.

This unrest sprang partly from economic conditions. But it was greatly intensified, especially in London, by the government's unwise handling of the reappearance in England of John Wilkes and his election as MP for Middlesex in March 1768, to the acclaim of boisterous crowds. Once again, Wilkes demonstrated his brilliant flair for publicity and libertarian rhetoric at every opportunity – even though in prison from June 1768 to April 1770 for the seditious libel of 1763. Gravely provoked, and urged on by the king, the administration decided to use Wilkes's conviction as grounds for his expulsion from the Commons. Between February and April 1769 he was three times expelled and three times re-elected until, on the third occasion, the Commons declared the badly defeated rival candidate elected instead.

This time, Wilkes's defiance and the government's persistence had created a major constitutional issue concerning freedom of election.[85] The intermittent public discontents of the 1760s now came to a climax of extra-parliamentary political activity of proportions unprecedented in Hanoverian times.[86] Controversy was intensified by pungent criticism of the ministry through 1769 in the celebrated Junius letters in the *Public Advertiser*. Crowd disorder in the metropolis was almost continual, while the City elected Wilkes an alderman in January. When parliament was prorogued in May, opposition leaders came together to plan a campaign which, by January 1770, produced more than 30 petitions, from perhaps 60,000 petitioners across the country, against the 'unconstitutional' disqualification of the elected representative of the Middlesex freeholders.

Despite this significant wider support, the leading edge of the surge of activity remained the metropolitan area, and at the heart of it were men with strong connections to Chatham. Even before Wilkes's reappearance, William Beckford had promoted a bill to prevent bribery in elections; a year later, shorter parliaments and a place and pension bill were added, creating from longstanding 'patriot' demands a 'radical' programme of parliamentary reform with wide metropolitan support.[87] In December 1768, a by-election in Middlesex brought into parliament another Chathamite, the lawyer Sergeant Glynn. In February 1769, supporters of Wilkes formed the Society of Supporters of the Bill of Rights, with an agenda wider than its immediate objective of paying Wilkes's debts. Prominent among them were James Townsend and John Sawbridge, both just beginning careers in metropolitan politics as agents of Shelburne's attempt, after his resignation, to build up a City interest. Both were influential in the petitioning campaign, especially its extension in Middlesex to include grievances far broader than the denial of electors' rights. In June 1769, as Beckford engineered their election as sheriffs in the City, the liverymen of Common Hall, with great applause for Beckford, seized the opportunity to push forward a similarly wide-ranging petition from the City.[88] Rounds of summer visiting cemented links and brought in Temple, who may have had a hand earlier in the City petition.[89] In October, the growing patriot 'ferment' in the City came to a peak with Beckford's controversial election, on Townsend's nomination, to a second term as Lord Mayor; this set observers recalling ominous seventeenth-century precedents. Temple and Shelburne graced Beckford's mayoral feast, otherwise 'miserably attended' by the usual 'good-company'.[90]

No wonder that by the summer of 1769 Walpole thought circumstances ripe for a Chatham reappearance.[91] Of the 'Chathamites', only Temple was close to Chatham through 1769,[92] and he, with Chatham's neighbour near Hayes, John Calcraft[93] – whose knowledge and skills as political 'man of business' were rapidly to become invaluable to Chatham – seemed to be managing Chatham's gradual 'coming forth again'. Immediately after his reconciliation with Chatham (assisted by Calcraft), Temple had declared their 'political differences . . . in a great degree over'.[94] With Calcraft's help, Temple fed Chatham a constant stream of information, spiced with reports and rumours of his return to office.[95] At first there were thoughts on both sides that Chatham might rejoin his old colleagues. When the soldier of Seven Years War fame, the Marquess of Granby, visited Chatham in April as an emissary from Grafton, and allegedly was told that 'Lord Chatham did not refuse to act with them', Grafton, according to Temple, meekly agreed 'to do as Lord Chatham should direct them when he came forth'. The king was hardly likely to be so complaisant, especially as it was increasingly clear that Chatham fully shared his supporters' disapproval of the administration's actions over the Middlesex election.[96] And it was, it seems, the growing turmoil evident in the City by late June that at last brought Chatham out to express his indignation in person to the king.[97]

Quite what Chatham expected from his sudden appearance at court on 7 July is not clear. At the time, observers were perplexed. However, his forthright criticism, in the private conversation he was granted with the king, of a number of recent measures, put an invitation to return to office out of the question. Chatham made much of his poor health and lack of ambition.[98] But there was increasing evidence of full recovery – he was said to be 'brisk and boyish' yet 'grown fat'. And restoration of 'perfect harmony' with Grenville soon suggested that Chatham's *wonderful resurrection* would put him in full 'pursuit of Power and Popularity' again, by a change of men as well as measures. Indeed, he declared as much in July in a contrived meeting with a Rockinghamite neighbour.[99]

Those of Chatham's supporters still remaining in office – chiefly Camden, still Lord Chancellor, and Granby – were put in 'great distress' by continuing pressure to declare themselves. The mayoral election in October was greeted warmly by Chatham, who gave his blessing to Temple's attendance at Beckford's feast.[100] By November, the cautious and sceptical Rockinghamites knew he was 'exceedingly animated' against the ministry. More surprisingly, he was wooing them with long-forgotten but now much-repeated compliments to the 'antient Whigg families' and Rockingham's 'knot of *spotless* friends, such as ought to govern this kingdom'.[101]

Scenting the possibility of a real crisis to exploit, yet genuinely appalled by the implications of the Middlesex election decisions, Chatham – politician to the core as he was – had, it seems, the whiff of earlier full-blooded oppositions in his nostrils again. His wooing of the Rockinghams showed recognition that success would demand more than Grenvillite support. Committing himself to an unprecedented effort at co-operation and throwing the caution of the early 1760s to the wind, Chatham was about to embark, with another characteristic burst of tremendous energy, on two sessions of the most remarkable opposition of his career.

. . .

'UNITED' OPPOSITION: THE LAST GREAT BID FOR POWER, 1770–71

By late November, Chatham had declared for 'three grand points' of opposition, 'Corsica for foreign affairs; America for home Policy; The right of Election as a constitutional Principle'.[102] It was soon clear, when parliament opened belatedly on 9 January while the king was still receiving petitions, that to Chatham the first two matters 'bore no comparison to . . . the notorious dissatisfaction expressed by the whole English nation' over the 'violation' of their rights. The 'internal disorder of the constitution' was 'the grand capital mischief', which demanded fundamental remedy. Otherwise, 'MAY DISCORD PREVAIL FOR EVER', he proclaimed. Moving a provocative amendment to the address-in-reply promising immediate enquiry into grievances, Chatham allowed the Lords no privileges but those that rested 'upon the broad bottom of the people' and urged them to defend the 'liberties of our fellow-subjects' over the Middlesex election, regardless of the risk of a clash with the Commons. A fortnight later, he suggested that the proper relationship 'between the constituent and representative body of the people' needed fundamental restoration through a measure of parliamentary reform: not the violent amputation of 'rotten' boroughs, but the 'gentler' remedy he had first briefly suggested in 1766, that of strengthening the representation of 'the soil' by allowing an additional member to each county.[103]

This championing of the people at the expense of the Commons added a new, full-blooded, populist dimension to the old Pitt patriot rhetoric. But the opposition Chatham had thus launched was never his alone. The Rockinghams, having played a major, if cautious, part in the petitioning campaign that Chatham had largely ignored, were also very keen to exploit the new issues in parliament. Moreover, having survived the attrition of return to opposition in 1766, they were fast developing a confident sense of distinctive identity already being distilled in Burke's classic manifesto, *Thoughts on the Cause of the Present Discontents*, to be published in April 1770. Tracing all the 'present discontents' to the influence of a secret court cabal through the 1760s which had undermined ostensible ministers, not least the Rockinghams, Burke proposed, as the only possible defence, the principled unity of a party devoted to the constitution. The Rockinghams, of course, were that party – the only true Whigs, the constitution's natural guardians. So, for these reasons as well as bitter experience, those to whom Chatham had already declared himself 'united body and soul' were reluctant now, as they would not have been before 1766, to respond to his wooing.[104]

Thus Chatham began his parliamentary campaign with only his own supporters in the Lords.[105] However, his second speech on 22 January 1770 gave warm support to a motion of Rockingham's as a 'public demonstration of that cordial union, which . . . subsists between us'.[106] The 'united opposition' had emerged. It went on to a joint thrust in the Lords on the Middlesex election issues on 2 February, in a debate which lasted until two in the morning and substantially cut the administration majority. Two 'warm protests' from the opposition declared 'they would never rest till the nation should obtain satisfaction on the Middlesex

election'.[107] Rockingham's confidence in Chatham warmed
and the two men worked together with remarkable harmony
for the rest of the session.[108]

The 'united opposition', of course, also operated in the
Commons. There already the government majority had been
uncomfortably cut in two critical divisions.[109] There, on all
issues in these two sessions, parallel campaigns were mounted
in which the Rockinghamites generally played a larger part
than did Chatham's small band.[110] Indeed, to concentrate
on Chatham's role – as this account must – cannot help but
underestimate other contributions. In the Lords, even Rockingham was bestirred into unusual activity in an attempt to
match his leadership to Chatham's, while the Duke of Richmond, a recruit of the mid-1760s increasingly valued by Rockingham for his reliability and judgement, began to make his mark.

The first attacks of the opposition further weakened
Grafton's tottering administration. In an unusually open
display of ministerial disunity, Camden and Granby supported Chatham on 9 January. Continuing relentless pressure at last secured Granby's resignation in mid-January,
while Camden was dismissed. But Grafton was brought to
resignation, announced on 30 January, less by these losses
than by difficulty in replacing the Chancellor. Without
Charles Yorke's sudden death as he agonized over deserting
his Rockinghamite friends for that coveted prize, Grafton
might well have recovered with the help of North's skills in
the Commons.[111] Certainly the king would not readily have
turned to those who publicly opposed the Middlesex election decisions and urged a dissolution.[112] He was becoming
implacable against Chatham, who had 'deserted' him in need
only to lecture him on subsequent 'mistakes'.[113]

The king found an alternative in Lord North. On 28 January, heartened by the narrow but sufficient victories in the
Commons, North agreed to take the Treasury. He came
with experience and much respect in the Commons. Within
weeks, he had stabilized parliamentary support and was well
on the way to consolidating the hold on office he was to
enjoy for twelve years – on the same bases as those enjoyed
by Walpole and Pelham – until dislodged by the dire crisis
of unsuccessful war with America.

However, in February 1770 North's success was far from
clear. He brought no new party support to give immediate

strength to slim government majorities. With some optimism the opposition campaign continued.[114] In the Lords on 2 March, urged by Chatham,[115] they moved a surprise motion for more seamen. Chatham's speech on this occasion drew attention not so much by his alarmist talk on the situation abroad,[116] but by the new extremism with which he flattered his Rockinghamite allies on their theme of the evils of 'secret influence'. This, he claimed, had 'occasioned all the present unhappiness and disturbances in the nation', and by it, he 'confessed', he had, in his own administration, been 'duped and deceived'. This was arrant nonsense, reckless of offence to the king. To Chatham's intense annoyance, it was not unreasonably refuted by Grafton as the product of 'a distempered mind'.[117] Twelve days later, Chatham took up a promising issue from the last session which the Rockinghams and Grenville had revived with some success in the Commons – that of over-expenditure on the civil list.[118] But Chatham was again diverted from a 'very able recapitulation' on the issue into further flaming exchanges and even more extreme insinuations of corruption which reflected directly on the king. No wonder one opponent thought he 'acted like a man mad'.[119]

In 'his old brilliant style', Chatham was indeed giving a cutting edge in the Lords to the joint opposition as he returned to the reckless opposition of his youth. No wonder they thought him 'supernatural'.[120] In this and the next session, he recurred repeatedly to violent insinuations of secret influence 'near the palace', influence which allegedly had misled the king and enslaved the Commons.[121] In return, for the time being and somewhat uneasily, the Rockinghamites accepted his radical rhetoric and supported his moves on the Middlesex election issue, as he sought 'to rouse his country to a just sense of the blessings' of the constitution and 'to give the people a strong and thorough sense' of its 'great violation' by 'those unjust and arbitrary proceedings'.[122] With few of the Rockinghamites' qualms about the royal prerogative, he joined the petitioners in calling for a dissolution of the parliament which had, he claimed, forfeited the people's confidence. Indeed, in both sessions he moved to address the king for such a dissolution.[123] But, instead of rousing the Lords, he now bored them by talking 'on the Middlesex election till nobody [would] answer him'.[124]

Meanwhile, Chatham was moving – with Calcraft's ever-active and indispensable help – to foster links with the City much more deliberately than ever before and more confidently than did the Rockinghams. In March, Beckford was in the thick of moves which produced an outspoken remonstrance to the king over the lack of response to the City's petition.[125] At the same time, with Chatham's approval, Beckford planned a great dinner to seal the union between the City and the parliamentary opposition. Chatham secured Rockingham's attendance and, when gout prevented his own presence, sent his wife and son to the very impressive and much noted occasion.[126] There were also rumours, not only that he helped to draft the City remonstrance, but of his active support for one from Westminster.[127] While thus encouraging out-of-doors protest, Chatham took steps to keep it within bounds acceptable to Rockinghamites. He firmly prevented plans to use Beckford's dinner to get assent to the City's emerging programme of parliamentary reform.[128] With Sawbridge's help, Calcraft forestalled an angry protest at the Middlesex meeting against half-hearted Rockinghamite support for remonstrances. Beckford, Townsend, and even Shelburne – whose City contacts they chiefly were that Chatham was exploiting – had also to be humoured.[129] Little wonder that observers began to see 'a crisis of very great moment' in this conjunction of London, press and parliamentary opposition – especially with Wilkes about to be released from prison.[130] In fact, the City's provocative remonstrance produced a markedly hostile reaction in the Commons, and opposition votes began to decline.[131] Chatham pressed on regardless. Predictably defeated in an attempt to initiate further parliamentary action on the Middlesex election, he proposed a motion of censure on those who had advised the king's hostile answer to the City remonstrance. This allowed him vigorously to defend the City's action, and to answer the Lords' sneers with praise of the dignity of City freemen.[132]

As the parliamentary session closed, Chatham's influence in the City reached its height. On 14 May, apparently on his suggestion, the Common Council agreed to another relatively moderate remonstrance which had his prior approval.[133] When, in presenting the remonstrance, Beckford took the unprecedented and much resented step of replying verbally to the king's answer, he was ecstatically congratulated by

Chatham. But, again, Chatham kept his supporters within bounds. He prompted them against their wishes into the usual dutiful address on the birth of a princess.[134] And when, in a vote of thanks for his 'zeal' in supporting the rights of election and petition, they sought again to commit him to parliamentary reform, he made quite clear his opposition to more frequent elections – while renewing in the Lords his suggestion of additional county members.[135] Beckford's sudden death on 21 June was undeniably a setback. Nevertheless, with Wilkes so far quiescent, two Rockinghamites were elected as sheriffs and another to serve out Beckford's mayoralty. The radicals who had attacked Burke's *Thoughts on the Cause of the Present Discontents* on its publication appeared to be under control, while Chatham's moderation on parliamentary reform was welcome to parliamentary allies.[136] While he developed his connection with Sawbridge and Townsend, he and Rockingham remained in touch over the summer, and Chatham was repeatedly reported 'in great health and spirits'.[137]

Chatham was buoyed through the summer by the emergence of an issue seemingly made for him. In June 1770, following six months of tension on the South Atlantic Falklands Islands, the Spanish carried out their longstanding determination to evict the British settlers.[138] As news of events reached Britain, Calcraft was quick to suggest they would 'turn confidence, towards those who, only, can save this country', and Chatham as quickly responded with war-like talk.[139] When Britain's firm response provoked a three-months' stand-off from October, just as the parliamentary session approached, the situation seemed even more promising for Chatham.

The opposition began their campaign strongly on this new issue in both Houses. George Grenville's death on the opening day after a distressing illness was both a family and, at this stage, a political blow to Chatham. Nevertheless, he was soon more energetically involved than ever in planning and rallying support in both Houses, with Shelburne now his chief ally. In the Lords, he spoke as he had in the 1750s, 'to save an injured, insulted, undone country'. Enlarging on his long experience of Spain, he urged that a 'patched up peace will not do'. As the great war minister, he discoursed on the proper use of the navy – and, less responsibly, on inadequate defences.[140] He seemed to invite the war that looked increasingly likely, attempting both to prompt and exploit the cry rising outside 'that there was nobody fit to conduct it but Lord Chatham'.[141] And, when government peers moved to defuse the opposition by excluding 'strangers' from debates, Chatham was provoked into leading an impotent protest 'in a violent emotion of rage'.[142]

Now, however, the intervention of the king and Lord North had turned Britain towards negotiation and, over the Christmas recess, the fall of Choiseul in France clinched the preservation of peace. A convention was reached just as parliament reassembled. The opposition's bubble burst. It was reduced to criticizing earlier 'neglect' and picking holes in the convention. Chatham took the lead in castigating 'an ignominious compromise', secured, he suggested, by suspicious 'interference' from France. Because the convention acknowledged no 'right' to the Falklands, it was, he claimed, offensive to British sovereignty and 'the inherent and essential dignity' of the Crown, and hence illegal. He explicitly hoped that Spain would be provoked to break the convention.[143] But opposition votes remained much lower than in the previous session and Chatham chafed impotently at 'the silly drama' of being reduced by the continued exclusion of 'strangers' to talking to 'the *Tapestry*' on the walls of the Lords' chamber.[144] Only on a move to amend an address to the king on the convention was there some resurgence. The story was the same in the Commons.[145] North's authority was decisively confirmed.

Meanwhile, in the City, Chatham's connections were now meeting difficulties. Townsend, although nominated, did not win the mayoralty, while Shelburne's attempts to shape further City protests failed.[146] The Falklands crisis added further friction when Wilkes, clashing with Sawbridge in a 'tumultuous' Westminster meeting, proposed the impeachment of North and, to Chatham's indignation, encouraged resistance to impressment for the navy in the City. Chatham's outspokenness in parliament on this sensitive issue weakened hopes of influence with the new Lord Mayor, Brass Crosby, and exacerbated the breach.[147] Attempting to heal it, Chatham initiated action in both Houses on an issue which interested the City, the rights of juries in seditious libel cases, recently highlighted by a case over one letter of the provocative publicist, Junius. Following recent precedent, Mansfield had directed the jury to decide only on the facts of publication and not whether the publication breached the law. Chatham, encouraged by Camden's contrary opinion, construed Mansfield's judgment as yet another subversion of 'our dearest rights, our most invaluable liberties'. Vehemently pursuing the attack, he vowed to press for parliamentary enquiry after Christmas.[148]

His vow was not fulfilled, largely because this issue brought the parliamentary alliance to breaking point. At the beginning of the session, Chatham had been equivocal about co-operation – indeed, he reverted to form by kicking and cuffing both 'friend and enemy' and declaring he was 'connected with nobody'.[149] Although he was quickly drawn into co-operation again, there were continuing tensions over his apparently self-interested exploitation of the Falklands crisis.[150] When the juries' rights issue came to the point of action in February 1771, differences could not be controlled. Chatham wanted a parliamentary enquiry, to lead to a declaration of what he maintained the law had always been. When the Rockinghams went ahead with a bill aimed rather at clarifying the law for the future, Barré reported almost exultingly the open disagreement of the opposition in the Commons which destroyed any hopes for it.[151] This disagreement prevented Chatham from supporting Rockinghamite plans to keep the Falklands issue alive; not even its suggested importance to 'our navigation in those seas' and to hope of discoveries 'of great consequence to . . . a commercial nation' could placate him.[152] He fell silent for two and a half months, kept in touch only by Calcraft and Barré.

In this time, the City careered further out of control over the famous printers' case. The Commons, attempting to enforce their standing order prohibiting the publication of accounts of debates, became embroiled with the City authorities who, at Wilkes's instigation, protected the printers. The case went to extremes. The Lord Mayor and Alderman Oliver (Beckford's successor as alderman and MP) were imprisoned in the Tower and popular feeling was brought to fever pitch again.[153] Chatham was torn two ways. He was very soon convinced that the Commons had gone too far in punishing the City officers but was equally uneasy about the challenge to the 'established jurisdiction of the House' and subversion of 'the parliamentary constitution'.[154] Yet Chatham's closest City friends, Townsend and Sawbridge, were persuaded to declare their full support for the City's action, after Chatham had praised them for standing apart. Even in the Commons, Chathamites were divided among themselves, most going further than Chatham approved at the time. Unlike Rockingham, Chatham did not encourage visits to the imprisoned officers. 'The scene is dreadful', reported Calcraft. 'Opposition are in great want of a leader, and a general system.'[155]

Such disarray disheartened Chatham – though he had done little to prevent it.[156] But, as the session drew to a close, he was spurred, especially by Shelburne, to one last effort. He resumed contact with Rockingham, supported a further move on the Middlesex election, and attempted somewhat half-heartedly to remove Rockingham's objections to another motion for a dissolution.[157] But most strikingly, he now came out in full support of the City on the printers' case, treating it as an issue of 'the liberty of the press' – as others had from the beginning. Despite his earlier views, he bitterly attacked all the Commons' actions, condemning them as 'bare-faced tyranny' more fitted to a French king. And, declaring that a dissolution was no longer a sufficient remedy when the 'whole constitution' was 'giving way', he solemnly declared himself 'a convert to triennial parliaments'.[158] His populist rhetoric had come to full fruition.

But to no avail. Chatham, thinking initially of his proposal of additional county representation, had delayed too long in responding to Shelburne's promptings to co-ordinate with Sawbridge, who had just moved in the Commons the first of what were to become his annual motions for shorter parliaments. Parliament was about to be prorogued.[159] More important, the recent open breach between 'constitutional radicals' and 'Wilkites' in the Society of Supporters of the Bill of Rights[160] destroyed any remaining hope of controlling metropolitan opinion. Even had Beckford lived, it is unlikely that even the constitutional radicals (whose programme was widely advertised in these years) would have been convinced by Chatham's belated and half-hearted conversion to shorter parliaments.

The tumultuous constituency awakened by Wilkes was quite another matter. He had never wanted success for the 'damned aristocracy' of the united opposition.[161] His followers agitated for a far more inclusive and accountable political and legal system than Chatham ever contemplated.[162] City and press might continue to show respect for Chatham, but Wilkes, not he, was now the 'hero of the Mob' and the 'middling' people who had formerly lionized Chatham.[163] Never again would extra-parliamentary politics be so readily harnessed to a parliamentary opposition as Pitt had harnessed them in 1756–57.

Nevertheless, the opposition of 1770–71 was indeed remarkable. Chatham's extremism left several experienced observers gasping.[164] In appealing against a supposedly discredited parliament to the people as the foundation of the constitution and envisaging a larger role for them, he had gone further in developing his 'patriotism' – if only in rhetoric – than any other leading politician. It was this extremism in deference to out-of-doors admirers that helped to breach Chatham's alliance with the generally more moderate Rockinghams. Nevertheless, the alliance had been on Chatham's part a remarkably sustained exercise in co-operation, suggesting he now recognized the need for 'Whig' allies. Most fundamental to the breach, when it came, was neither issues nor even Chatham's autocratic personality, but his long-standing fear of Old Corps 'connection' now in the new form of the confident party solidarity preached by Burke. To this he retorted that 'he was the oldest Whig in England and could not now submit to be called only an *ally* of the Whigs. He was *a Whig*'.[165]

This remarkable opposition was, however, a disastrous failure. True, free from the restraints of office, Chatham's oratory rose to something like his old brilliance in the new forum, 'far superior to all his other adversaries', at least when Mansfield was silent.[166] In this sense, perhaps, and shrinking instinctively from the burdens of office, he was, as Jeremy Black has argued,[167] most at ease in opposition. But, much as Chatham often dwelt theatrically on his age and infirmities, the whole tenor of his words and behaviour – most clearly over the Falklands crisis – leaves no doubt that he, like others in opposition, wanted office.[168] However, the two moments passed at which a call might have come – in the wake of Grafton's resignation and when a Falklands war seemed likely. North's strengthening majorities demonstrated that the 'sober and respectable' part of the nation was no more convinced than the king that redress of petitioners' grievances was essential to the renewed 'peace and quietness' they so much wanted.[169] Nor, much as some might dislike aspects of the convention reached with Spain, did they think that war over some tiny Atlantic islands was essential to Britain's interests. As Walpole quipped, although Chatham might have been called for had war been declared, 'nobody was desirous of making war only to make him necessary'.[170] Both Rockinghamites and Chathamites came out of the opposition weakened. North reaped the harvest for eleven long years.

Chatham's disillusionment with contemporary politics, always latent and growing through the 1760s, came to a peak in these years of opposition. Yet with some tact and skill, he could have dominated the decade, eased problems and possibly bridged the widening gap between parliamentary and popular politics. Instead, he developed no coherent strategy to cope with new circumstances, swinging rather from extreme to extreme. From lofty disengagement, he came too late to offer co-operation to the Rockinghams, when they had developed a solidarity of their own. Having skilfully recovered the confidence of the king, he threw it away and came to provoke him beyond endurance. He did nothing to ease Britain's international isolation or the British situation in America or India. He was part cause of the very weaknesses that disillusioned him. Chatham, too, had lost his way.

. . .

NOTES

1. To Montagu, 10 July 1766, *Correspondence*, X, p. 222: 'he will want the thorough-bass of drums and trumpets, and is not made for peace'; cf. *Memoirs George III*, II, p. 259.
2. Burke to O'Hara, 29 July 1766, in Thomas W. Copeland (ed.), *The Correspondence of Edmund Burke* 9 vols (Cambridge, 1958–70), I, p. 263; cf. Mitchell to Yorke, n.d., *Chatham Correspondence*, III, p. 43n.
3. Expressions are conveniently gathered in *A genuine collection of the several pieces of political intelligence extraordinary* . . . (1766).
4. Chesterfield to his son, 1 Aug. 1766, in Bonamy Dobrée (ed.), *The Letters of Philip Dormer Stanhope, fourth Earl of Chesterfield* 6 vols (New York, 1932), VI, pp. 2752–3.

5. Hampden to Grenville, 31 July, Grenville to Trevor, 10 Aug., HL, Stowe Papers, STG22/34, ST7, vol. 2; Walpole to Mann, 1 Aug., *Correspondence*, XXII, pp. 442–3; Wray to Hardwicke, 5 Aug., Hardwicke Papers, Add. MSS 35401, f. 302, cf. *Memoirs George III*, II, p. 255; Lord Townshend to Bute, 14 Aug. 1766, Bute Papers, HP.

6. Porter to Weston, 29 Aug. 1766, HMC, *Weston Underwood*, p. 401, quoted in Paul Langford, *The First Rockingham Administration 1765–1766* (Oxford, 1973), p. 265; Rigby to Bedford, 25 Sept. 1766, in Lord John Russell (ed.), *Correspondence of John, Fourth Duke of Bedford* 3 vols (1842–6), III, p. 346.

7. Lord Townshend to Bute, 14 Aug., HP; Lyttelton to Elizabeth Montagu, 24 Aug., HL, Montagu Papers, MO1339; cf. Burke to Rockingham, 21 Aug. 1766, in Copeland (ed.), *Burke Correspondence*, I, p. 266.

8. Title page, *E[ar]l of Ch[atha]m's apology* (1766); cf. e.g. *London Evening Post*, 5–7 Aug 1766, *A genuine collection*, pp. 10–13, 18, 25, 34.

9. Lyttelton to Elizabeth Montagu, 24 Aug. 1766, MO1339, and e.g. *A genuine collection*, pp. 13, 37, 38, 40, 64, 88–9.

10. See above, p. 160 and n. 146, and *An enquiry into the conduct of a late right honourable commoner* (1766), *An examination of the principles and boasted disinterestedness of a late right honourable gentleman* (1766), *A genuine collection*, passim.

11. Walpole to Mann, 1 Aug. 1766, *Correspondence*, XXII, p. 443.

12. *A genuine collection*, p. 84; cf. *London Evening Post*, 5–7 Aug. 1766.

13. Lord Edmond Fitzmaurice, *The Life of William, Earl of Shelburne afterwards First Marquess of Landsdowne*, 3 vols (1875–6), I, p. 412; Hume to the Marquise de Barbentane, in John Y. Greig (ed.), *The Letters of David Hume* 2 vols (Oxford, 1932), II, p. 85; Lyttelton to Elizabeth Montagu, 24 Aug. 1766, HL MO1339; *Memoirs George III*, II, p. 291.

14. Newcastle's second-hand account of a conversation with Chatham, 7 Sept., Newcastle Papers, Add. MSS 32977, ff. 41–2; C. Townshend to Sackville, 1 Aug., Sackville to Irwin, 20 Aug. 1766, HMC, *Stopford-Sackville*, I, pp. 67, 114.

15. Walpole to Montagu, 10 July 1766, *Correspondence*, X, p. 222; cf. above, p. 159. Most notable was the loss of William Dowdeswell, the Rockinghams' Chancellor of the Exchequer, who was keen to stay; Langford, *Rockingham Administration*, pp. 259–60, 279.

16. John Brooke, *The Chatham Administration 1766–1768* (1956), pp. 53–61; Langford, *Rockingham Administration*, pp. 272–4.

17. Barrington to Mitchell, 14 Dec. 1766, *Chatham Correspondence*, III, p. 138n.; Brooke, *Chatham Administration*, pp. 13–15, 38–42, 62–7.

18. Barrington to Mitchell, 14 Dec. 1766, *Chatham Correspondence*, III, pp. 138–9n.; Sackville to Irwin, 9 Dec. 1766, HMC, *Stopford-Sackville*, I, pp. 116–17.
19. [26 Nov. 1766], Sir William R. Anson (ed.), *Autobiography and Political Correspondence of Augustus Henry, Third Duke of Grafton* (London, 1898), p. 107.
20. Newcastle's account, 7 Sept. 1766, Add. MSS 32977, f. 42.
21. Grafton to Chatham, 17 Oct., *Chatham Correspondence*, III, pp. 110–12; Chatham to Grafton, 19 Oct. 1766, in Anson (ed.), *Grafton*, pp. 108–9.
22. Hardwicke to C. Yorke, 2 Dec., Add. MSS 35362, f. 53; John Pringle to Walter Scott, 11 Dec. 1766, HMC, *Polwarth*, V, p. 365.
23. Simmons and Thomas, II, p. 90 (14 Jan. 1766), cf. Langford, *Rockingham Administration*, p. 85; Pitt to Lady Stanhope, 20 June 1766, PRO 30/8/86, f. 320.
24. Bedford's private journal, 24 Oct., in Russell (ed.), *Bedford Correspondence*, III, p. 349; Chatham to Mitchell, 8 Aug., cabinet minute, Conway to Mitchell, 8 Aug. 1766, *Chatham Correspondence*, III, pp. 30, 31n., 29–30n.
25. Stanley to Grenville, in William James Smith (ed.), *The Grenville Papers* 4 vols (1852–3), III, pp. 284–5; Conway, Mitchell to Pitt, 29, 30 July, *Chatham Correspondence*, III, pp. 15–20; Stanley to Pitt/Chatham, 26 July, 2 Aug. 1766, PRO 30/8/57, ff. 168–76.
26. Mitchell to Chatham, Conway, 21 Aug., 17 Sept., to Yorke, [n.d.], *Chatham Correspondence*, III, pp. 46–50, 67–71 and nn., 42n.
27. Conway, Grafton, Stanley to Chatham, 26 Sept., 1 Oct., Conway to Mitchell, [30 Sept. 1766], *Chatham Correspondence*, III, pp. 77–80, 82–7, 82–4nn.; cf. Anson (ed.), *Grafton*, p. 105.
28. Mitchell to Chatham, Conway, 6 Dec. 1766, *Chatham Correspondence*, III, pp. 139–43 and nn.; Stanley to Chatham, 2, 21 Jan. 1767, PRO 30/8/57, ff. 191–4.
29. Cabinet minute, 15 [Nov.] 1766, PRO 30/8/71, ff. 210–11; Geoffrey W. Rice, 'Great Britain, the Manila ransom, and the first Falklands dispute with Spain, 1766', *International History Review* 2 (1980), esp. pp. 401–5; H.M. Scott, *British Foreign Policy in the Age of the American Revolution* (Oxford, 1990), pp. 102–7; Basil Williams, *The Life of William Pitt Earl of Chatham* 2 vols (1913), II, pp. 223–4. But see Margaret M. Escott, 'Britain's relations with France and Spain 1763–1771', Ph.D. thesis, University of Wales, 1988, esp. pp. 104–5, 231–2, 501, for a more positive view of Chatham's personal contribution.

30. Thomas Price, James Boswell to Chatham, 7–12 Aug., 18 Sept. 1766, PRO 30/8/53, ff. 242–7, vol. 3, f. 129; Boswell to Pitt/Chatham, 19 Feb. 1766, 3 Jan., 8 April 1767, *Chatham Correspondence*, II, pp. 388–9, III, pp. 159, 244–5; cf. Beckford to Shelburne, 1 Oct. 1766, Lansdowne Papers, HP.

31. Shelburne to Chatham, 18 Oct., Chatham to Shelburne, 19 Oct, Rochford to Chatham, 28 Nov. 1766, *Chatham Correspondence*, III, pp. 113–15, 131.

32. Langford, *Rockingham Administration*, pp. 87–8.

33. Williams, *The Life of William Pitt*, II, p. 220, cf. PRO 30/8/79, ff. 298–9, vol. 85, ff. 368–9, vol. 93, ff. 240–1 (state of ships in the English, French and Spanish navies, all 10 Sept. 1766), Bedford's private journal, 24 Oct. 1766, in Russell (ed.), *Bedford Correspondence*, III, p. 349; Brooke, *Chatham Administration*, pp. 13–16, 65.

34. Scott, *British Foreign Policy*, pp. 109–10.

35. Anson (ed.), *Grafton*, p. 105.

36. Cf. Scott, *British Foreign Policy*, pp. 97, 99, 101.

37. For detailed references for what follows, see Marie Peters, 'The myth of William Pitt, Earl of Chatham, great imperialist. Part II', *Journal of Imperial and Commonwealth History* 22 (1994), pp. 393, 399–402.

38. See above, pp. 102–3.

39. *Memoirs George III*, II, p. 278; *Chatham Correspondence*, III, p. 59n.

40. Chatham to Grafton, [23] Aug., in Anson (ed.), *Grafton*, p. 102; Grafton to Chatham, 28 Aug. 1766, *Chatham Correspondence*, III, p. 59.

41. Thomas Walpole to Chatham, 9 Sept. 1766, *Chatham Correspondence*, III, pp. 61–4, gives one trenchant view of the problems.

42. Chatham to Grafton, 7 Dec., in Anson (ed.), *Grafton*, p. 110, cf. Pringle to Scott, 11 Dec. 1766, 5 Jan. 1767, HMC, *Polwarth*, V, pp. 365–6.

43. Anson (ed.), *Grafton*, pp. 109–10; Pringle to Scott, 11 Dec. 1766, HMC, *Polwarth*, V, p. 365.

44. *Memoirs George III*, III, pp. 277, 279–80, 287–90; Chatham to Grafton, 7 Dec. 1766, in Anson (ed.), *Grafton*, pp. 110–11; Philip Lawson, 'Parliament and the first East India inquiry, 1767', *Parliamentary History* 1 (1982), pp. 101–4.

45. Chatham to Townshend, [24 Sept. 1766], *Chatham Correspondence*, III, p. 73; Philip Lawson, 'Parliament, the constitution and corn: the embargo crisis of 1766', *Parliamentary History* 5 (1986), pp. 17, 24, 28.

46. Lawson, 'Embargo crisis', pp. 25–32.

47. Lyttelton to Elizabeth Montagu, 22 Nov., HL, MO1343; *Chatham Correspondence*, III, pp. 125–7nn. (11 Nov. 1766); Lawson, 'Embargo crisis', pp. 29–30.

NOTES

48. P.D.G. Thomas, *British Politics and the Stamp Act Crisis* (Oxford, 1975), pp. 287–9.
49. Newcastle's account, 7 Sept. 1766, Add. MSS 32977, f. 41.
50. Thomas, *Stamp Act*, pp. 293–5.
51. Bedford's private journal, 19, 24, 31 Oct. 1766, in Russell (ed.), *Bedford Correspondence*, III, pp. 348–51.
52. There is an almost total absence of official material (except on America in 1766 and matters of patronage) in the Chatham Papers for the Chatham administration – a marked contrast to the war years.
53. Albemarle to Rochford, 23 Jan., William L. Clements Library, Pitt Papers, vol. 1; Gascoyne to Strutt, 24 Jan. 1767, Strutt Papers, HP.
54. *Chatham Correspondence*, III, pp. 149–58 (quotation, p. 153); Pringle to Scott, 5 Jan. 1767, HMC, *Polwarth*, V, pp. 366–7; Sir Lewis Namier and John Brooke, *Charles Townshend* (1964), pp. 161–2; H.V. Bowen, *Revenue and Reform. The Indian Problem and British Politics 1757–1773* (Cambridge, 1991), pp. 58–9; Lawson, 'East India inquiry', pp. 104–5.
55. Grenville to Buckinghamshire, 27 Jan. 1767, HL, Stowe Papers, ST7, vol. 2; Lawson, 'East India inquiry', p. 105.
56. Chatham to Shelburne, 31 Jan., 3 Feb., to Grafton, 16 Feb., to Grafton and Shelburne, 17 Feb., *Chatham Correspondence*, III, pp. 181–2, 189, 212, 214; Chatham to Grafton, 23 Jan., 9 Feb. 1767, in Anson (ed.), *Grafton*, pp. 113–14, 116–17 (quotation); 'East India Plan of Motion', Clements Library, Lansdowne Papers, vol. 90, f. 441 (dated 6 March by Bowen, *Revenue and Reform*, p. 60, n. 45).
57. Bowen, *Revenue and Reform*, pp. 59–66; Peters, 'Myth', pp. 401–2.
58. Gascoyne to Strutt, [11–25 Feb.], HP; cf. Charlemont to Flood, 19 Feb., [T. Rodd, ed.], *Original Letters . . . to the Right Hon. Henry Flood* (1820), p. 31; Sackville to Irwin, 13 Feb 1767, HMC, *Stopford-Sackville*, I, p. 119.
59. Belasyse to Fauconberg, 28 Feb., Belasyse Papers, HP; Walpole to Mann, 2 March 1767, *Correspondence*, XXII, p. 488.
60. Simmons and Thomas, II, pp. 410–11; cf. Grenville's diary [wrongly dated 21 Jan.], in Smith (ed.), *Grenville Papers*, IV, p. 211, Charlemont to Flood, 29 Jan. 1767, in Rodd (ed.), *Flood Letters*, p. 11; Thomas, *Stamp Act*, pp. 338–40.
61. Shelburne to Chatham, 1 Feb. 1766, *Chatham Correspondence*, III, pp. 184–5.
62. Burke to O'Hara, 2 Dec. 1766, in Copeland (ed.), *Burke Correspondence*, I, p. 284.
63. Chatham to Shelburne, 3, 7, 17 Feb., *Chatham Correspondence*, III, pp. 188–9, 193–4, 215; Chatham to Shelburne, 10,

23 March 1767, Bowood Muniments, Bodleian Library microfilm, Box S12, ff. 70–1, 78–9; Peters, 'Myth', pp. 398–9.

64. Cf. his explanation recounted by Walsh to Clive, 22 Nov. 1766, quoted in Peters, 'Myth', p. 401, and see above, p. 58.

65. Grafton, Shelburne to Chatham, 13 March 1767, *Chatham Correspondence*, III, pp. 232–6; Peters, 'Myth', p. 399; Thomas, *Stamp Act*, ch. 16.

66. Hume to [Hertford], 8 May 1766, HL, HM7203; e.g. Eliot to Hollis, 13 May 1767, 'Letters from Andrew Eliot to Thomas Hollis', *Collections of the Massachusetts Historical Society* fourth series, 4 (1858), p. 404.

67. Brooke, *Chatham Administration*, pp. 111–12.

68. Grafton, Shelburne to Chatham, 13 March 1767, *Chatham Correspondence*, III, pp. 232–6.

69. Chatham to George III, [3], 7, 12 March 1767, ibid., pp. 228, 230–1.

70. Walpole to Mann, 2 March, *Correspondence*, XXII, p. 490; Sandwich to Rochford, 22 March, Pitt Papers, vol. 1; Belasyse to Fauconberg, 16 April 1767, HP.

71. Bristol conveyed frequent messages: *Chatham Correspondence*, III, pp. 226–7, 237, 240–1, 247–8, 250.

72. Grafton to Chatham, Chatham to Grafton, 27, 29 May, Chatham to George III, [2 June] 1767, ibid., pp. 255–60, 268; Anson (ed.), *Grafton*, pp. 138–9.

73. *Memoirs George III*, II, p. 320 [c. 30 March].

74. Anson (ed.), *Grafton*, p. 137.

75. Whately to Grenville, 29 July, in Smith (ed.), *Grenville Papers*, IV, pp. 123–4; Nuthall to Camden, [5 Aug.], Camden Papers, HP; James Harris, memoranda, 12 July 1767 (Lyttelton reporting a Beckford visit to Chatham), Hampshire Record Office, Malmesbury Collection, 9M73/G748; Lady Chatham to Nuthall, 17 Aug. 1767, *Chatham Correspondence*, III, p. 282n.

76. George III to Camden, 6 Aug., in Sir John Fortescue (ed.), *The Correspondence of King George the Third from 1760 to December 1783* 6 vols (1927–8), I, p. 501; George III to Chatham, 23 Jan., 14 Oct. 1767, *Chatham Correspondence*, III, pp. 318, 343.

77. *Chatham Correspondence*, III, pp. 334–44, cf. Anson (ed.), *Grafton*, pp. 213–24; Brooke, *Chatham Administration*, pp. 375–84.

78. Burke to O'Hara, 30, 31 March [1767], in Copeland (ed.), *Burke Correspondence*, I, p. 303; Northington to Shipley, 11 March 1770, Northington Papers, HP.

79. E.g. *Gazetteer*, 3 Dec.; *London Chronicle*, 2–4 Dec. 1766, 14–17, 17–19 March; *London Evening Post*, 5–7, 26–8 March 1767.

80. E.g. *London Chronicle*, 4–7 April; *Gazetteer*, 4, 10 April 1767.
81. E.g. *Gazetteer*, 17, 18, 19 Oct. 1768.
82. Anson (ed.), *Grafton*, p. 103, cf. 91.
83. Edward to Elizabeth Montagu, 29 Sept. 1767, Elizabeth Montagu to Pepys, cf. to Elizabeth Carter, 23, 25 May 1778, HL, MO2034, 4036, 3448; *Memoirs George III*, II, p. 320 (March 1767), cf. pp. 272–4 (Nov. 1766), III, pp. 30–1 (May 1767) and, e.g., Burke to Rockingham, 30 July 1769, in Copeland (ed.), *Burke Correspondence*, II, p. 52.
84. Grenville diary, 26 Nov., in Smith (ed.), *Grenville Papers*, IV, p. 404; Lady Chatham to Beckford, 9 Dec., PRO 30/8/10, f. 55; Harris, memoranda, 13 Dec. 1768, 16 March 1769, 9M73/G750.
85. Pitt was apparently wiser over George II's wish to see Lord George Sackville expelled in 1759: Fitzmaurice (ed.), *Shelburne*, I, p. 356.
86. Lucy S. Sutherland, *The City of London and the Opposition to Government, 1768–1774* (1959), and George Rudé, *Wilkes and Liberty* (Oxford, 1962) are still indispensable, together with John Brewer, *Party Ideology and Popular Politics at the Accession of George III* (Cambridge, 1976), ch. 9, and Peter D.G. Thomas, *John Wilkes. A Friend to Liberty* (Oxford, 1996), chs 5–8.
87. William Maitland, *The History of London from its Foundation to the present Times . . . continued . . . by the Rev. John Entick* 2 vols (1772), II, pp. 85–6; Brooke, *Chatham Administration*, p. 337 and n.; Sutherland, *City of London*, pp. 11–12, 22–3.
88. Rudé, *Wilkes and Liberty*, pp. 61–2, 108–10, 153; John Norris, *Shelburne and Reform* (1963), pp. 58–68; Sutherland, *City of London*, p. 21; R. Burke to E. Burke, [24 June 1769], in Copeland (ed.), *Burke Correspondence*, II, p. 34.
89. Lyttelton to Grenville, 25 July, in Smith (ed.), *Grenville Papers*, IV, pp. 429–30, cf. Lyttelton to Elizabeth Montagu, 21 Aug. 1769, HL, MO1357; drafts in Temple's hand, Add. MSS 57033, ff. 59–64; Sutherland, *City of London*, p. 27, n. 3.
90. Beckford to Shelburne, 24 Oct., HP; C. Yorke to Hardwicke, 9 Oct., Wray to Hardwicke, 14 Nov., Add. MSS 35362, f. 264, 35402, f. 45; Gascoyne to Strutt, 27 Oct., HP; Rigby to Bedford, 10 Nov. 1769, in Russell (ed.), *Bedford Correspondence*, III, p. 410; Sutherland, *City of London*, p. 21.
91. *Memoirs George III*, III, pp. 249–50; cf. Walpole to Mann, 14 Jan. 1769, *Correspondence*, XXIII, p. 82.
92. Surviving correspondence suggests that, in 1769, Beckford was closer to Shelburne, who had no direct contact with Chatham.

93. See above, p. 146.

94. Grenville to Suffolk, 25 Nov., Grenville diary, 23 Nov. 1768, in Smith (ed.), *Grenville Papers*, IV, pp. 398, 403.

95. [Temple] to [Lady Chatham], [24 Jan.], 28 March, list of minority, [April 1769], PRO 30/8/62, ff. 147–8, 161, vol. 74, f. 107, vol. 83, ff. 140–6; cf. *Chatham Papers*, III, pp. 349–54, 356–61.

96. Granby to Chatham, Chatham to Granby, 27 April, Temple to Lady Chatham, 6 May 1769, *Chatham Correspondence*, III, pp. 354–6; Harris, memoranda, 18 July 1769, 9M73/G751 (first quotation); cf. Almon to Wilkes, [?Feb. 1769], Wilkes Papers, Add. MSS 30870, f. 107.

97. Cf. anon. to Hardwicke, 8 July, Add. MSS 35609, f. 10; Walpole to Mann, 19 July 1769, *Correspondence*, XXIII, p. 132.

98. Chatham's account to Temple, 7 July, in Smith (ed.), *Grenville Papers*, IV, pp. 426–7, reveals little except vanity, but Anson (ed.), *Grafton*, pp. 236–7, provides a reliable account.

99. Campbell to Holland, 9 Sept., in Earl of Ilchester (ed.), *Letters to Henry Fox, Lord Holland* (1915), p. 287; *Memoirs George III*, III, p. 248; Hardwicke to C. Yorke, 30 July, Add. MSS 35362, ff. 251–2; Harris, memoranda, 12 Aug., 9M73/G751; Rockingham to Burke, 15 Oct. 1769, in Copeland (ed.), *Burke Correspondence*, II, pp. 90–1 (quoting Camden).

100. Wray to Hardwicke, 4 Oct., Add. MSS 35402, f. 38, cf. e.g. Whately to Grenville, 3 Aug., in Smith (ed.), *Grenville Papers*, IV, p. 433, Calcraft to Chatham, Chatham to Calcraft, 25 Nov., *Chatham Correspondence*, III, pp. 364–5, [Temple to Lady Chatham], n.d., PRO 30/8/62, f. 149; Beckford to Chatham, 16 Oct., PRO 30/8/19, f. 101, to Shelburne, 24 Oct., HP; Chatham to Temple, 8 Nov. 1769, in Smith (ed.), *Grenville Papers*, IV, p. 278.

101. Burke to Rockingham, 6, [24] Nov., in Copeland (ed.), *Burke Correspondence*, II, pp. 105, 112–13; Fitzwilliam to Rockingham, 1 Dec. 1769, in Earl of Albemarle (ed.), *Memoirs of the Marquis of Rockingham and his Contemporaries* 2 vols (1852), II, p. 142; Frank O'Gorman, *The Rise of Party in England. The Rockingham Whigs 1760–82* (1975), p. 246.

102. Burke to Rockingham, [24] Nov., 1769, in Copeland (ed.), *Burke Correspondence*, II, p. 112.

103. *Chatham Correspondence*, III, pp. 369–74nn., 377–87nn. (9 Jan.), 401–8nn. (22 Jan. 1770), quotations from pp. 372, 404, 401, 473, 406–7nn.; cf. Simmons and Thomas, II, pp. 86, 150 (14 Jan., 3 Feb. 1766). Henry Grattan's account of the first speech emphasizes its forcefulness (Henry Grattan (ed.), *Memoirs of the Life and Times of the Rt Hon. Henry Grattan* new edn, 5 vols (1849), I, pp. 230–4).

NOTES

104. Portland to Rockingham, 3 Dec. 1769, in Albemarle (ed.), *Rockingham*, II, p. 343; *Memoirs George III*, IV, pp. 22–3; John Yorke to Hardwicke, 5 Jan. 1770, Add. MSS 35375, ff. 19–20.
105. *Memoirs George III*, IV, pp. 23–4.
106. *Chatham Correspondence*, III, pp. 408–9nn.
107. *Parl. Hist.*, XVI, cols 813–29, cf. 820 and 665; *Memoirs George III*, IV, pp. 58–9 (quotations).
108. John Yorke to Hardwicke, 5 Jan., Add. MSS 35375, ff. 19–20; cf. Rockingham to Lady Chatham, 24 Jan. 1770, *Chatham Correspondence*, III, pp. 401–10; *Memoirs George III*, IV, pp. 22, 39.
109. O'Gorman, *Rise of Party*, pp. 256–7.
110. Ibid., ch. 12, and W.M. Elofson, *The Rockingham Connection and the Second Founding of the Whig Party, 1768–1773* (Montreal and Kingston, 1996), chs 4–6, provide full accounts.
111. North's title was a courtesy one as son of the Earl of Guilford.
112. *Chatham Correspondence*, III, pp. 396–8 and nn.; *Memoirs George III*, IV, pp. 28–30, 40–1; Walpole to Mann, 30 Jan. 1770, *Correspondence*, XXIII, pp. 181–3 and n. 9.
113. George III to Chatham, 14 Oct. 1768, *Chatham Correspondence*, III, p. 343; Harris, memoranda, 8 Dec. 1770, 9M73/G767.
114. Burke to Nagle, 8 Feb., in Copeland (ed.), *Burke Correspondence*, II, p. 123; Calcraft to the Chathams, 22 Feb. 1770, PRO 30/8/25, f. 35.
115. Temple to Lady Chatham, [18], [19] Feb., PRO 30/8/62, ff. 192, 194–5.
116. Harris, memoranda, 8 March, 9M73/G754; J. Yorke to Hardwicke, 13 March 1770, Add. MSS 35369, f. 129; *Memoirs George III*, IV, pp. 77–8.
117. *Parl. Hist.*, XVI, cols 441–3; *Memoirs George III*, IV, pp. 62–3.
118. O'Gorman, *Rise of Party*, pp. 274–5; Elofson, *Rockingham Connection*, pp. 83–4.
119. Lloyd to Grenville, 15 March, in Smith (ed.), *Grenville Papers*, IV, p. 509; *Parl. Hist.*, XVI, cols 849–52; *Memoirs George III*, IV, pp. 67–8; Harris, memoranda, 15 March 1770, 9M73/G754.
120. Walpole to Mann, 22 Jan., *Correspondence*, XXIII, p. 180; Grattan to Broome, 19 April 1770, in Grattan (ed.), *Memoirs*, I, p. 163.
121. *Parl. Hist.*, XVI, col. 959 (1 May 1770, when Chatham was called to order); cf. XVII, cols 220–22 (1 May 1771).
122. *Parl. Hist.*, XVI, col. 924 (5 April), cf. col. 957 (1 May 1770); O'Gorman, *Rise of Party*, pp. 275–6; Elofson, *Rockingham Connection*, pp. 86–7.
123. *Parl. Hist.*, XVI, cols 978–9 (14 May 1770), XVII, cols 220–4 (1 May 1771).

124. Walpole to Mann, 6, cf. 24 May 1770, *Correspondence*, XXIII, pp. 208–9 and n. 4, 215.

125. Maitland, *History of London*, II, pp. 104–5.

126. Chatham to Beckford, 10 March, *Chatham Correspondence*, III, p. 431n.; *Memoirs George III*, IV, p. 77; Beckford to Chatham, 21 March, Rockingham to Chatham, 25 March, PRO 30/8/19, f. 103, vol. 54, f. 201; Walpole to Mann, 23 March, *Correspondence*, XXIII, pp. 199–200; Gascoyne to Strutt, 29 March 1770, HP.

127. Harris, memoranda, 31 March, 9M73/G754; cf. Calcraft to Temple, 18 March 1770, *Chatham Correspondence*, III, p. 430 and n., cf. p. 434.

128. Alexander Stephens, *Memoirs of John Horne Tooke* 2 vols (1813), I, pp. 187–8; Chatham to Beckford, 10 March, *Chatham Correspondence*, III, p. 431n.; Beckford to Rockingham, 12 March 1770, in Albemarle (ed.), *Rockingham*, II, p. 172.

129. Calcraft to Chatham, 29, 30 March, 10 April, Chatham to Calcraft, 30 March 1770, *Chatham Correspondence*, III, pp. 436–9, 441.

130. Joseph Yorke to Hardwicke, 20 March, cf. 27 March, 3 April, Add. MSS 35369, ff. 131, 133, 135; Walpole to Mann, 15 March 1770, *Correspondence*, XXIII, pp. 195–8.

131. Elofson, *Rockingham Connection*, pp. 84–5.

132. *Parl. Hist.*, XVI, cols 957–9, 966 (1 May), 966–8 (4 May); *Memoirs George III*, IV, pp. 81–2 (4 May 1770).

133. Shelburne to Chatham, [May 1770], PRO 30/8/56, ff. 106–7, 108; drafts in Lady Chatham's hand, variously amended, ibid., vol. 74, ff. 109–10, HL, HM31583; Maitland, *History of London*, II, pp. 113–14.

134. Chatham to Beckford, Beckford to Chatham, 25 May, Townsend to Chatham, 23, 25 May, Chatham to Townsend, 23 May 1770, *Chatham Correspondence*, III, pp. 462–4, 459–61.

135. *Chatham Correspondence*, III, pp. 464–5nn., 457n.; Townsend to Chatham, n.d., PRO 30/8/64, f. 129.

136. Ian R. Christie, *Wilkes, Wyvill and Reform* (1962), pp. 40–4; Thomas, *Wilkes*, pp. 117–20; Burke to Shackleton, [before 15 Aug. 1770], in Copeland (ed.), *Burke Correspondence*, II, p. 150.

137. E.g. Townsend to Chatham, [June 1770], PRO 30/8/64, ff. 131, 133; Chatham to Calcraft, 10, 15 Sept., 28 July, Chatham–Calcraft Papers, Add. MSS 43771, ff. 58–9, 60–1, *Chatham Correspondence*, III, p. 469; John Yorke to Hardwicke, 1 Aug., Add. MSS 35375, f. 25, cf. Grenville to Lyttelton, 9 Sept. 1770, Grenville Papers, Add MSS 57827, f. 148.

138. Scott, *British Foreign Policy*, pp. 140–56, describes the ensuing crisis.

139. Calcraft to Chatham, 10 June, 8 Sept., PRO 30/8/25, ff. 47, 55; John Yorke to Hardwicke, 1 Aug. 1770, Add. MSS 35375, f. 25.
140. *Parl. Hist.*, XVI, cols 1091–1108 (22 Nov. 1770 – quotations, cols 1092, 1098).
141. Cf. ibid., col. 1322 (11 Dec.), *Memoirs George III*, IV, p. 139 (28 Nov.); Burke to Rockingham, [18 Dec. 1770], in Copeland (ed.), *Burke Correspondence*, II, p. 173 and n. 4.
142. *Memoirs George III*, IV, pp. 144–5 (10 Dec. 1770).
143. *Parl. Hist.*, XVI, cols 1339–41 (25 Jan.), 1355 (5 Feb.); *Memoirs George III*, IV, p. 179 (8 Feb. 1771).
144. Chatham to Barré, 22 Jan., to Lady Chatham, 25 Jan. 1771, *Chatham Correspondence*, IV, pp. 73, 86.
145. *Parl. Hist.*, XVI, cols 1379–80 (14 Feb. 1770); O'Gorman, *Rise of Party*, p. 280; Elofson, *Rockingham Connection*, pp. 113, 115.
146. Calcraft to Chatham, 13 Sept. (enclosure), 18 Sept., Shelburne to Chatham, [Oct., Nov.], PRO 30/8/25, ff. 59, 57, vol. 56, ff. 112–13, 92–5; Chatham to Shelburne, 24 Sept., [4 Oct.], 11 Nov., Shelburne to Chatham, 11 Nov., Calcraft to Chatham, 19 Oct., Chatham to Calcraft, 20 Oct. 1770, *Chatham Correspondence*, III, pp. 471–3, 484–5, 474–5; Thomas, *Wilkes*, p. 120.
147. Chatham to Calcraft, 10 Nov., to Shelburne, 11 Nov., Shelburne to Chatham, [26 Nov.], *Chatham Correspondence*, III, pp. 480 and n., 485, IV, p. 22 and n. (22 Nov. 1770); *Memoirs George III*, IV, pp. 120–2, 180–1 (11 Feb. 1771), but cf. p. 139 (28 Nov. 1770).
148. Shelburne to Chatham, [1 Dec.], *Chatham Correspondence*, IV, pp. 35–6 and nn.; *Parl. Hist.*, XVI, cols 1305–6 (5 Dec.), cf. 1302, 1313–17, 1321–2; *Memoirs George III*, IV, p. 146 (11 Dec. 1770).
149. Walpole to Mann, 26 Nov., *Correspondence*, XXIII, p. 251; *Memoirs George III*, IV, p. 134 (22 Nov. 1770).
150. Elofson, *Rockingham Connection*, pp. 112–15.
151. *Memoirs George III*, IV, pp. 148–9, but cf. O'Gorman, *Rise of Party*, pp. 281–3 for a more impartial account and Elofson, *Rockingham Connection*, pp. 120–5 for detail; Barré to Chatham, 8 March 1771, *Chatham Correspondence*, IV, pp. 109–12.
152. Richmond to Chatham, 19 Feb. 1771, PRO 30/8/54, ff. 124–5.
153. The definitive account is now Thomas, *Wilkes*, ch. 8 (cf. its n. 1, p. 254).
154. Chatham to Calcraft, 26 March, 7 April, to Barré, 17, 26 March 1771, *Chatham Correspondence*, IV, pp. 129–30, 141–2, 117–18, 136–7.
155. Barré to Chatham, 17, 21, 26 March, Chatham to Barré, 17, 26 March, Calcraft to Chatham, 26 March 1770, ibid., pp. 116,

121, 131–6, 118, 137, 125–7; Albemarle (ed.), *Rockingham*, II, pp. 207–9.

156. Chatham to Calcraft, 7 April 1771, *Chatham Correspondence*, IV, p. 142.

157. Chatham to Rockingham, 25 April, Rockingham to Chatham, 26 April, ibid., pp. 165–70, cf. 154–8, 160–5; Chatham to Rockingham, [1 May 1771], Sheffield Central Library, Wentworth Woodhouse Muniments, R1–1374.

158. *Parl. Hist.*, XVII, cols 220–4, quotations cols 221, 222–3 (1 May); Thomas, *Wilkes*, p. 128. Chatham seems to have reverted later to his original views on the printers' case: Chatham to Shelburne, 29 Nov 1772, *Chatham Correspondence*, IV, p. 230.

159. Shelburne to Chatham, [9 April], Chatham to Shelburne, 22 April 1771, *Chatham Correspondence*, IV, pp. 146–7, 156–7.

160. Thomas, *Wilkes*, pp. 114–15, 121–4, 140–4.

161. Wilkes to [Suard], 2 March 1770, William L. Clements Library, Wilkes Papers, vol. 3.

162. See e.g. John Brewer, 'English radicalism in the age of George III', in J.G.A. Pocock (ed.), *Three British Revolutions: 1641, 1688, 1776* (Princeton, NJ, 1980), esp. pp. 342–58; idem, 'The Wilkites and the law, 1763–74: a study of radical notions of governance', in John Brewer and John Styles (eds), *An Ungovernable People. The English and their Law in the Seventeenth and Eighteenth Centuries* (1980), pp. 128–71.

163. Burke to O'Hara, [11 April 1768], in Copeland (ed.), *Burke Correspondence*, I, p. 349; cf. Wilkes to Suard, 8 Aug. 1769, Clements Library, Wilkes Papers, vol. 4.

164. Northington to Shipley, 14 Jan., 11 March, HP; Rigby to Bedford, 14 May, in Russell (ed.), *Bedford Correspondence*, III, p. 412; Holland to J. Campbell, 21 June 1770, Holland House Papers, Add. MSS 51406, f. 171.

165. Richmond to Rockingham, 12 Feb. 1771, Wentworth Woodhouse Muniments, R1–1358 (a letter which clarifies thinking on both sides); cf. Chatham to Rockingham, 15 Nov. 1770, in Albemarle (ed.), *Rockingham*, II, p. 194, *Parl. Hist.*, XVI, col. 1108 (22 Nov. 1770).

166. Cf. *Memoirs George III*, IV, p. 159, and Mansfield on the old theme of inconsistency, *Parl. Hist.*, XVI, col. 1304 (5 Dec. 1770).

167. Jeremy Black, *Pitt the Elder* (Cambridge, 1992), p. 280.

168. Cf. Scott, *British Foreign Policy*, p. 150, on Secretary of State Weymouth's calculations, and the incident in the summer of 1770 recounted by Elofson, *Rockingham Connection*, p. 109.

169. Belasyse to Fauconberg, 17 May, cf. 24 April, 1 May 1770, HP.

170. *Memoirs George III*, IV, p. 179.

Chapter 6

CHATHAM AGONISTES, 1772–78

By May 1771, Chatham's last sustained burst of political energy was spent. For the last seven years of his life, his interventions, if sometimes intense and significant, particularly on American questions, were to be sporadic. At last he adopted the role of the retired elder statesman to which he had merely pretended a decade earlier.

It took some months, however, for disillusionment to sink in. Further rumours of ministerial changes and war circulated through the summer and autumn, while agitation continued in the City, where Calcraft maintained links.[1] At the end of the year, Shelburne returned from abroad ready for action in Chatham's interest, and the Rockinghams cautiously considered renewing contacts.[2] By then, however, bitter divisions in the City between Wilkites and Shelburne's friends had allowed the election of a ministerial supporter as Lord Mayor.[3] By the eve of the parliamentary session in January 1772, Chatham was complaining of a 'headlong, self-willed spirit' that had 'sunk the City into nothing', and of 'the narrow genius of old-corps' connection' that had 'weakened Whiggism', rendering impossible the 'national union on revolution principles' which alone could 'withstand present corruption'. So, he concluded, not 'the smallest good' could result from attendance in the House.[4] For their part, the Rockinghams were increasingly convinced that their 'steady and temperate adherence to ... principles' contrasted sharply with the Chathamites' readiness to 'raise clamour' solely out of anxiety for 'the profits of office'.[5] The two groups went their own ways entirely for the next three years.

Chatham's decision was perhaps confirmed by the attrition of his small political group. Temple, already disillusioned with politics, had been driven into retirement by the death of his brother, George Grenville. Camden, having differed with Chatham over almost every recent issue, now declared himself 'a single man, detached from all party'.[6] Any hope of George Grenville's erstwhile followers was lost when they defected to the ministry as a group early in 1771. At the same time, the Falklands crisis caused uneasiness to two peers normally friendly to Chatham, Lords Huntingdon and Northumberland.[7] Lyttelton, personally on good terms with Chatham again from 1770, was largely retired and died in 1773. Much worse, Calcraft, by far the most active aide Chatham ever had, was struck with serious illness in 1772, and died in August. Of prominent supporters, only Shelburne remained to be Chatham's chief ally and political informant in the following years. In the Commons, the few remaining 'Chathamites' were led by Shelburne's followers – Barré, increasingly prominent in recent debates, and John Dunning, the lawyer pivotal in Shelburne's City contacts, whose legal skills more than compensated for the loss of Camden.[8]

. . .

POLITICS FROM AFAR: FARMING AND FAMILY, 1772–74

This time, Chatham's retirement from politics was not that of a shattered recluse. His health, he boasted, was better 'than I have known these twenty years' and continued generally good.[9] These were years of withdrawal into enjoyment of the rural delights hitherto usually restricted to summers and the family pleasures that had always absorbed his private moments. Soon he was busy 'farming, hunting, and planting', spending 'many hours every day in the field', and was far too occupied to visit Lyttelton at Hagley Hall.[10] His time was spent mostly at Burton Pynsent, in Somerset, the property he had inherited in 1765 with other assets, variously estimated but certainly considerable, from the eccentric 'old Whig', Sir William Pynsent. Pynsent had never met Chatham but, according to one account, saw in his opposition to the Peace of Paris a parallel to his own vote long

before against the Treaty of Utrecht (1713).[11] The inheritance had only recently been secured on appeal against other
claimants in a Lords' judgment that won unusual praise
from Chatham for Mansfield's 'sagacity' and 'justice'.[12] But
Chatham had long before begun extensive development of
both house and estate. He added a new wing and in 1771–
72 was occupied in acquiring portraits of selected heroes of
the Seven Years War – Saunders, Granby, Boscawen – to
hang in the ballroom, together with those of Temple, Lady
Chatham and himself.[13] In the grounds, he built a lofty
column, dedicated to his benefactor. Its viewing platform
allowed even greater enjoyment of the rich, rolling countryside, with vistas to the sea beyond, than did the house in its
commanding situation. The column was designed with the
help of the famous landscape gardener, Lancelot ('Capabil-
ity') Brown, who became a warm admirer. The development
of the estate went on apace, with animals of prime bloodstock
searched out and thousands of trees planted – including
cedars from Lebanon and other species from America.[14] For
Chatham, Burton Pynsent became 'replete with rural delights'
– 'dairy enchanting, pillar superb, terrace ravishing'. There,
he wrote,

Herds, flocks, and smiling Ceres deck our plain,
And, interspersed, an heart-enlivening train
Of sportive children frolic o'er the green.[15]

The early 1770s were probably the Chathams' happiest
family years. Each of the children, all carefully educated at
home to avoid the rigour Chatham had endured at Eton
and now in their teenage years, drew comments reflecting
genuine affection from their 'old doting daddy'. The preco-
cious and delicate William, born in the *annus mirabilis* of
1759 and aged seven when news came of his father's peerage, had rejoiced that, as the second son, he would still be
able 'to serve the country in the House of Commons like
papa'.[16] Now he practised oratory under his father's eye. At
Lyme Regis, on the Dorset coast no great distance from
Burton Pynsent, on an extended holiday in 1773, the 'two
philosophers' – William and the children's tutor, the Rev.
Edward Wilson – swam in the sea, while the 'Soldier Citizen'
– the eldest son, Lord Pitt, preparing with a military engineer

there for his career – danced until two in the morning. From Lady Chatham, left at Burton Pynsent, came an account of 'Boy [James, the youngest son] on the dear grey mare, and the girls [Hester and Harriot] in their chaise . . . trotting over the lawn'.[17] When together at Burton Pynsent, the children delighted in amateur theatricals, while in 1775, in London with their mother for Harriot's 'coming out' season, the two girls enjoyed the opera, balls and the pleasure gardens at Ranelagh.[18]

Just weeks before, in December 1774, Hester, the eldest child, had been married, to the family's delight, to Charles, Lord Mahon, son of Chatham's cousin, Philip, Earl Stanhope, at whose estate at Chevening the family had spent a delightful summer in 1769. By late 1773, plans were under discussion for Pitt to join the army, his father eventually deciding that the British force in Canada under General Carleton would be more suitable to his youth than 'the large and obnoxious intercourse of a great foreign army'. He left, followed by his parents' anxious thoughts, early in 1774. By this time, William, aged fourteen, had gone up to Cambridge, where an illness in his first term caused grave anxiety, and James, 'the Tar', at twelve, had begun his naval training.[19] Of the 'many fair stars' that had shone round Chatham at Burton Pynsent,[20] only Harriot and Lady Chatham were left.

But all was not happy, even in these halcyon years. Despite Chatham's facility in amassing 'legacies from old men and old women' and 'pensions . . . from Courts', his income, even at perhaps £7,000 a year now, was never sufficient for his tastes. His love of display of status, not only through building, farming and gardening but also in servants and lavish appurtenances of all kinds, was not unusual in the period, but in Chatham it seemed inordinate, even to contemporaries. Shelburne thought him 'naturally ostentatious to a degree of ridicule; profuse in his house and family beyond what any degree of prudence could warrant'.[21] The expense of developments at Burton Pynsent had already required, in 1765–66, the sale of Hayes (in Kent), the home of the early married years and to Lady Chatham 'so loved a place', only for it to be repurchased, at great cost and inconvenience, at Chatham's urgent demand during his illness in 1767. When attempts to sell it again in 1772 failed, continued expense at Burton Pynsent required the sale of outlying lands there. In 1770, creditors raised an outcry against Chatham. Time and again he was rescued by loans, large and small, from admiring and compliant relatives and friends. Captain Alexander Hood and his wealthy wife, Molly, Lady Chatham's cousin, were large and willing creditors over many years, but by 1776 Hood feared the strain on family relationships and insisted that Chatham's children should know the details of loans secured on the Burton Pynsent estate.[22]

The burden of all this – with much else to do with family organization – fell on Lady Chatham.[23] She needed all the business acumen she possessed, acumen which surprised the family solicitor, Thomas Nuthall, when he first encountered it in 1767 but was recognized by a neighbouring farmer and the London banker, Thomas Coutts, alike.[24] In 1773 demands for payment from a surveyor and a London bookseller left her struggling with 'horrid addition sums'; a little earlier, she had decided not to visit the family party at Lyme Regis again 'because of oeconomicals'.[25] William's Cambridge letters were regularly punctuated with requests for money to meet tutors' and college bills. Much worse were the debts that James ran up in Gibraltar in 1777, which required an appeal to Chatham's nephew, Thomas, for a loan of £1,000. 'This accâblement, after the trials I have had so long to contend with, makes me like one astonished by a blow', she wrote. Her sons were taking after their father, and his father and grandfather before him. As poignant was the letter to Temple in 1775, when Chatham was believed at the point of death, asking for £1,000 to meet 'the diversity of calls' occasioned by 'an illness of such length'. The sudden onset of illness, she pleaded unconvincingly, had prevented Chatham's making provision for it. By 1778, the family's finances were in a parlous state.[26] And while Chatham took a real interest in his children's education, daughters' as well as sons', his wife always conducted the correspondence with the family's tutor, the Rev. Edward Wilson, when parents and children were separated. Even in the best of times, Chatham demanded the possibility of seclusion from the children which extensions at Hayes and the new wing at Burton Pynsent allowed. When he was ill in 1767–68, they were relegated to the London house, while in 1775 William was persuaded not to come home in the summer vacation because of his father's 'nervous state'.[27]

In the early 1770s, Chatham may have represented himself withdrawn from politics, with

> Ambition cured, and an unpassioned mind;
> A statesman without power, and without gall,
> Hating no courtiers, happier than them all;[28]

but at his own request he was kept fully informed, chiefly by Shelburne,[29] on the disparate issues of these rather less contentious years, and his disillusionment did not mellow. His claim to be 'Vot'ry . . . to freedom'[30] received some substantiation when he abandoned his recent retirement to support an unsuccessful bill to relieve dissenting ministers and teachers from the need to subscribe to the Church of England's Thirty-Nine Articles as required by the Toleration Act of 1689. He welcomed first news of the bill, conveyed by Shelburne.[31] Then a careful case – larded with compliments that support might increase 'the glory of even the Earl of Chatham' – was put to him by the dissenting minister, Dr Richard Price, introduced by Shelburne.[32] Chatham responded to Price's appeal for help against expected opposition from the bishops by coming to speak with 'as much oratory and fire as, perhaps, he ever did'. With much irony, he contrasted the bishops with the 'poor, humble, despised Fishermen' – their distant predecessors, Christ's disciples – who 'pressed hard on no man's conscience'.[33] Illness apparently prevented active support for a further bill the next year, on which Chatham elicited detailed information from Price. The 'whole constitution is now a shadow!' he commented indignantly on Price's report that in debate ministers had avowed '*enslaving*' the dissenters to keep them under control. By the time Price asked advice about another move in 1775, Chatham had exhausted himself in other causes.[34]

Otherwise, on matters Shelburne reported to him in these years of retirement in the early 1770s, Chatham responded only with comment from the sidelines. Like much opposition and popular sentiment, he was scathing about the most contentious issue of 1772, the 'new-fangled and impudent' Royal Marriages Act, and the 'wanton and tyrannical' powers it gave George III, after the clandestine marriages of his libertine brothers, to control the marriages of all descendants of George II under the age of 25.[35] Late the following year,

he made his principles clear on the Irish parliament's proposal to tax absentee landlords. This proposal aroused the
ire of many Rockinghamites and, initially, Shelburne too,
because they were substantial absentee landholders themselves. Rockingham hoped for a 'general union' to urge the
Crown to reject the bill, even hinting that Chatham might
be drawn 'from the country' over it, and, according to
Shelburne, the City, too, was roused against the measure.
Chatham, on the other hand – admittedly with much less at
stake – was quite clear that a bill which was 'the genuine
desire of the Commons of Ireland . . . exercising their inherent, exclusive right, by raising supplies in the manner they
judge best' should not be opposed in England. His stand
for this 'most sacred, fundamental right of the Commons'
did something to justify his hitherto largely unearned reputation with the Irish 'patriots', who were trying to relieve
Ireland's constitutional subordination to England. Certainly,
his views contrast with the Rockinghamites' implicit assump-
tion of subordination. Shelburne was won round – and saw
the connection with American issues.[36]

Chatham was much less constructively involved in the
matters on which Shelburne most frequently reported in
these years. These were the whole range of issues concerning the East India Company's operations in India and at
home which kept attention on its affairs even in the hectic
years of 1769–71.[37] Chatham had alluded to Indian questions at some length in his interview with the king in July
1769.[38] But in the vigorous opposition that followed in 1770–
71, these questions – too complex for 'raising a storm' –
were wholly ignored. They were grist only to the mill of
Chatham's developing ideas about 'corruption', in this case
by the 'influx' of the riches of Asia, and (in private only)
about constitutional 'tyranny' (if 'sovereign power' to raise
troops in England were allowed to the Company).[39] Even in
the crisis of 1772, Chatham at first avowedly averted his gaze
when the Company was threatened with bankruptcy, and its
affairs engrossed most of the long parliamentary session with
two committees of enquiry and the passage of North's Regulating Act.[40]

Chatham's attention was fully engaged only from late May
1773, well after the main lines of a 'Chathamite' response had
been defined by Barré in March. Only then were Chatham's

earlier ideas of 1766–67 on the state's interest clarified in new terms of a 'mixed right to the territorial revenues between the state and the Company, as joint captors'. He also strongly asserted the right of parliament to intervene, especially to reform abuses of Company power in India. But at the same time he feared the effects of unlimited state intervention at home, particularly if it were to give to the Crown the riches of India and thus supposedly facilitate the subversion of liberty by secret influence.[41]

In the major part they took in debates on these lines, often in support of the administration, Shelburne and Barré undoubtedly saw themselves as followers of Chatham – who warmly welcomed Barré's contribution as conforming to his views.[42] Yet their initiatives and Chatham's late response suggest that not only did his followers prompt Chatham's interest in this major crisis of Company power and state–Company relations, they probably also helped to shape his ideas.[43] His sentiments were undoubtedly nobly expressed. They were certainly more constructive than those of the Rockinghamites, who fully shared his resistance to increasing 'the influence of the Crown' (fast becoming their major objective) but insisted on outright opposition to North's legislation as an invasion of chartered rights.[44] However, Chatham's ideas simply followed the trend of developments and opinion and hardly suggested constructive solutions. Certainly, he did not feel compelled to intervene in person. Domestic issues raising questions of liberty still aroused him more than imperial problems.

. . .

AMERICA, 1775–78

Within a year, however, Chatham – no longer a man 'sure he can do no good'[45] – had embarked on the last campaign of his life, his attempts to avert a mortal breach in relations with the American colonies.

In 1769, America had been one of his avowed planks of opposition[46] – and was another issue he failed to develop. He certainly gave it more public attention than India, but this attention was only incidental to his overriding domestic preoccupations; he saw American policy as further proof of invasions of liberty. Such treatment did nothing to resolve the earlier contradiction between his partiality for the American cause, dominant early in 1766, and the authoritarian emphasis increasingly noticeable later in that year. 'I love the Americans', Chatham said, 'because they love liberty' and 'for the noble efforts they made in the last war'. But 'they must be subordinate', especially in 'all laws relating to trade and navigation'.[47] No more than anyone else, including the Rockinghams,[48] did Chatham appreciate how far American opinion had already moved since the mid-1760s in expanding the 'liberty' they required from Britain.

In March 1770, the North ministry brought to parliament the decision made the year before to repeal all the Townshend duties except that on tea. Although 'having it much in his heart to express his earnest wishes for the Total Repeal', Chatham was absent when the proposal was debated in the Lords in April. He was again absent on 18 May, when a series of Rockinghamite motions earlier debated in the Commons allowed a general attack on American policy since 1767 without clarifying any alternative. Chatham had gout at the time. Nevertheless, it is hard to avoid Walpole's conclusion that he deliberately 'kept away' on these occasions, when the Rockingham, Chatham and Grenville groups in opposition were likely to be divided and the issues provided less 'combustible matter' than other grievances.[49]

Thereafter, while the Rockinghamites continued to avoid the issues, Chatham, too, was almost completely silent on America until the autumn of 1773. Then, the implementation of a recent act, intended to help the East India Company by reducing British duties on tea re-exported to America, brought cheap tea to America. For the British government, this linking of two problems was quite coincidental. To many Americans, it seemed a plot to induce them to pay the one remaining duty on imported goods. Their attitudes were typified in the famous Boston Tea Party on 16 December 1773, when the first cargo under the new Act was dumped in Boston harbour.[50] After three years of relative quietude, this renewed resistance and British reactions to it were to precipitate a crisis of unprecedented severity.

Shelburne was among the very few who immediately recognized the likely response to shipments of tea. He was equally quick to appreciate the probable effects of the government's proposed plans to punish Massachusetts for the

Tea Party as they were unfolded in March and April 1774 and eventually became the so-called Coercive or (to the Americans) 'Intolerable' Acts.[51] In contrast, for Chatham this 'most serious and alarming perspective' in America at first merely increased his longstanding mood of general foreboding that 'England has seen her best days'.[52] 'America sits heavy upon my mind', he might say, but his first detailed comment, in March, showed him still condemning American violence while supporting American rights as long as they obeyed the laws of navigation and trade – the same old formula, clarified only with the proviso that these laws should be 'for regulation not for revenue'. And he was seemingly reluctant to add his 'no-weight' to Westminster debates – in which, indeed, general hostility towards the Americans was obvious.[53]

Nevertheless, Chatham came up from Burton Pynsent to Hayes early in April and, at last, on 26 May, he appeared dramatically in the Lords as an invalid for the first time since the early 1760s, 'his legs wrapped in black velvet boots' and leaning on a black-covered crutch, to speak on the last stages of the American legislation.[54] His speech – among the best-reported of his speeches – appears to have been so contradictory in drift as to allow reporters to take from it what they chose.[55] It was, according to Walpole,

> a long feeble harangue, in which on one side he blamed the violence of the Bostonians, and on the other every step that had provoked them or been taken to chastise them. He talked high of the sovereignty of this country, but condemned the taxes.

The confusion about Chatham's views is summed up in two well-attested but contradictory dicta soon circulating. He was reported to have claimed 'that this country had no right under heaven to tax America', but also to have stated privately that he wanted 'no more statues erected [of him in America]'.[56] The confusion was not just in the minds of listeners. The crisis had called Chatham out of retirement but his dilemma was still unresolved. He did nothing to clarify the ambivalence of both Barré and Dunning and the Rockinghamites, as some battled as best they could for a more conciliatory approach against the tide of opinion for assertion of a parliamentary authority in which they also believed.[57]

Chatham's inclination to interpret the crisis in vague terms of tyrannical conspiracy was strengthened in reaction to the Quebec Act, which settled the government of Canada and was by coincidence passed at the same time. The concessions to Roman Catholicism and French law and the generous definition of Canadian boundaries in this well-considered measure provoked a militantly prejudiced parliamentary and popular opposition. At a late stage, Chatham joined in with full fury, thundering more vehemently than leading Rockinghamites against 'popery and arbitrary power' and revealing not only the antiquated sterility of his thought on the new responsibilities 'his' war had brought but also the limits of his toleration. Soon he was at one with many Americans in seeing the measure as further proof of a 'whole system of American oppression'.[58]

Through 1774, the American crisis deepened as, in response to the 'intolerable' Acts, the colonies prepared to send delegates to a 'continental congress' in Philadelphia in September. By the middle of the year, Chatham had begun an uncharacteristically active search for information about American views from a handful of Americans resident in London, notably those with links with radical groups in the City such as William Lee and Stephen Sayre, and the much more eminent Benjamin Franklin. They led him to believe that the attempt to raise revenue in America was still the root of the problem. Far from seeking independence, as was now widely feared, Americans would, they assured him, still accept a fair regulation of commerce. These contacts were inevitably out of touch with the complexity and rapid evolution of American opinion. So, when news began to arrive in December of the proceedings of the congress, reports were filtered to Chatham in such a way as to confirm him further in his growing conviction: what the congress wanted was a settlement along the lines of his policy of nine years earlier.[59]

On two occasions in the early weeks of 1775, as the political world absorbed the news from the congress and Chatham feared that any day 'the doom against America' would 'be pronounced from the treasury bench',[60] he clarified his views publicly. On 20 January, he moved unsuccessfully for the withdrawal of British soldiers from Boston as a necessary preliminary to conciliation; on 1 February he proposed what he called a 'Provisional Act for Settling the Troubles in America'.[61] His move seized the initiative, not only from the administration but also from the Rockinghamites, as Burke, increasingly prominent in their ranks, goaded them into activity in face of the growing threat of war.

At first, as in 1770–71 in response to issues of liberty at home, Chatham seemed to go over wholeheartedly to the radical cause. He abandoned criticism of the Americans for lavish praise of their uncorrupt congress and their true Whiggism, heaping criticism instead on British ministers. Although there was no statement to this effect in his 'act', his 20 January speech explicitly affirmed the right of Americans not to be taxed without consent as a right given not only by 'the constitution', but by 'God and nature', and on 1 February he avowed these 'former arguments'.

However, the 'act' declared that the colonies were 'of right' subordinate to the British Crown and parliament. The colonies were required to recognize this authority; only then did the 'act' provide that there should be no taxation without consent (to be expressed through the colonial assemblies); on the same condition depended other generous concessions, notably the repeal of all the legislation since 1763 about which the congress had complained. And Chatham's fundamental reason for insisting on imperial authority – not preoccupation with empire, but his abiding concern with security against the Bourbons – was apparent: the 'act' explicitly recognized the importance to the navy of imperial regulation of commerce; it also required British control of the disposition of the army and the allocation of the perpetual revenue envisaged from the colonies.[62]

Chatham's proposal – on which he had worked hard[63] – was a constructive and genuine attempt to reconcile the two aims which had for so long jostled in his thinking: 'to secure to the colonies property and liberty, and to insure to the mother country . . . subordination'.[64] But its presentation suffered from his usual political faults. Advice from his American contacts was ignored or overridden; potential supporters among the Rockinghamites, his own colleagues, even Shelburne, were notified only at the last minute.[65] Certainly, no attempt was made now to mobilize the outside opinion in favour of conciliation that emerged in City and country as the crisis deepened.[66] More fundamentally, the act's elements of 'concession', as Chatham called them, went much too far for majority British opinion, especially in parliament – Chatham was lucky to secure support from 32 peers (against 68) for its introduction.[67] On the other hand, the aspects of 'assertion' were quite unacceptable to most American opinion, which had now moved beyond acceptance of any parliamentary authority.

There was, perhaps, a brief window of opportunity for conciliation at this crucial point in Anglo-American relations. However, Chatham's proposals illuminate the almost insuperable difficulty of bridging the gap across the Atlantic. This was even less likely to be achieved by North's conciliatory proposals, put to parliament on 20 February, which simply offered freedom from parliamentary taxation to those colonies that would pay their share of civil and military expenses. The next month, Burke, whose views had been powerfully stated the previous April, produced a more generous and imaginative vision of a free association of peoples. The power to tax would be transferred to colonial assemblies, contentious legislation repealed and a veil drawn over parliamentary supremacy. Yet Burke's scheme was still, like the others, stuck in the thinking of the 1760s in seeing taxation as the crucial issue and had, like Chatham's, no hope of parliamentary approval. North's scheme, after being carefully steered through the Commons, was doomed when it arrived in America just as news was circulating of the bloodshed at Lexington and Concord. The course was set for confrontation[68] – and there is nothing at all to suggest that Chatham could have altered it, had there been the change of ministry some dreamed of.

After the rejection of his 'act', Chatham was much more open to the co-operation the Rockinghams now also welcomed, but illness prevented his attendance in the latter part of the session. Predictably, he dismissed North's conciliatory proposals as 'mere verbiage, a most puerile mockery'.[69] Then, from the summer, as sporadic encounters through 1775 turned to full-scale war with the colonists in 1776 (while they declared independence and approached France for aid), Chatham slipped into another two years of often completely incapacitating illness, sometimes coming near death.[70] Only occasionally and indirectly, when brief improvements in his health permitted, could he show distaste for developments – by withdrawing his son from service with General Carleton in Canada in February 1776 and, in July, reaffirming in a statement to his doctor, Addington, made public in November, the views 'which stand so fully explained in the Provisional Act'.[71] Meanwhile, as patriotic sentiment cohered around the administration, the Rockinghams sank into despair. They could wish neither for victory – which they believed would vastly increase their bogey, 'the influence of the Crown' – nor for the defeat from which Britain's enemies would benefit. They could only dither between secession from parliament and seemingly factious opposition.[72]

In 1777, however, the opposition took on more life when in May, and again at the end of the year, Chatham was able to return to 'thunder and lighten'[73] on the war as the threat of French help to the Americans grew. Five speeches in these months[74] brought the themes of his later years to a climax in a crescendo of impending doom. The 'gathering storm may break', he proclaimed, even while the war was still going well. Then, after the startling news of General Burgoyne's defeat at Saratoga was received in December 1777, Chatham feared 'prospects full of awe, terror, and impending danger; . . . a cloud . . . ready to burst and overwhelm us in ruin'. In higher terms than ever, he declared the value of the colonies – 'the great source of all our wealth and power'. Despite the war and the overwhelming hostility of most British opinion to the Americans, his sympathy for them was still plain, and his calls for generous measures of conciliation – on lines similar to those of 1775 – even more insistent. He forcefully reiterated his old theme, the impracticability and, more, the undesirability of subduing the Americans by force. 'If you conquer them, what then?' he asked in May. 'You cannot make them respect you; you cannot make them wear your cloth.'[75]

Burgoyne's defeat simply made Chatham's appeals the more urgent.[76] Enthusiastically co-operating with the Rockinghams,[77] he took the lead in a fury of activity, attacking the whole conduct of the war and making wholesale criticism of ministers. In bitter disillusionment he returned pointedly to the theme of pervasive secret influence, which, he alleged, had broken 'all public and family connection' and extinguished 'all public and private principle'. Repeatedly, he 'contrasted the fame and renown we gained in the last war, with the feats and disgraces of the present', especially as he criticized the use of Indians and German mercenaries. 'Was it by means like these', he asked, 'that we arrived at that pinnacle of fame and grandeur, which . . . established our reputation in every quarter of the globe?'[78]

In these critical years, Chatham was obviously driven by a searing despair about the imperial crisis. When his age and health might well have excused him, he pushed himself to unusual efforts in a courageous stand against the tide of British opinion. More than this: as his reminders of the achievements of 'his' war suggest, his overweening self-confidence was far from extinguished. Certainly, in May 1774, Walpole believed that Chatham 'meant to insinuate . . . that he alone could assert the authority of England, and compose the differences in America'.[79] There is much to suggest – notably his choice of intermediary in arranging his reappearance[80] – that he then had the scent of office in his nostrils again. There were more rumours at the end of the year, when Burke certainly thought that hopes 'that the Closet door stands a jarr' lay behind Chatham's approaches to Rockingham.[81] And again in late 1777, it seems from the tone of Chatham's flurry of letters as well as his speeches that he believed that 'the vengeance of a much injured and afflicted people' might at last be awakened to 'fall heavily on the authors of their ruin'.[82] And then it was not merely the political innocents – those who claimed that '[e]very rank looks up to him with the only gleam of hope that remains' – but others better informed who believed that Chatham might, and should, be called to office.[83]

These hopes were quite unfounded. The king was the great obstacle. In 1775, he rejected out-of-hand even a modi-fication of the terms of Chatham's pension 'least it should be wrongly construed a fear of him'. The king went on: 'his political conduct last Winter was so abandoned, that he must in the eyes of the dispassionate, have totally undone all the merit of his former conduct'; he was now simply 'a trumpet of Sedition'.[84] Quite apart from his feelings, the king did not need Chatham. North's parliamentary majority was more than secure.

That majority wavered as political tensions heightened in 1777, after Saratoga, and again in March 1778, when the long-expected news came of a Franco-American treaty. North – his nerves, never strong, quite shattered by mounting difficulties – seemed to totter. Very reluctantly, the king now allowed an indirect approach to Chatham. North might well have given way. Negotiations broke down, however, on the unbridgeable gulf between Chatham's unnegotiable demand, in his old manner, to 'be a dictator' and the king's equally unrelenting refusal to allow more than an accessory role to 'that perfidious man'.[85] Yet still Chatham continued to wait 'to be call'd upon by the King, and a pretty general power put in his hands' and wondered why the call did not come.[86]

Perhaps partly influenced by these hopes, late in December Chatham had suddenly dropped his co-operation with the Rockinghams to adopt again the pose of the disillusioned recluse. Uppermost in his mind, however, was his utter aversion to the idea that the Rockinghams had already begun to explore and now avowed more openly: that only acknowledgement of constitutional independence for America could mitigate Britain's crisis.[87] 'I will as soon *subscribe to Transubstantiation* as to *Sovereignty, by Right*, in the Colonies', Chatham wrote to Shelburne in December.[88] In vain the Duke of Richmond, for the Rockinghamites, attempted to persuade him to explore the possibility of some intermediate position 'between the *sovereignty* and *allegiance* of America'. To him the difference was absolute. And it was 'to express the indignation he felt at an idea which he understood was gone forth, of yielding up the sovereignty of America' that he came once more, clearly ill, to the Lords on 7 April, to answer Richmond on this question.[89]

Chatham's speech – a defiant cry of injured national pride at 'the dismemberment of this ancient and most noble monarchy!' – was a 'sort of enthusiastic rapture', incoherent to most listeners, leaving them divided over his intentions about the war.[90] He struggled to rise again to answer Richmond – only to fall in 'a sudden fit'.

'You may conceive better than I can describe', wrote Camden to his daughter,

> the hurry and confusion the expression of grief and astonishment that broke out and actuated the whole assembly. Every man seemed affected more or less except the E[arl] of M[ansfield] who kept his seat and remained as much unmoved

as the poor man himself who was stretched senseless across a bench.

Two sons and his son-in-law 'in speechless agony stood by him', Elizabeth Montagu reported. As the Lords adjourned in respect, doctors were called and Chatham was removed to a nearby house. By evening, he had 'recovered his senses perfectly' and soon it was being reported that the fit was no worse than one of the previous summer from which he had completely recovered. But by the end of the month he was 'past all hope of recovery, dying rather of weakness than distemper'.[91] He died at Hayes on 11 May.

. . .

DEMISE, 1778

Chatham was already 'politically dead'. The court, as Walpole scathingly observed, would now 'scarce inoculate a half-dead skeleton on their other infirmities'. Even Camden admitted that, after such 'public and notorious an exposure of his decline, no man will look up to him' nor France any longer fear him. Reportedly, Camden came to see the death as 'a fortunate event'.[92] In fact, Chatham's inadequacies before his collapse are patently evident in retrospect. If he favoured continuing the war against the Americans as well as France, it was quite unrealistic to expect a sick old man to repeat the apparently miraculous reversal of fortunes of the last war, especially if Spain were to join France (as she did a year later). Even had Chatham adopted the policy Shelburne was advocating of a defensive holding operation in America combined with generous offers of conciliation – by no means an unviable policy – there was little to suggest he could have mobilized British support or won over the Americans.[93] It was a measure of North's desperation and the bankruptcy of British politics that Chatham should be expected to 're-place us once more on the throne of Neptune'.[94] In fact, Saratoga was more shock than disaster. The war was as yet far from lost. But nothing in Chatham's career since 1761 suggests he had the necessary political or strategic vision to turn the tide this time. Walpole was right to see his death as 'of no great consequence'.[95] The king was able to sustain

North's failing nerve for four more years, the Rockinghamites and a Chathamite remnant under Shelburne isolated in the wings.

Official reactions to Chatham's death were mixed. The Commons unanimously agreed to the immediate suggestion of his friends for a funeral at public expense and a monument in Westminster Abbey and began moves for a perpetual annuity to his heirs and a vote of £20,000 to pay his debts. But Shelburne's motion that the Lords should attend the funeral was narrowly defeated.[96] There was also some worrying opposition in the Lords to the annuity bill, and some sarcastic comment outside that the family were indeed fortunate that Chatham died while parliament was still sitting.[97] On the other hand, 'the first commercial city in the empire' competed for the honour of burying Chatham at St Paul's, and, when that was refused by the king because of the Commons' prior recommendation, the Common Council pointedly set up a committee to consider a memorial 'to that excellent and disinterested Statesman in the time of whose Administration the Citizens of London never returned from the Throne dissatisfied'. The membership of the committee, which deliberated over the next eighteen months between a painting and a sculpture, amply reflected the City radicals' appropriation of Chatham's reputation.[98] The funeral on 9 June, preceded by two days' lying-in-state in the palace of Westminster which drew great crowds, was undoubtedly magnificent. The procession included a banner of the family crest with Britannia mourning over it.[99] But many eminent people apparently shared Walpole's determination to 'go to no puppet-shows'; only two court peers or relatives with court connections and a mere handful of Rockinghamite peers attended.[100]

The dramatic collapse and lingering death in such a crisis provoked an intense burst of 'Chathamania'.[101] The newspapers were 'filled with accounts of preparations for his funeral, and verses to his memory', Elizabeth Montagu reported. His dying 'as it were in a Patriot act' had, she claimed, 'revived all the colours of popularity' tarnished by the pension. Unsympathetic although she usually was, she caught the 'mania' herself, and while Chatham's recovery was still possible hoped that his coming to office might still give the administration 'credit at home, and respect abroad'.

At the time when we are insulted by our enemies it is terrible to think that quenched in dark clouds of slumber lie the terror of his beak [the hooked nose], and lightnings of his eye. I hoped he would pounce on the Gallick foe and spoil his pert crowing.[102]

'All England' was brought by Chatham's death to think him essential, acknowledged Walpole, himself unmoved. There were valedictory odes and verses. However, the mood was brief.[103] Later in the year, there was a bout of public controversy, drawing in both families, over whether Chatham had countenanced recent attempts to bring him back to office with Bute.[104] After that, little more. New perils left no time or inclination to dwell in vain on vanished glories. Surprisingly, only one medal was struck to mark Chatham's passing.[105]

Chatham was gone.

. . .

NOTES

1. Temple to Lady Chatham, 21 July, PRO 30/8/62, f. 222; Elizabeth to Edward Montagu, [?23 Aug.], Montagu Papers, HL, MO2770; [Almon to Calcraft, draft], 26 Sept., notes, [Oct.] 1771, William Perkins Library, Duke University, Almon Papers.
2. Chatham to Addington, 23 Nov., *Chatham Correspondence*, IV, p. 185; Hood to Lady Chatham, 30 Dec., PRO 30/8/21, f. 21; Rockingham to Dowdeswell, 19 Dec. 1771, in Earl of Albemarle (ed.), *Memoirs of the Marquis of Rockingham and his Contemporaries* 2 vols (1852), II, p. 213.
3. Almon to Calcraft, 5, 26 Sept. (draft) 1771, Almon Papers; *Memoirs George III*, IV, pp. 216–18, 229–30; Peter D.G. Thomas, *John Wilkes. A Friend to Liberty* (Oxford, 1996), pp. 145–6.
4. Chatham to Shelburne, [10 Jan. 1772], *Chatham Correspondence*, IV, p. 187.
5. Dowdeswell to Rockingham, 18 July 1773, William L. Clements Library, Dowdeswell Papers; cf. W.M. Elofson, *The Rockingham Connection and the Second Founding of the Whig Party, 1768–1773* (Montreal and Kingston, 1996), pp. 130–1, 183–5, 188–9.
6. Calcraft to Chatham, 1 Sept., PRO 30/8/25, f. 53; Temple to Chatham, 3 Dec., Camden to Chatham, 28 Nov., 3 Dec.

1770, *Chatham Correspondence*, IV, pp. 29–30, 37–8, cf. 46, 90, 98, 141, 145 and n.; [Almon to Calcraft, draft], 10 Nov., Almon Papers; Richmond to Rockingham, [22 Jan. 1771], Sheffield Central Library, Wentworth Woodhouse Muniments, R1–1352.

7. Elofson, *Rockingham Connection*, pp. 116–17; Richmond to Rockingham, 1 Feb. 1771, Wentworth Woodhouse Muniments, R1–1354.

8. Shelburne to Chatham, 12 Jan. 1772, *Chatham Correspondence*, IV, pp. 188–9, cf. 242–9, 253, on Barré.

9. Chatham to Shelburne, [10 Jan. 1772], ibid., p. 186, cf. pp. 181, 233, 264.

10. Chatham to Calcraft, 22 Sept., to Addington, 23 Nov. 1771, ibid., pp. 183, 185; Chatham to Lyttelton, 22 July 1772, Hagley Hall, Lyttelton Papers, vol. 6, f. 312.

11. Elizabeth to Edward Montagu, [15] Jan. 1765, HL, MO2556; Walpole to Mann, 13 Jan. 1765, *Correspondence*, XXII, pp. 276–7 and nn.; *Memoirs George III*, II, pp. 32–3.

12. Chatham to Lyttelton, 7 May 1771, Lyttelton Papers, vol. 6, ff. 292–3; *Memoirs George III*, IV, pp. 149–50, 214.

13. Chatham to Lady Chatham, 6 Aug. 1770, Chatham to Calcraft, 18 Dec. 1771, PRO 30/8/5, ff. 251–2, vol. 6, f. 17; Saunders to Chatham, 10 Dec. 1772, *Chatham Correspondence*, IV, pp. 231–2 and n.

14. E.g. Calcraft to Chatham, 17 May 1771, *Chatham Correspondence*, IV, p. 178, cf. Warburton, quoted on p. 221n.

15. Ibid., p. 197n.

16. Chatham to Lady Chatham, 9 April 1772, ibid., p. 206; Basil Williams, *The Life of William Pitt Earl of Chatham* 2 vols (1913), II, p. 288.

17. Chatham to Lady Chatham, 8 June, *Chatham Correspondence*, IV, p. 267, 15 July, [Sept.], Lady Chatham to Chatham, [1773], PRO 30/8/5, ff. 289–91, vol. 9, ff. 176–7.

18. Shelburne to Chatham, 17 Jan. 1773, *Chatham Correspondence*, IV, p. 238, cf. 240n.; Lady Chatham to Chatham, [29 Jan. 1775], PRO 30/8/9, f. 207; Williams, *The Life of William Pitt*, II, p. 290.

19. Williams, *The Life of William Pitt*, II, pp. 290–2; *Chatham Correspondence*, IV, pp. 287–94, 308–12; Chatham to Lady Chatham, 22 Dec. [1773], PRO 30/8/5, ff. 296–7.

20. Lyttelton to Chatham, 20 Feb. 1772, *Chatham Correspondence*, IV, p. 196.

21. Elizabeth to Edward Montagu, [15] Jan. 1766, cf. Elizabeth Montagu to [Elizabeth Carter], 25 May 1778, HL, MO2556, 3448 [p. 5]; Lord Edmond Fitzmaurice (ed.), *Life of William,*

Earl of Shelburne afterwards First Marquess of Landsdowne 3 vols (1875–6), I, p. 75; cf. *Memoirs George III*, III, p. 30.

22. *Chatham Correspondence*, II, pp. 328, 335, 423–4; Lady Chatham to Pitt, 10 May 1766, Hood to Lady Chatham, 15 March 1776, PRO 30/8/9, f. 12, vol. 23, ff. 164–6; *Memoirs George III*, III, pp. 31–2; Williams, *The Life of William Pitt*, II, pp. 283–5.

23. See e.g. her correspondence, especially in these years (PRO 30/8/47, ff. 102ff.), with Peter Jouvencel, a Privy Council clerk and tenant on the Hayes estate.

24. *Memoirs George III*, III, p. 32; Williams, *The Life of William Pitt*, II, p. 287; Stanley Ayling, *The Elder Pitt Earl of Chatham* (1976), p. 406.

25. Lady Chatham to Chatham, 23 Sept., 1 July 1773, PRO 30/8/9, ff. 151–3, 140.

26. Lady Chatham to Thomas Pitt, 8 April 1777, Dropmore Papers, Series II, Add. MSS 69288, no. 32; Lady Chatham to Temple, 3 Aug. 1775, HL, HM31577; Temple to Lady Chatham, 22 Feb. 1778, PRO 30/8/63, ff. 121–2.

27. William to Lady Chatham, 10, 19 July 1775, PRO 30/8/11, ff. 119–22.

28. Verse, [Feb. 1772], *Chatham Correspondence*, IV, p. 197n.

29. Shelburne to Chatham, 20 Feb. 1772, PRO 30/8/56, ff. 118–21.

30. Verse, [Feb. 1772], *Chatham Correspondence*, IV, p. 197n.

31. Shelburne to Chatham, 18 March, Chatham to Shelburne, 3 April 1772, ibid., pp. 199–201, 204–5.

32. Price to Chatham, 13, 16 May 1772, PRO 30/8/53, ff. 211–12, 206.

33. *Parl. Hist.*, XVII, cols 440–1; Horace Walpole, *Journal of the Reign of King George the Third, from the Year 1771 to 1783*, ed. Dr Doran, 2 vols (1859), I, pp. 95–6 (19 May 1772).

34. Price to Chatham, 23 Feb., 11 March, 3 April 1773, 9 Feb. 1775, PRO 30/8/53, ff. 220–1, 218–19, 213, 210; Chatham to Shelburne, 14 April 1773, *Chatham Correspondence*, IV, p. 259.

35. Chatham to Shelburne, 3 April 1773, *Chatham Correspondence*, IV, pp. 203–4; Elofson, *Rockingham Connection*, pp. 133–40, 144.

36. Shelburne to Chatham, 31 Oct. cf. 17 Oct. 1773, 8 Jan. 1774, Chatham to Shelburne, 24 Oct. 1773, 10 Jan. 1774, cf. 4 Nov. 1773, *Chatham Correspondence*, IV, pp. 303–4 (quotation), 296–7, 317–19, 299–301 (quotation), 319–21 (quotation), cf. 305–8; Elofson, *Rockingham Connection*, pp. 158–63.

37. H.V. Bowen, *Revenue and Reform: The Indian Problem in British Politics 1757–1773* (Cambridge, 1991), chs 5–11.

38. See Ch. 5, n. 98.

39. Debate, 22 Jan. 1770, Chatham to Calcraft, 21 Feb. 1771, *Chatham Correspondence*, III, p. 405n., IV, p. 104.

40. Chatham to Shelburne, 29 Nov., cf. Shelburne to Chatham, 26 Nov. 1772, ibid., IV, pp. 230, 227–9.

41. *Parl. Hist.*, XVII, cols 823–7 (23 March 1773); Chatham to Shelburne, 24 May, 17 June, 17 July 1773, *Chatham Correspondence*, IV, pp. 264–5 (quotation), 276–8, 283–5; Marie Peters, 'The myth of William Pitt, great imperialist: Part II', *Journal of Imperial and Commonwealth History* 22 (1994), pp. 402–4.

42. Chatham to Shelburne, 17 June, 14 April 1773, *Chatham Correspondence*, IV, pp. 278, 258.

43. Shelburne's visit to Burton Pynsent in Jan. 1773 (ibid., p. 238) may have allowed greater influence by Chatham than the correspondence suggests.

44. Elofson, *Rockingham Connection*, ch. 8.

45. Chatham to Shelburne, 29 Nov. 1772, *Chatham Correspondence*, IV, p. 230.

46. See above, p. 187.

47. W.S. Johnson to J. Trumbull, 6 March 1770, quoted in Simmons and Thomas, III, pp. 206–7 (the only account of the 2 March debate to indicate any attention to America).

48. Paul Langford, 'The Rockingham Whigs and America, 1767–1773', in Anne Whiteman *et al.* (eds), *Statesmen, Scholars and Merchants. Essays in Eighteenth-Century History presented to Dame Lucy Sutherland* (Oxford, 1973), pp. 137–50.

49. Chatham to Shelburne, [3 April], Bowood Muniments, Bodleian Library microfilm, Box S13, f. 142; Rockingham to Lady Chatham, 15, 17 May 1770, PRO 30/8/54, ff. 207, 209; *Memoirs George III*, IV, p. 99; cf. Peters, 'Myth', p. 404 and nn. 105–8.

50. For background to this and what follows, see Peter D.G. Thomas, *From Tea Party to Independence* (Oxford, 1991).

51. Shelburne to Chatham, 26 Sept. 1773, 27 March 1774, PRO 30/8/56, f. 130, Bowood Muniments, Box S13, f. 81; cf. Chatham to Shelburne, 6 April 1774, *Chatham Correspondence*, IV, p. 342.

52. Chatham to Shelburne, 24 Oct. 1773, 20 March 1774, cf. 29 Nov. 1772, *Chatham Correspondence*, IV, pp. 301, 337, 230–1.

53. Chatham to Shelburne, 6, 20 March, 6 April 1774, ibid., pp. 331, 336–8, 342–3.

54. Walpole, *Journal*, I, p. 369.

55. Cf. Ian R. Christie, 'The Earl of Chatham and American taxation, 1774–5', *The Eighteenth Century* 30 (1979), pp. 247–50, with Peters, 'Myth', pp. 405–6 and nn.

56. Walpole, *Journal*, I, p. 369; Simmons and Thomas, IV, p. 440; T. Hutchinson to Chief Justice Oliver, in Peter Orlando Hutchinson (ed.), *The Diary and Letters of His Excellency Thomas Hutchinson* 2 vols (1883–6), I, p. 203.

57. Thomas, *Tea Party*, chs 4, 5; Elofson, *Rockingham Connection*, pp. 168–9; Frank O'Gorman, *The Rise of Party in England. The Rockingham Whigs 1760–82* (London, 1975), pp. 311–14.

58. Simmons and Thomas, IV, p. 230 (17 June 1774); Chatham to A. Hood, n.d., Bridport Papers, Add. MSS 35192, f. 19.

59. Peters, 'Myth', pp. 406–7.

60. Chatham to Stanhope, 31 Jan. 1775, *Chatham Correspondence*, IV, p. 388.

61. *Parl. Hist.*, XVIII, cols 150–60 and nn., 165–6 (20 Jan.), 198–204, 210–12 (1 Feb. 1775 – quotations, cols 165, 199). Following quotations are from this source unless otherwise indicated.

62. Cf. Peters, 'Myth', pp. 407–9.

63. Chatham to Lady Chatham, 18 Jan. 1775, *Chatham Correspondence*, IV, p. 370; drafts, PRO 30/8/74, ff. 161–76.

64. Chatham to Carleton, n.d., *Chatham Correspondence*, IV, p. 407.

65. Peters, 'Myth', p. 409.

66. Thomas, *Tea Party*, pp. 181–6; John Sainsbury, *Disaffected Patriots. London Supporters of Revolutionary America 1769–1782* (Kingston, 1987), ch. 3; James E. Bradley, *Popular Politics and the American Revolution in England. Petitions, the Crown, and Public Opinion* (Macon, GA, 1986), esp. chs 1–3.

67. Comparable to minority votes in the 1770 session and much better than 18 for his 20 Jan. 1775 motion.

68. Thomas, *Tea Party*, pp. 217–19, ch. 10; O'Gorman, *Rise of Party*, pp. 337–40.

69. Chatham to Mahon, 20 Feb. 1775, *Chatham Correspondence*, IV, p. 403.

70. Excerpts, William Pitt, James Grenville to Lady Chatham, May 1775–Nov. 1776, Jan.–June 1777, ibid., pp. 427–8nn.

71. Lady Chatham to Carleton, 14 Feb. 1776, cf. to Major Caldwell, July 1775, Lady Chatham to Addington, with memorandum, 17 Nov., to Camden, 22 Nov., Shelburne to Lady Chatham, 23 Nov. 1776, ibid., pp. 420, 410–12, 423–5 (quotation), 427–9.

72. O'Gorman, *Rise of Party*, ch. 16.

73. Philip Yorke to Hardwicke, 29 May 1777, Hardwicke Papers, Add. MSS 35613, f. 315.

74. *Parl. Hist*, XIX, cols 316–20, 343–4 (30 May), 360–75 and nn., 409–11 (20 Nov.), 474–8 (2 Dec.), 485–91, 507–8, 509, 510, 512 (5 Dec.), 596, 597–602 (11 Dec. 1777); cf. Peters,

'Myth', n. 152, and pp. 409–10 for further references for what follows.

75. *Parl. Hist.*, XIX, cols 316, 597, 319, 317.
76. Ibid., cols 599–602 (11 Dec. 1777).
77. *Chatham Correspondence*, IV, pp. 450–79; Albemarle (ed.), *Rockingham*, II, pp. 324–5; Wentworth Woodhouse Muniments, R1–1746, R151; Bowood Muniments, Box S13, ff. 116–19, Box S28, ff. 26–7.
78. *Parl. Hist.*, XIX, cols 487, 488–9, 371.
79. Walpole, *Journal*, I, pp. 367–8.
80. Not Shelburne, but the second Lord Lyttelton, who had recently voted for the administration's American measures and believed many wanted Chatham in office: Lyttelton to Temple, 17, 18 May 1774, *Chatham Correspondence*, IV, pp. 344–8, 354n.; cf. Thomas, *Tea Party*, p. 84.
81. Burke to Rockingham, 5 [Jan. 1775], in Thomas W. Copeland (ed.), *The Correspondence of Edmund Burke* 9 vols (Cambridge, 1958–70), III, p. 89.
82. *Parl. Hist.*, XIX, col. 602.
83. T. Coutts to Lady Chatham, 21, 25 March, *Chatham Correspondence*, IV, pp. 511–12 (quotation), 515; cf. e.g. Noailles to Vergennes, 12 Dec., Vergennes to Montmorin, 13 Dec. 1777, Beaumarchais to Vergennes, 24 Feb. 1778, in B.F. Stevens, *Facsimiles of MSS in European Archives relating to America, 1773–83* 25 vols (1889–98), XX, nos 1772, 1776, XXII, no. 1870; Camden to Lady Elizabeth Pratt, 9 April 1778, Kent Archives Office, Pratt Papers, C173/30. Cf. O'Gorman, *Rise of Party*, p. 366.
84. George III to North, 9 Aug. 1775, in Sir John Fortescue (ed.), *The Correspondence of King George the Third* 6 vols (1927–8), III, p. 242.
85. Lord John Russell (ed.), *Memorials and Correspondence of Charles James Fox* 4 vols (1853–7), I, pp. 180–7 (quotation, p. 182); correspondence of North and George III, [15]–22 March 1778, in Fortescue (ed.), *Correspondence of George III*, IV, pp. 54–72 (quotation, p. 59); Andrew Stockley, 'The allure of Lord Chatham: attempts to reconstruct the ministry in March 1778', B.A. (Hons) research essay, University of Canterbury, 1989.
86. North to George III, 16 Feb., in Fortescue (ed.), *Correspondence of George the Third*, IV, p. 38; Lady Chatham to Coutts, 22, 26 March 1778, *Chatham Correspondence*, IV, pp. 512n., 515n.
87. O'Gorman, *Rise of Party*, pp. 351, 354–5, 361–2, 372; *Parl. Hist.*, XIX, cols 608, 609 (Richmond, 11 Dec. 1777).

88. Chatham to Shelburne, 18 Dec. 1777, Bowood Muniments, Box S13, ff. 122–7.
89. Mahon to Chatham, 11 Feb., Richmond to Chatham, 5 April, Chatham to Richmond, 6 April 1778, *Chatham Correspondence*, IV, pp. 497–506, 516–18, 519n. (quotation); *Parl. Hist.*, XIX, col. 1023.
90. *Parl. Hist.*, XIX, col. 1023; *London Chronicle*, 7–9 April 1778; cf. Peters, 'Myth', p. 410 and nn. 165–9.
91. Camden to Lady Elizabeth Pratt, 9 April, to R. Stewart, 30 April, Pratt Papers, C173/30, C173/31; Camden to Grafton, [9] April, in Sir William R. Anson (ed.), *Autobiography and Political Correspondence of Augustus Henry Third Duke of Grafton* (1898), pp. 300–1; Elizabeth Montagu to [Elizabeth Vesey], 9 April, HL, MO3444; John Hinchcliffe to Grafton, 8 April 1778, Suffolk Record Office, Grafton Papers, 423/773.
92. Walpole to Mason, 8 April, *Correspondence*, XXVIII, pp. 379–80, cf. George III to North, 8 April, *Correspondence of George the Third*, IV, p. 102; Camden to Grafton, [9] April 1778, in Anson (ed.), *Grafton*, p. 302; Portland to Rockingham, 9 June 1778, Wentworth Woodhouse Muniments, R1–1782.
93. *Parl. Hist.*, XIX, cols 853–4, 1051, 1052, 1056–8; Fitzmaurice (ed.), *Shelburne*, III, pp. 25–8.
94. Walpole to Mason, 15 May 1778, *Correspondence*, XXVIII, p. 394.
95. Ibid.
96. *Annual Register* 21 (1778), pp. 186–9, 207, 238–40.
97. T. Walpole to Grafton, 3 June, Grafton Papers, 423/181; Camden to Lady Elizabeth Pratt, 8 June, Pratt Papers, C173/36; Sir B[eaumont] H[otham] to W. Eden, 3 June 1778, in Stevens, *Facsimiles*, V, no. 495.
98. *Annual Register* 21 (1778), pp. 240–1 (quotation); resolution, 6 June 1778 (quotation), Corporation of London Record Office, minutes of committee, 1778–83, MSS 55.28.
99. *Annual Register* 21 (1778), pp. 243–4; *London Chronicle*, quoted in *Correspondence*, XXXIII, p. 19, n. 4.
100. Walpole to Mason, 31 May, *Correspondence*, XXVIII, p. 401; Walpole, *Journal*, II, p. 220; Clarendon to T. Pitt, 10 June 1778, and answer, Add. MSS 69288, no. 68; Albemarle (ed.), *Rockingham*, II, p. 356.
101. Hotham to Eden, 3 June, 1778, in Stevens, *Facsimiles*, V, no. 495.
102. Quotations from Elizabeth Montague to Elizabeth Vesey, 20 May, to Elizabeth Carter, 17 May, 24 April, 8 May, cf. 9 April, 17, 23, 25 May, HL, MO6518, 3447, 3444, 3446, 6516, 6030, 4036, 3448.

103. Walpole to Mann, 31 May, cf. 7 July, 8 Oct. 1778, *Correspondence*, XXIV, pp. 383, 393, 415, Elizabeth Montagu to Pepys, 23 May 1778, MO4036.
104. *Annual Register* 21 (1778), pp. 244–64.
105. Lawrence Brown, *A Catalogue of British Historical Medals 1760–1960* (1980), p. xiv. There was no post-death cult like that of his son; cf. J.J. Sack, 'The memory of Burke and Pitt: English conservatism confronts its past, 1806–1829', *Historical Journal* 30 (1987), pp. 630–9.

CONCLUSION

The heroic status given to Chatham by many contemporaries is perpetuated in two splendid monuments. In Westminster Abbey, Chatham stands in his parliamentary robes, in speaking pose, above Britannia flanked by figures representing the earth and ocean. In the City's Guildhall monument, Chatham appears as a Roman senator. At his right, commerce pours the riches of the world into Britannia's lap, while Chatham is addressed by the figure of the City, above the symbols of industry. Inscriptions on both monuments join in celebrating – the City's at great length – the heights of 'prosperity and glory' bestowed by divine providence on Britain during his administration.[1] And in 1781, crowds flocked to see a painting which made the fame and fortune of the American painter, J.S. Copley, recently arrived in London. In the style just becoming popular as a celebration of the exploits of empire, Copley portrayed Chatham's collapse in the Lords as the death scene of a military hero. Like the generals and admirals who fought 'his' war, Chatham was dying – the picture is misleadingly called 'the Death of Chatham' – to preserve the empire he had won. This heroic image – an image to sustain the nation in new tribulations – was eventually popularized by a long-delayed and rather expensive engraving by Franceso Bartolozzi, published in 1791.[2]

The reality of Chatham's political life is, of course, far more complex. Two important stages of his career – the wartime coalition and the period 1770–71 – still need more work.[3] Nevertheless, this brief study has been able to depict a Pitt who, after the first enthusiasms of youth, developed an early interest in exploring the exercise of Britain's recently acquired power abroad. That exploration was, however, no smooth path of discovery showing superior insight. Pitt's education in the realities of foreign policy was complicated by volatile circumstances, at home as well as abroad, and was subordinated to his highly political manoeuvres for recognition and power – manoeuvres often necessitated by his own recklessness, particularly in inviting sharp royal displeasure. Against these odds, his chief strength was his developing gift of oratory, a gift which won him a reputation at least as much for inconsistency (sometimes later disarmingly admitted) as for patriotism.

By chance even more than by skill, Pitt's particular qualities allowed him to seize the opportunities offered by domestic and foreign crisis in 1755–57. In the coalition of 1757–61, he rose magnificently to the challenge of war. He did not manage and win the war single-handed or show any particular originality in strategy, diplomacy or administration. But, if nothing else, he infused a spirit and determination recognized almost unanimously by the military and naval commanders and foreign princes with whom he worked. Shortly after his death, one of the commanders remembered him 'as an illustrious example, how one great man, by his superior ability, could raise his drooping country from the abyss of despair to the highest pinnacle of glory, and render her honoured, respected, revered, and dreaded by the whole universe'. In the cooler estimate of Horace Walpole at the same time, 'A minister that inspires great actions must be a great minister'.[4] Not for nothing – much as they overestimated Pitt in his later years – did French statesmen continue to fear his return to office.

Pitt's reputation was never free from an undercurrent of criticism and distrust bred by his opportunism and apparent inconsistencies. This counter-view was virulently expressed in the Earl of Egmont's fragmentary unpublished account of Pitt's career to 1755.[5] For many others, the status won in wartime was tarnished by the pension of 1761 and the title of 1766. Pitt's maverick behaviour in the 1760s exposed deeper flaws to closer observers. In 1766, the second Earl of Hardwicke pronounced him 'absolutely Impracticable, Invidious, and Mischievious [sic]'; by 1771, David Hume could see no talent in him but a disordered oratory.[6] The record of the Chatham administration did nothing, of course, to modify such criticism. Chatham never recognized its failure, and it was sad to see him resort, in explaining it, to the myth of secret influence. No wonder Walpole saw in him a decline which paralleled that of the nation and sighed 'to think how he and we are fallen'.[7]

Nevertheless, as the fleeting ministries of the 1760s, and even North's in the 1770s, seemed incapable of handling Britain's difficulties, memories of Pitt's wartime glories burned the brighter in retrospect. 'We are no longer great in any way', exclaimed Walpole in 1769, remembering 'glory under Mr Pitt'. 'We are afraid to meddle in little Corsica, though the French have so woefully miscarried there; and we enjoy half the empire of the Mogul only to traffic in India stock!' To Bishop Warburton in 1771, Chatham was 'the greatest statesman this country ever produced: how exceedingly great was he in the last war! and the splendour of his ministry has been illustrated ever since by the wretched administrations that have followed him'. That splendour shone as brightly as ever in the crisis in which he died. The second Lord Lyttelton, looking back in 1777, reminded the Lords of how Chatham had 'inspired himself, then very young, and the nation at large, with the most exalted and heroic ideas'. For Elizabeth Montagu, his 'spirited' last speech 'made the lustre of his setting sun equal to the glories of his brightest meridian hour'. To Walpole, 'comparison with his predecessors and successors' would always make Chatham appear great.[8]

So Pitt carried with him into postwar politics 'his name, his successes, his eloquence, the cry of the many'.[9] But never could he capitalize on these advantages to rise to the same heights again for his or his country's advantage. The 1760s were painfully to reveal his shortcomings in playing the levers of power. Indeed, he was sometimes so inept that it is not surprising that he was suspected of 'political gout' as an escape from difficulties. He could act the courtier with the exaggerated obsequiousness shown in his letters to George III. It was said 'that at the levee he used to bow so low, you could see the tip of his hooked nose between his legs', and he burst into tears of gratitude in his final inter-view with the king in 1761.[10] But, time and again, he quite failed to understand the personalities and political needs of George II and his grandson. George II was only briefly reconciled, if at all, just before his death.[11] In the mid-1760s, Pitt showed some adroitness in repairing his breach with George III, only to revert, by 1770, to the reckless insouciance of his youth. By 1770, George III came to dislike Chatham more than any other politician; by 1778 the king was driven to declare that he would rather lose his throne than submit to him as minister.[12] It is true that, over the eighteenth century, there was a shift of the centre of decision-making from closet to cabinet. And in this shift, the strength of the wartime coalition – which owed so much to Pitt – was something of a milestone, dealing as it did, first, with a tired old king and, then, with an inexperienced young one. But still the closet was important, and Chatham suffered for much of his career because he did not 'stand well' there.

Pitt's greatest strength, his command of the Commons, protected by the grant of the 1761 peerage to his wife, was abandoned for the sake of his health and pride in 1766 – and in any case was never conventionally exercised to lead in the normal sense of strengthening a ministry by linking closet and Commons. His oratory notwithstanding, it could never be said of Pitt, as Chesterfield said of Sir Robert Walpole, that he 'was both the ablest Parliament man, and the ablest manager of a Parliament, that I believe ever lived'.[13]

Fearful always for his independence, Pitt showed himself at his most opportunist – even disingenuous – in his exploitation of the political support party could give. Having asserted exclusive Whiggism or courted the Tories as suited his needs, he then won praise in the wartime coalition for uniting all parties 'for the common Good' – praise that was an important part of his patriot reputation.[14] He had no compunction, nevertheless, in renewing, in the 1760s, an ideological claim to true Whiggism – or 'Revolution Principles' – while standing disdainfully aloof from the co-operation and business necessary to create a successful political group. Only Calcraft, in 1770–71, came anywhere near to making Chatham's 'personal party' carry weight. The alternative slogan 'measures not men' was a fine aspiration to tap a potent disillusionment with mid-century politics – his own and the young king's included – but, by itself, it was no formula for effective administration.

If Pitt was careless about party, he was also ambivalent about the newer influences in politics generated from a widening political nation. Certainly 'popularity' came – somewhat fortuitously – to help both to lift his early career and to shape his wartime reputation. But its cultivation owed nothing to Pitt directly (if something to the *Monitor*, organ of Pitt's City intermediary, William Beckford), and for most of the 1760s he was apparently indifferent to, even disdainful of, the fluctuations of reputation suggested by commentary in the press. The City might regard him as their hero for the benefits 'his' war brought many citizens, but, apart from Beckford, he made no attempt to develop contacts there, except in 1770–71, and then the links had been established, and continued to be developed, much more by Shelburne than by him. The sorts of constituencies he represented meant that, except in 1763 in Bath, over the peace, he never had to cope with the force of opinion in them. Even in 1770–71, when he turned more to 'the people' than at any other stage in his career, the populist edge to his rhetoric remained condescending in a way that Wilkes's was not. Not only was he hesitant about freedom of the press; only belatedly and half-heartedly was he converted to specific measures of reform.[15] So, despite his unique status, he could not engage new constituencies or bridge gaps between parliamentary and popular politics, let alone contribute to the evolution of a genuine radicalism. Despite North's apparent reconstruction of the Walpole–Pelham model of political power, the mould of earlier Hanoverian politics was being reshaped by new forces in Chatham's last two decades. But he contributed more to breaking that mould by the impact of the wartime administration in weakening the hold of parties than by incorporating new forces.

Chatham was a politician to his very core – if never a conventional one – and there was some sound political sense in his detachment from extra-parliamentary politics. As he well knew, courting new political forces was a two-edged sword, more likely to offend kings and 'respectable' men in parliament than to make those forces effective. However, in this case as so often, the political instincts which drove him were not, except briefly, a matter of skill or insight but, above all, of ambition. The political tenets he evolved with some skill in the 1760s were directed solely to supreme power for himself; the slogan 'measures not men' was in large part a mask for megalomania. He was never free, even in his last campaign, from the suspicion that he was merely out to 'raise a storm' for his own benefit. As Burke saw then, the 'least peep into that Closet intoxicates him, and will to the End of his Life'.[16] And, while ambition is natural and necessary in a politician, claims to patriotism seem compromised when they are subordinated to ambition. Furthermore, as a constructive politician attuned to a changing world, Chatham's record bears no comparison with the twenty years' dominance of Sir Robert Walpole – the other 'great man' of the century in contemporary eyes.

Nevertheless, contemporaries clearly sensed in Chatham an intellectual power and vision.[17] It was a perception shaped primarily by the speeches of 'the most admired orator of the age'[18] in a period which valued rhetoric as a supreme form of expression. Those speeches conveyed a vision which others – without instigation from him – amplified in the printed word to shape the reputation Pitt won and, as Lord Chatham, never entirely lost. When he spoke as a 'patriot' in the mid-1750s, he seemed to bring renewal to tired Pelhamite politics, promising respite from 'corruption' and attention to the country's true interests. From the early 1760s, he conveyed a similar vision by identifying himself as a Whig of 'Revolution principles'. These principles led Pitt to recognize genuine issues of liberty in the Wilkes affairs – so he argued against the legality of general warrants in 1763–64 and for the rights of electors and petitioners in 1770–71. In the cause of liberty, he defended a broad definition of the rights of juries in libel cases and, over the question of the publication of parliamentary debates, came – albeit briefly – to expound a positive concept of freedom of the press based not merely on the absence of legal restraint but on the right of the people to be informed. His tolerant Whig religious principles[19] led him to support easier naturalization for foreign Protestants and Jews in the 1750s and an extension of the religious liberty of Dissenters in the 1770s – although his tolerance certainly did not extend to Catholics.[20] On the basis of the principle of representation, Pitt vigorously defended the right of American colonial assemblies and the Irish parliament to determine their own taxation. And by 1775 he claimed that this 'great, fundamental, essential maxim of our liberties' was given by 'God, and nature' as well as 'the constitution'.[21]

Above all, with Pitt's Whiggism went an almost mystical veneration of the role of parliament. He was convinced of the importance of parliamentary privilege to liberty and, over the publication of debates, abandoned it only at the last minute and perhaps for tactical reasons. One of the most consistent characteristics of his thought is his readiness, from the 1740s to the 1770s, to submit issues for resolution by parliamentary enquiry, a readiness based, it seems, on ideas of the representative nature of the Commons and the status of the Lords as 'the hereditary great council'.[22] And, more conventionally, he envisaged the authority of parliament as essential to the unity of the empire.

Thus the vision Pitt's oratory communicated to contemporaries certainly identified him as a champion of liberty – despite the political motivation, too often underrated by historians, which so often shaped his stands. However, there was a gap between vision and realization. 'His views were great and noble ... but they were too visionary.' 'If struck with some great idea, he neither knew how nor had the patience to conduct it.'[23] All too seldom did he apply his mind more than briefly to the investigation that might have evolved principles into constructive new ideas. Only slowly did he come to terms with imperial problems and never did he seem to appreciate the changing context of European relations. There is little reason to suppose that, had he been in office longer in the 1760s, he would have managed either the foreign or the domestic sphere more effectively than others did. He had no appreciation of postwar economic and financial problems. His populist rhetoric contributed little to the transformation of the 'country' ideology in which it was rooted into the radicalism of the later part of the century. He could pose no fundamental solutions for the 'corruption' or the supposed infractions of the role and rights of 'the people' on which he dwelt so eloquently, no clear answers to the questions that radicalism posed about the nature of representation, where the voice of the people was properly to be heard, where sovereignty ultimately resided.

Indeed, the very nature of his oratory reflects the gap between vision and realization. All agree that its power was enforced by all the arts of voice, eye and facial expression, felicitous language derived from a rich imagination, an authoritative bearing mellowing in age the terrible invectives of the Commons days, and superb acting skills without which, some thought, he would have appeared ridiculous. The famous actor, David Garrick, is reported to have said that Pitt would have outshone all on the stage.[24] But many noticed, too, that (in marked contrast to Lord Mansfield) 'his matter was never ranged, it had no method'; there was 'nothing wanting but a plan or order, of which there not being the least trace, tis impossible to record anything but glowing scraps, or splendid morsels'. The Earl of Sandwich, answering Chatham in the Lords in his last year, justly remarked, 'Oratory is one thing, my Lords, and truth, reason and conviction another.'[25] Careful exposition and argument were no more Chatham's way than systematic investigation and thought. In truth, he was no minister for peacetime, not only because he no longer had 'the thorough-bass of drums and trumpets', but much more because he lacked these and other qualities of 'a great civil minister'.[26]

The key to why intellectual power and vision were not translated into solid achievement must be sought in those recesses of Chatham's scarred personality into which the biographer can barely penetrate. This study, however, has tentatively suggested that a public persona with a hard protective shell was shaped by inherited traits, the effects of harsh schooldays, the effort to have his talents recognized by the narrow circle of the 'great Revolution families' to which he did not belong, and the struggle with persistent illness that was part cause, part consequence of the personality. From early in Pitt's political life, his arrogance was conspicuous. Success and adulation shaped in him a sense of invulnerable superiority. By the height of his career, he was not unfairly characterized as 'most arbitrary and despotic' in manner, 'in principle a friend to liberty, but in his temper a tyrant'.[27] So often his letters on public matters show a verbosity and pomposity that masks real meaning. With success came an ostentation that accorded ill with his supposed 'patriot' indifference to money.[28] There was always an artifice about his public front. As Shelburne's often-quoted description puts it, Pitt was 'always acting, always made up, and never natural, . . . constantly upon the watch, and never unbent. . . . I was in the most intimate political habits with him for ten years . . . without drinking a glass of water in his house or company, or five minutes' conversation out of the way of business'.[29] To many Pitt seemed incapable of friendship.[30]

This studied distance increasingly shaped Pitt's relations with colleagues. Cultivating men created 'an incumbrance'.[31] Of his youthful associates, only the amiable James Grenville maintained an uninterrupted relationship. Lyttelton (Pitt's oldest friend), George Grenville, Temple, were used and ruthlessly discarded, with contact resumed when circumstances suited – just as, later, Wilkes was repudiated, Grafton was first implored to take office in 1766, only to be virulently abused in 1770, and Camden was consulted or ignored as Chatham pleased. Even in Chatham's last decade, he oscillated between Shelburne – valuable when the time seemed ripe for opposition and out-of-doors support – and Temple, who was usually at his elbow when office was in mind. He was utterly unable to bring out and benefit from the talents of others. His own qualities could have been usefully complemented by the business-like system of George Grenville or the foresight, capabilities and indefatigability of Shelburne – who, in his 'Bowood circle', developed the following sometimes misleadingly called Chathamite. Instead, Pitt broke with or demanded the subordination of colleagues and allies and chose to rely more on men of second rank like Thomas Potter, William Beckford and John Calcraft. Potter and Calcraft were able men, no mere stooges, but were content not to challenge Pitt's superiority in their relatively brief associations. Beckford was different. Vain, impetuous, ostentatious, little respected in the Commons for his frequent ill-considered, ill-delivered speeches, 'without principles, without decency, without fear',[32] Beckford was more handicap than help to Pitt – with the major exception of his influence in the City. Yet he was Pitt's most longstanding political friend, enjoying privileged access to offer advice, his loyalty quite unshaken by passing differences or shifts in City opinion.[33] Pitt's public persona encouraged him to cultivate admiring deferential associates like Beckford, rather than the colleagues and allies who could aid constructive achievement.

The private man was very different. The lively friendships of youth might give way in middle life to the warmth of family relationships, yet there were still friendships of some intimacy in later life with men as diverse as the writer, radical and Harvard benefactor, Thomas Hollis, a neighbour in the West Country,[34] Garrick, the actor, and the Chatham family's doctor, Anthony Addington. Pitt took a close and affectionate, if somewhat autocratic, interest in the welfare and university education of his nephew, Thomas (which did not win his lasting affection)[35] and, much later, chose a tutor for and advised on the education of his orphaned godson, the younger William Beckford.[36]

However, there was always a strong element of superiority and adulation in these relationships of private life – including the closest family ones. Chatham's wife, Hester, had grown up in a highly political family amid constant talk of politics; the marriage was, to a considerable degree, a political alliance and, in some senses, she was her husband's partner in politics. She did not merely copy documents or keep her ear to the ground for political gossip; she often managed his correspondence and received reports from Temple or Calcraft in his lieu. Yet only occasionally do any hints of her views surface in her correspondence with her husband.[37] Generally, the letters are rapturously admiring, and on one occasion at least Chatham condescendingly corrected the grammar of a letter to Elizabeth Montagu.[38] It seems as if the marriage fulfilled the latter's prophecy at the time of the engagement: 'there is an authority in the character of Mr P[itt] that will secure him the deference and obedience of his wife; proud of him abroad she will be humble to him at home'.[39] 'She was his nurse, his flatterer, his housekeeper and steward', wrote Chatham's nephew, and, in their retired lives, part chosen, part enforced by illness, they 'fed each other's prejudices'. In this largely conventional role – '[t]o be your second self is my sole ambition', she wrote – both Hester's correspondence and her memorial urn to Chatham leave no doubt that she found 'Felicity inexpressible'.[40]

The children, too, learnt from a young age, from the plaudits that followed the war, to see their father as a hero, an attitude which carried over into William's reports to his mother on his father's speeches. The mood was reinforced by members of Hester's wider family such as James Grenville and Hester's cousin, Molly Hood, wife of Captain, later

Admiral, Alexander Hood. This private circle of friends and family provided a necessary respite from public life, as well as solace for Chatham's often strained relations with his own family, even with his favourite sister, Ann. But, as his nephew aptly noted, its close atmosphere of cloying devotion did nothing to restrain Chatham's egotism and hardly encouraged a realistic assessment of the demands of the outside world.

At the crux of any explanation of the disjunction between public and private man, between vision and lack of achievement, must lie Chatham's deep-seated debilitating illness, which so shaped his personality and hampered his career. Illness could make him both the tragic hero and the comic – in both the 'mummery' of public appearances as an invalid and also in private, in the picture drawn of him in his later years, sitting up in bed, 'his meagre jaws and uncouth habiliments' – he was wearing 'a duffil cloak, without arms, bordered with a broad purple lace. On his head he had a nightcap, and over that a hat with a broad brim flapped all round' – resembling nothing more than the defeated Don Quixote.[41]

Yet, however deep the paradoxes, Chatham's impact on contemporaries must always be recognized. Camden, often alienated in later years, mourned Chatham's death: 'I am now a mere insignificant individual. With L[or]d C[hatham] I was something as his shadow; but now my substance being gone, I am nothing.' At the same time, Elizabeth Montagu, so often a critic, acknowledged 'a certain sublimity about him at all times, and on all occasions, not merely such as captivates the vulgar, but that which wins mankind in general'. Horace Walpole, who observed his whole career, attempted to capture the mixture of the man: 'Lord Chatham I have described in all the lights in which he appeared, sometimes a capital statesman, sometimes an empiric, sometimes a lunatic'. Burke, whose distaste for Chatham grew with closer acquaintance, nevertheless was a pall-bearer at Chatham's funeral and composed the glowing tribute of the Guildhall monument. Nearly fifteen years after Chatham's death, annotating a letter of his to Rockingham, Burke commented bitterly on the difference between 'the *real*' and 'the ostensible public man' in 'that grand artificer of fraud'. But he was compelled to add a postcript: 'Oh! but this does not derogate from his great, splendid side. God forbid!'[42]

What was this 'great, splendid side' that so lived in the minds of contemporaries? Central to it was Chatham's vision of national greatness, projected through the great drama of the struggle against the Bourbons. This, coupled with a deep sense of Britain's frailty, was the most consistent theme of his rhetoric, dwelt on from his earliest years in parliament. It undergirded the anti-Hanoverianism that bridled at the thought of England as a province of the electorate. It rose to a crescendo in the Seven Years War when, as Walpole summed it up, Pitt seemed determined 'that his administration should decide which alone should exist as a nation, Britain or France'.[43] It rose again in desperation in his last speech. 'My Lords', he said then,

> His Majesty succeeded to an Empire as great in its extent as its reputation was unsullied. Shall we tarnish the lustre of this nation by an ignominious surrender of its rights and fairest possession? . . . Shall a people that seventeen years ago was the terror of the world, now stoop as low as to tell its ancient inveterate enemy, take all we have only give us peace?[44]

He had 'aspired to redeem the honour of his country, and to place it in a point of giving law to nations. His ambition was to be the most illustrious man of the first country in Europe.'[45]

This was the vision of themselves and their place in the world which, for contemporaries, transmuted Pitt's ambition and 'political elasticity' above the 'ridiculous mixture of avarice and vanity' in other men[46] and, more than anything, gave him power over their minds – in the process doing much to unite them. The vision was deeply imperialist, giving the nation a sense of 'pride, . . . pride of *conquest*' and grandeur – depicted, for example, in Francis Hayman's massive history paintings of victories in America, India and at sea, painted during the war for the Vauxhall Gardens rotunda, or, more soberly, in the temple of Bellona at Kew[47] – and seeing no limits to the areas in which this great battle would be fought out. It was authoritarian, not least in its emphasis on the role of parliament. It exalted national grandeur over liberty, thus contributing more to that assertive nationalism which came to attach patriotism to the state rather than to radicalism.[48] In the last resort, despite

Chatham's real sympathy with the American colonists, his vision ruled out any imaginative solution of the breach with them.[49]

Thus Chatham's rhetoric constructed the heroic image that the monuments to him perpetuate. Whether it out-weighs the reality of his political life – the rampant ambi-tion, the superficiality of thought and limited achievement, the pompous 'theatrical stuffing and raised heels', the down-right hypocrisy, which so enraged Burke[50] – is questionable. Chatham himself defined 'just patriotism' as 'large and comprehensive sentiments for the common happiness of the whole'. In another context, Elizabeth Montagu wrote: 'I cannot believe any wise man who truly loves his country wishes to excite a hurley burley. True patriotism is first pure, then peaceable, without partiality, and without hypocrisy'.[51] Chatham hardly qualifies as a patriot by either definition.

Furthermore, in so many (if not all) respects, his ways of thinking were essentially old-fashioned and nostalgic. He claimed for himself 'old fashioned Whig principles'; his maxims and principles of a 'British' foreign policy were learnt, he said, from the disciples of the great patriots of King William's reign.[52] The major gap in his religious tol-eration, his vehement anti-Catholicism, betrays an attitude that was becoming outdated, at least among the educated. His preferred mode of parliamentary reform, allowing an additional member to each county, was deliberately chosen because it would strengthen representation of 'the soil', not urban interests that so lionized him. He never welcomed the opening of politics to wider opinion by the publication of parliamentary debates as Burke did, by publishing accurate versions of his own speeches (although he took steps to repress some misleading ones). In fact, his instinctive sym-pathies always lay, not with the newer, expanding com-mercial world and the popular opinion of growing cities, but with the still predominant landed elite into which he and his family married and whose preoccupations success allowed him to emulate in his rural retreat at Burton Pynsent.[53]

Indeed, Chatham did not understand, let alone welcome, change – unlike Shelburne, who was freed by Chatham's death to develop his own ideas. Chatham's oratorical gift was particularly appropriate to a time when 'cutting a figure', playing a role on that stage where he excelled, the House of Commons, was of the essence of politics – although it had only recently, in the generation or so before his birth, become a way to stake a claim to power. In his lifetime, however, that essence changed. Much remained the same. Superficially it might be true that North and the Younger Pitt worked on the model shaped by Walpole, linking court and Commons in a parliamentary monarchy. But by the 1760s and 1770s, economic and social diversification was producing a much greater range and variety of interests to be accommodated by politics, the need to do so driven home by the ever-growing appreciation of the importance of commerce to the power of the state. More was demanded of the state – in which, as the American crisis so clearly demonstrated, parliament's role was growing – in adjusting to these interests, expressed by increasingly effective lobbying by pressure groups, as well as in meeting the problems and responsibilities of empire. A vigorous press had made political information – not least parliamentary debates – much more widely available. Popular politics were more continuously active and more sophisticated in organization and expression.

The international stage, on which Chatham aspired so successfully to cut a figure for himself and his country, changed too. The concerns of continental European states, as they turned eastwards, slipped away from those of Britain. The world-wide dimension of conflict with France grew and the European diminished as France turned to a blue-water strategy to wreak vengeance for humiliating defeat.

The range of new problems, while entrenching the shift of decision-making from closet to ministers, required an increased professionalism of politicians, and with it the definition of politics changed. The concept of national welfare and the amelioration of problems by the gathering of information and the evolution of policies became more important. And the papers of Charles Townshend, Shelburne, the Rockinghams, pre-eminently Burke, to say nothing of the career of Chatham's son, the Younger Pitt, bear witness to much greater application to these tasks than do those of Chatham. He was a great man, perhaps, but one of flawed greatness who only briefly was able to rise to the challenge of his age. By his last decade, time had passed him by.

NOTES

1. Both monuments are described in [John Almon], *Anecdotes of the life of the Right Honourable William Pitt, Earl of Chatham* 3rd edn, 3 vols (1793), III, pp. 313–15, 323–4 (cf. the eulogies at pp. 358–61, 362–5); the City monument is reproduced, with its inscription attributed to Burke, as the frontispiece of Marie Peters, *Pitt and Popularity. The Patriot Minister and London Opinion during the Seven Years' War* (1980). A wax death mask is also held in the Abbey, depicting the softened features of old age.
2. Jules David Prown, *Jonathan Singleton Copley* 2 vols (Cambridge, MT, 1966), II, pp. 284, 287–8, 289–90; Linda Colley, *Britons. Forging a Nation 1707–1837* (New Haven, CT, 1992), pp. 178–80.
3. The wartime coalition deserves a study which fully integrates domestic and foreign sources, including the correspondence of Frederick the Great; the remarkable opposition of 1770–71 deserves further exploration, especially in relation to developments in London and the press. Further, Pitt's attitudes to Ireland have not been fully elucidated.
4. Admiral Sir George Rodney to Lady Chatham, 3 Dec. 1779, PRO 30/8/54, ff. 236–7; Walpole to Mann, 8 Oct. 1778, *Correspondence*, XXIV, p. 415.
5. Egmont Papers, HP.
6. Hardwicke to C. Yorke, 19 Jan. 1766, quoted by Paul Langford, *The First Rockingham Administration 1765–1766* (1973), p. 147; Hume to Strahan, 25 March 1771, in G. Birkbeck Hill (ed.), *Letters of David Hume to William Strahan* (Oxford, 1888), p. 185; cf. Hume to [Hertford], 8 May 1766, HL, HM7203, and below, p. 242.
7. Walpole to Mann, 14 Jan. 1769, *Correspondence*, XXIII, p. 82.
8. Walpole to Mann, 14 Jan. 1769, 8 Oct. 1778, ibid., XXIV, p. 415; Wilson to Lady Chatham, Dec. 1771, *Chatham Correspondence*, IV, p. 221n.; *Parl. Hist.*, XIX, col. 332 (30 May 1777); Elizabeth Montagu to Pepys, 23 May 1778, Montagu Papers, HL, MO4036.
9. Manchester to Rockingham, 18 Jan. 1775, in Earl of Albemarle (ed.), *Memoirs of the Marquis of Rockingham and his Contemporaries* 2 vols (1852), II, p. 266.
10. Chase Price, reported in Albemarle (ed.), *Rockingham*, II, p. 83; George F.S. Elliot, *The Border Elliots and the Family of Minto* (Edinburgh, 1897), p. 368; but cf. Lyttelton's 1763 comment, see above, p. 145.

11. See above, p. 110; there is no direct evidence from George II.
12. James Harris, memoranda, 8 Dec. 1770, Hampshire Record Office, Malmesbury Collection, 9M73/G767; George III to North, [?15 March 1778], in Sir John Fortescue (ed.), *The Correspondence of King George the Third* 6 vols (1927–8), IV, p. 58.
13. Colin Franklin, *Lord Chesterfield. His Character and* Characters (Aldershot, 1993), p. 114.
14. John Entick *et al.*, *The General History of the Late War* 5 vols (1763–4), dedication; cf. above, pp. 137–8.
15. See above, p. 195.
16. Burke to Rockingham, 5 [Jan. 1775], in Thomas W. Copeland (ed.), *The Correspondence of Edmund Burke* 9 vols (Cambridge, 1958–70), III, p. 89.
17. E.g. Charles Townshend in 1766, Sir William R. Anson (ed.), *Autobiography and Political Correspondence of Augustus Henry Third Duke of Grafton* (1898), p. 105; Shelburne to Chatham, 12 Jan. 1772, *Chatham Correspondence*, IV, p. 189; Elizabeth Montagu to Pepys, 23 May 1778, HL, MO4036.
18. *Memoirs George III*, IV, p. 23.
19. The 'detached sentences' in his handwriting, printed in *Chatham Correspondence*, IV, pp. 238–53, illustrate his own religious beliefs.
20. P.J. Marshall draws attention to the stinging rebuke Pitt delivered to Bedford in 1760, when, as Lord Lieutenant, he suggested, following serious riots in Dublin, that 'New Light Presbyterians or Twaddlers' were 'at least equally with the Papists to be guarded against'; 'A nation defined by empire, 1755–1776', in Alexander Grant and Keith M. Stringer (eds), *Uniting the Kingdom? The Making of British History* (1995), p. 217.
21. Simmons and Thomas, V, pp. 273–4, 278 (20 Jan. 1775).
22. See above, pp. 58, 181; Marie Peters, 'The myth of William Pitt, Earl of Chatham, great imperialist: Part II', *Journal of Imperial and Commonwealth History* 22 (1994), pp. 398, 401, 414–15.
23. Anson (ed.), *Grafton*, p. 91; *Memoirs George III*, II, p. 259.
24. Lord Rosebery, *Chatham: His Early Life and Connections* (1910), p. 499.
25. 'Family Characters and Anecdotes by Lord Camelford [Pitt's nephew, Thomas]', Dropmore Papers, Series II, Add. MSS 69333, f. 28; Harris, Parliamentary Memorials, 15 Nov. 1763, 9M73/G712; *Parl. Hist.*, XIX, col. 375 (20 Nov. 1777); cf. Hume as in n. 6 above.
26. Walpole to Montagu, 10 July 1766, *Correspondence*, X, p. 222; Elizabeth Montagu to Pepys, 23 May 1778, HL, MO4036.

27. Edward to Elizabeth, Elizabeth to Edward Montagu, 6, 9 July 1765, HL, MO1980, 2569.
28. See above, p. 183; Lord Edmond Fitzmaurice (ed.), *Life of William, Earl of Shelburne afterwards First Marquess of Landsdowne* 3 vols (1875–6), I, pp. 75–6; Camel-ford, 'Family Characters and Anecdotes', Add. MSS 69333, ff. 19, 31–2.
29. Fitzmaurice (ed.), *Shelburne*, p. 77.
30. Cf. above, p. 39; Shelburne to Fox, 26 Dec. 1761, Lansdowne Papers, HP; Harris, memoranda, 13 May 1767 (conversation with Robert Wood), 9M73/G745; Burke, note, in Copeland (ed.), *Burke Correspondence*, I, p. 265, n. 1; Hume to Strahan, 25 March 1771, in Birkbeck Hill (ed.), *Letters of Hume*, p. 185.
31. *Shelburne*, I, p. 76.
32. Elizabeth Montagu to Lyttelton, 2 Dec. 1766, HL, MO1450.
33. Peters, *Pitt*, pp. 12–13, 270, and passim; Beckford to Chatham, n.d. [1763], 9 Aug. 1766, PRO 30/8/19, ff. 78, 89.
34. E.g. Chatham to Lady Chatham, 16 June 1773, *Chatham Correspondence*, IV, pp. 273–4.
35. [Lord Grenville, ed.], *Letters written by the late Earl of Chatham to his nephew Thomas Pitt, Esq.* 2nd edn (1804); Sir Lewis Namier and John Brooke, *The House of Commons 1754–1790* 3 vols (1964), III, pp. 286–7. Thomas's dislike of his uncle permeates his 'Family Characters and Anecdotes', Add. MSS 69333.
36. The Rev. John Lettice to Chatham, 11 Dec. 1773, *Chatham Correspondence*, IV, pp. 313–16 and nn.; Basil Williams, *The Life of William Pitt Earl of Chatham* 2 vols (1913), II, pp. 288–9 and n.
37. See e.g. 25 Jan. 1771 (on the Falklands issue), [Jan. 1775] (some detail of various views about America), 21 Feb. 1775 (the last surviving dated letter, on North's American proposals), PRO 30/8/9, ff. 88–9, 199–200, 209–10.
38. Chatham to Lady Chatham, n.d., PRO 30/8/5, ff. 265–6.
39. Elizabeth Montagu to [West], 5 Nov. [1754], HL, MO6720.
40. Camelford, 'Family Characters and Anecdotes', Add. MSS 69333, ff. 31, 26; Lady Hester to Pitt, 20 Sept. [1755], PRO 30/8/7, ff. 76–8; inscription, Hoare (Pitt) Papers, PRO 30/70/7, f. 483; Camelford, ff. 30–1, is clearly wrong on this point.
41. Horace Walpole, *Journal of the Reign of King George the Third from the Year 1771 to 1783*, ed. Dr Doran, 2 vols (1859), I, p. 370.
42. Camden to R. Stewart, [12] May 1778, Kent Archives Office, Pratt Papers, C173/32; Elizabeth Montagu to Pepys, 23 May 1778, HL, MO4036; *Memoirs George II*, III, p. 176; Burke, 13 July 1792, in Albemarle (ed.), *Rockingham*, II, p. 195.

43. *Memoirs George II*, III, pp. 51–2.
44. *Parl. Hist.*, XVI, col. 1023 (7 April 1778).
45. *Memoirs George II*, III, p. 2.
46. Thomas Lyttelton to Elizabeth Montagu, 30 Aug. [1765], HL, MO1497.
47. Camden, 16 March 1775, in Simmons and Thomas, V, p. 545; Brian Allen, 'Rule Britannia? History painting in 18th-century Britain', *History Today* 45 (June 1995), pp. 15–17.
48. Cf. e.g. Linda Colley, 'Radical patriotism in eighteenth-century England', in Raphael Samuel (ed.), *The Making and Unmaking of British National Identity. I: History and Politics* (1989), esp. pp. 172–6, 181–4.
49. On this theme, cf. Marie Peters, 'The myth of William Pitt, great imperialist: Part I', *Journal of Imperial and Commonwealth History* 21 (1993), pp. 52–5, 'Myth, Part II', pp. 416–17.
50. See above n. 42.
51. Pitt to Lady Stanhope, 30 Nov. 1764, PRO 30/8/86, f. 322; Elizabeth Montagu to [Elizabeth Carter], 14 Sept. 1774, HL, MO3342.
52. Chatham to Shelburne, 10 Jan. 1774, *Chatham Correspondence*, IV, p. 321; Peter D. Brown and Karl W. Schweizer (eds), *The Devonshire Diary . . . Memoranda on State of Affairs 1759–1762* (1982), p. 111.
53. For other examples of this sympathy, see Peters, 'Myth, Part II', pp. 413–4 and n. 188.

FURTHER READING

Brief historiographical studies of writing on Pitt are to be found in Richard Middleton, *The Bells of Victory. The Pitt–Newcastle Ministry and the Conduct of the Seven Years' War, 1757–1762* (Cambridge, 1985), pp. 219–32, and Marie Peters, 'The myth of William Pitt, Earl of Chatham, great imperialist. Part I: Pitt and imperial expansion 1738–1763', *Journal of Imperial and Commonwealth History* 21 (1993), pp. 31–4. Karl W. Schweizer (ed.), *William Pitt, Earl of Chatham 1708–1778. A Bibliography* (Westport, CT, 1993) is comprehensive if sometimes undiscriminating.

Among biographies of Pitt, Basil Williams, *The Life of William Pitt Earl of Chatham* 2 vols (1913), is still unrivalled for insight and thorough knowledge of the Chatham Papers, although shaped by the 'great man' approach. Albert von Ruville's *William Pitt, Earl of Chatham* 3 vols (1907), while heavy going, brings a valuable European perspective. Stanley Ayling, *The Elder Pitt Earl of Chatham* (1976) is a creditable and readable attempt at a modern biography. The first modern scholarly study is Jeremy Black's *Pitt the Elder* (Cambridge, 1992), strongest for its use of newly available sources and on Pitt's earlier career. Romney Sedgwick, *The House of Commons 1715–1754* 2 vols (1971), II, pp. 355–6, and Sir Lewis Namier and John Brooke, *The House of Commons 1754–1790* 3 vols (1964), III, pp. 290–9, provide invaluable short accounts of Pitt's career, as of all other MPs. Marie Peters, 'William Pitt, First Earl of Chatham', in Robert Eccleshall and Graham Walker (eds), *A Biographical Dictionary of British Prime Ministers* (forthcoming) is a shorter account. Vere Birdwood (ed.), *So Dearly Loved, So Much Admired. Letters to Hester Pitt, Lady Chatham, from her Relations and Friends 1744–1801* (1994), by the compiler of the recent comprehensive calendar of the Chatham Papers, gives some insight into the family.

Specialist work on themes and periods of Pitt's career includes Marie Peters, 'The myth of William Pitt, great imperialist. Part I' (see above), 'Part II: Chatham and imperial reorganization, 1763–78', *Journal of Imperial and Commonwealth History* 22 (1994); idem, *Pitt and Popularity. The Patriot Minister and London Opinion during the Seven Years' War* (Oxford, 1980); Lucy S. Sutherland, 'The City of London and the Devonshire–Pitt administration', *Proceedings of the British Academy* 46 (1960), reprinted in Aubrey Newman (ed.), *Politics and Finance in the Eighteenth Century. Lucy Sutherland* (1984); Paul Langford, 'William Pitt and public opinion, 1757', *English Historical Review* 88 (1973); John Brooke, *The Chatham Administration 1766–1768* (1956). I.R. Christie, 'William Pitt and American taxation, 1766: a problem of parliamentary reporting', *Studies in Burke and His Time* 17 (1976) and idem, 'The Earl of Chatham and American taxation, 1774–1775', *The Eighteenth Century* 30 (1979) amply demonstrate the problem of recovering Pitt's words and ideas.

The best general account of the period of Pitt's career, among a wealth of useful textbooks, is Paul Langford, *A Polite and Commercial People. England 1727–1783* (Oxford, 1989), which includes a full and discriminating bibliography. John Cannon's *Samuel Johnson and the Politics of Hanoverian England* (Oxford, 1994) is a thematic study in context of a life which almost exactly coincided with Pitt's, and, especially in its perceptive and eminently judicious final chapter, 'The nature of Hanoverian politics', provides some alternative to Langford's view. Geoffrey Holmes and Daniel Szechi, *The Age of Oligarchy. Pre-industrial Britain 1722–1783* (1993), if not reliable in all respects, is valuable for its political chronologies and appendices summarizing a wealth of information.

Broad interpretations of the period which do much to integrate specialist work are John Brewer's *The Sinews of Power. War, Money and the English State 1688–1783* (1989) and Linda Colley, *Britons. Forging the Nation 1707–1834* (New Haven, CT, 1992). Two collections edited by Jeremy Black in Macmillan's 'Problems in Focus' series, *Britain in the Age of Walpole* (1984) and *British Society and Politics from Walpole to Pitt 1742–1789* (1990) include valuable essays on the economy and society, high and popular politics, party, the press, religion, foreign policy and empire. Roy Porter, 'English Society in the eighteenth century revisited', in the latter collection, assesses *inter alia* (as does Jeremy Black, 'England's "Ancien Régime"?', in *History Today* 38 [1988]) J.C.D. Clark's much-debated but not otherwise easily accessible argument that monarchy, aristocracy and church continued overwhelmingly to dominate Hanoverian society. To this thesis, Cannon (see above) is a balanced riposte.

Coverage of the themes of essays in the Black collections can be extended on popular politics by reference to H.T. Dickinson, *The Politics of the People in Eighteenth-Century Britain* (1994), a concise, comprehensive synthesis of specialist work, his own and that of others. Lucy Sutherland, 'The City of London in eighteenth-century politics', in Richard Pares and A.J.P. Taylor, *Essays Presented to Sir Lewis Namier* (1956) and reprinted in Newman (ed.) (see above), has not been surpassed as an overview. The seminal work of Nicholas Rogers can be sampled in his *Whigs and Cities. Popular Politics in the Age of Walpole and Pitt* (Oxford, 1989), which lists more in its comprehensive bibliography. Frank O'Gorman's rehabilitation of the electoral system in *Voters, Patrons and Parties. The Unreformed Electoral System of Hanoverian England 1734–1832* (Oxford, 1989) is more briefly foreshadowed in his 'Electoral deference in "unreformed" England', *Journal of Modern History* 56 (1984) and 'The unreformed electorate of Hanoverian England: the mid-eighteenth century to the Reform Act of 1832', *Social History* 11 (1986). Perhaps because historians' interests have moved on, there seems to be no recent concise survey of the minefield of argument about party, but the issues have not greatly changed from those adumbrated by William Speck, 'Whigs and Tories dim their glories: English political parties under the first two Georges', and Frank O'Gorman, 'Party in the later eighteenth century' (both in John Cannon (ed.), *The Whig Ascendancy. Colloquies on Hanoverian England*, 1981), Nicholas Rogers, 'Party politics during the Whig ascendancy', *Canadian Journal of History* 18 (1983) and Frank O'Gorman, *The Emergence of the British Two-Party System, 1760–1832* (1982). On the press, in addition to his essay in the first Black collection, Michael Harris provides an overview in Michael Harris and Alan Lee (eds), *The Press in English Society from the Seventeenth to the Nineteenth Centuries* (1986); John Brewer, *Party Ideology and Popular Politics at the Accession of George III* (Cambridge, 1976), especially chapter 8, is stimulating, and Marie Peters, 'Historians and the eighteenth-century English press: a review of possibilities and problems', *Australian Journal of Politics and History* 34 (1988) reviews the literature. On ideology and political ideas, H.T. Dickinson, *Liberty and Property. Political Ideology in Eighteenth-Century Britain* (1977) again gives a comprehensive survey and John Cannon, *Parliamentary Reform 1640–1832* (Cambridge, 1973) covers both ideas and organization. The simplest introduction to J.G.A. Pocock's extensive and seminal work is probably his '*The Machiavellian Moment* revisited: a study in history and ideology', *Journal of Modern History* 53 (1981). Isaac Kramnick, *Bolingbroke and his Circle. The Politics of Nostalgia in the Age of Walpole* (Cambridge, MT, 1968) further describes the ideological basis of opposition to Walpole, while Marie Peters, 'The *Monitor* on the Constitution, 1755–1765: new light on the ideological origins of English radicalism', *English Historical Review* 86 (1971), Linda Colley, 'Eighteenth-century radicalism before Wilkes', *Transactions of the Royal Historical Society* fifth series, 31 (1981), and idem, 'Radical patriotism in eighteenth-century England', in Raphael Samuel (ed.), *The Making and Unmaking of British National Identity. I: History and Politics* (1989) trace aspects of the transformation of the 'country' ideology; John Brewer, 'English radicalism in the age of George III', in J.G.A. Pocock (ed.), *Three British Revolutions: 1641, 1688, 1776* (Princeton, NJ, 1980) conveys something of the complexity of the radical outcome, while his *Party Ideology* (see above) has much on the 1760s.

Valuable introductions to foreign policy are provided by Paul Langford, *The Eighteenth Century* (1976) and Jeremy Black, *A System of Ambition? British Foreign Policy 1660–1793* (1991); the European context is described in Derek McKay and H.M. Scott, *The Rise of the Great Powers, 1648–1815* (1983), and the nature of Britain's empire crisply interpreted in Daniel Baugh, 'Maritime strength and Atlantic commerce. The uses of a "grand marine empire"', in Lawrence Stone (ed.), *An Imperial State at War* (1994), while Richard Pares, 'American versus Continental warfare, 1739–63', *English Historical Review* 51 (1936) (also in his *The Historian's Business and Other Essays*, Oxford, 1961) has hardly been surpassed in later writing on this important theme. The standard specialist works on the metropolitan aspects of imperial problems are Lucy S. Sutherland, *The East India Company in Eighteenth-Century Politics* (Oxford, 1952), complemented by H.V. Bowen, *Revenue and Reform: The Indian Problem in British Politics* (Cambridge, 1991) and P.D.G. Thomas's trilogy, *British Politics and the Stamp Act Crisis* (Oxford, 1975), *The Townshend Duties Crisis* (Oxford, 1987) and *From Tea Party to Independence* (Oxford, 1991). Broader introductions to the American question (on which there is a wealth of material) include Peter D.G. Thomas, *Revolution in America. Britain and the American Colonies 1763–1776* (Cardiff, 1992) (an outline), Ian R. Christie and Benjamin W. Labaree, *Empire or Independence 1760–1776* (Oxford, 1976) and the controversial and stimulating R.W. Tucker and D.C. Hendrikson, *The Fall of the First British Empire. Origins of the War of American Independence* (Baltimore, MD, 1982).

Much new work is appearing on two important aspects of the eighteenth century perhaps too lightly dealt with in this book: on religion, current debates can be sampled in John Walsh, Colin Haydon and Stephen Taylor (eds), *The Church of England c.1689–c.1833. From Toleration to Tractarianism* (Cambridge, 1993), Colin Haydon, *Anti-Catholicism in Eighteenth-Century England, c.1714–80. A Political and Social Study* (Manchester, 1994), and David Hempton, *Religion and Political Culture in Britain and Ireland From the Glorious Revolution to the Decline of Empire* (Cambridge, 1996); Jacobitism is dealt with in Bruce Lenman, *The Jacobite Risings in Britain 1689–1746* (1980), while Paul Kleber Monod, *Jacobitism and the English People 1688–1788* (Cambridge, 1989) is perhaps the best recent work.

Modern biographies of central figures whose careers coincide with much of Pitt's include Reed Browning, *The Duke of Newcastle* (New Haven, CT, 1975) and Philip Lawson, *George Grenville. A Political Life* (Oxford, 1984). Shelburne lacks a modern biographer, but Charles Stuart, 'Lord Shelburne', in Hugh Lloyd Jones, Valerie Pearl and Blair Worden (eds), *History and Imagination. Essays in Honour of H.R. Trevor-Roper* (1981) gives a very perceptive sketch.

The context of Pitt's earlier career can be explored further in J.H. Plumb's unfinished classic, *Sir Robert Walpole. The Making of a Statesman* (1956) and *Sir Robert Walpole. The*

King's Minister (1960), and much more briefly in H.T. Dickinson, *Walpole and the Whig Supremacy* (1973), Betty Kemp, *Sir Robert Walpole* (1976), and Brian W. Hill, *Sir Robert Walpole: 'Sole and Prime Minister'* (1989). Also invaluable are Paul Langford, *The Excise Crisis. Society and Politics in the Age of Walpole* (Oxford, 1975), J.B. Owen, *The Rise of the Pelhams* (1957), Linda Colley, *In Defiance of Oligarchy. The Tory Party 1714–60* (Cambridge, 1982), and Robert Harris, *A Patriot Press. National Politics and the London Press in the 1740s* (Oxford, 1993). There is no adequate biography of George II, but J.B. Owen, 'George II reconsidered', in Anne Whiteman, J.S. Bromley and P.G.M. Dickson, *Statesmen, Scholars and Merchants. Essays in Eighteenth-Century History presented to Dame Lucy Sutherland* (Oxford, 1973) is a judicious reassessment. Neither Pelham nor Henry Fox has received recent scholarly treatment in print, but John Wilkes, *A Whig in Power. The Political Career of Henry Pelham* (Evanston, IL, 1964) is useful, and P.A. Luff, 'Henry Fox and the "Lead" in the House of Commons 1754–1755', *Parliamentary History* 6 (1987) gives some illuminating conclusions from his Oxford D.Phil. thesis (1982), 'Henry Fox, the Duke of Cumberland and Pelhamite politics, 1748–57'.

On the Seven Years War period, Richard Middleton, *The Bells of Victory. The Pitt–Newcastle Ministry and the Conduct of the Seven Years' War, 1757–1762* (Cambridge, 1985) is essential, supplemented by his 'The Duke of Newcastle and the conduct of patronage during the Seven Years' War, 1757–1762', *British Journal of Eighteenth-Century Studies* 12 (1989). It is a pity that nothing from the somewhat different account in E.J.S. Fraser, 'The Pitt–Newcastle coalition and the conduct of the Seven Years' War, 1757–1760', D.Phil. thesis, Oxford, 1976, has been published. Karl W. Schweizer, *Frederick the Great, William Pitt, and Lord Bute. The Anglo-Prussian Alliance, 1756–1763* (New York, 1991) is the most satisfactory account available of wartime diplomacy, and Stanley McCrory Pargellis, *Lord Loudoun in America* (Princeton, NJ, 1933), with his editorial introduction to *Military Affairs in North America 1748–1765* (New York, 1936), still provides the best background to the American war.

The 1760s and 1770s are well served. John Brooke's *King George III* (1972) is a masterpiece, scholarly and readable. Sir Lewis Namier's great works, *The Structure of Politics at the Accession of George III* (rev. edn 1957) and *England in the Age of the American Revolution* 2nd edn (1966), still have much relevance for a study of this kind, especially read in the light of Linda Colley, *Lewis Namier* (1989), an invaluable introduction. The judicious insights of Richard Pares, *King George III and the Politicians* (Oxford, 1953) still carry much weight. Essential later works include Paul Langford, *The First Rockingham Administration 1765–1766* (Oxford, 1975), Frank O'Gorman, *The Rise of Party in England. The Rockingham Whigs 1760–82* (1975), Peter D.G. Thomas, *Lord North* (1976), and John Brewer, *Party Ideology and Popular Politics at the Accession of George III* (Cambridge, 1976), while recently W.M. Elofson, *The Rockingham Connection and the Second Founding of the Whig Party, 1768–1773* (Montreal and Kingston, 1996) has filled a gap admirably. Sir Lewis Namier and John Brooke, *Charles Townshend* (1964) captures its brilliant but wayward subject; Karl W. Schweizer (ed.), *Lord Bute. Essays in Reinterpretation* (Leicester, 1988) has much to offer; John Norris, *Shelburne and Reform* (1963), while slight in some respects, provides essential context for Chatham's later career. On extra-parliamentary politics of this period, Peter D.G. Thomas, *John Wilkes. A Friend to Liberty* (Oxford, 1996) is superb, but older works are still probably the best broad introduction: Lucy S. Sutherland, *The City of London and the Opposition to Government, 1768–1774* (1959), reprinted in Newman (ed.) (see above), George Rudé, *Wilkes and Liberty* (Oxford, 1962), and Ian R. Christie, *Wilkes, Wyvill and Reform* (1962). John Sainsbury, *Disaffected Patriots. London Supporters of Revolutionary America* (Kingston, 1987), and the more substantial James E. Bradley, *Popular Politics and the American Revolution in England* (Macon, GA, 1986) bear on the themes of this book.

CHRONOLOGY

1688–9	'Glorious' Revolution: accession of William III and Mary II
1689–97	War of the League of Augsburg
1702	Accession of Queen Anne
1702–13	War of the Spanish Succession
1708	Birth of William Pitt
1714	Accession of George I
1715	Jacobite rising
1721	Walpole ministry
1727	Accession of George II
1733	Excise crisis – serious challenge to Walpole
1734	General election
1735	Pitt enters parliament as MP for Old Sarum
1736	Pitt dismissed from his military commission (1731) for opposition in parliament
1737	Breach between George II and Frederick, Prince of Wales; Pitt made Groom of the Bedchamber to the prince
1739	Convention of the Pardo with Spain (Jan.) War of Jenkins' Ear against Spain in Caribbean
1740	War of the Austrian Succession
1742	Resignation of Walpole; Carteret Secretary of State
1743	Battle of Dettingen
1744	Granville (Carteret) dismissed; 'broad-bottom' ministry; Pitt not given office
1745	Jacobite rising Capture of Louisburg (French Canada)
1746	Pelham ministry; Pitt Vice-Treasurer for Ireland (Feb.), Paymaster-General (May)
1748	Peace of Aix-la-Chapelle; Louisburg returned
1751	Death of Prince of Wales
1754	Death of Pelham; Newcastle ministry Pitt marries Lady Hester Grenville

1755	British defeats by French in America
	Subsidy treaties with Hesse-Cassel and Russia
	Pitt dismissed for opposition in parliament
1756	First Convention of Westminster (Britain and Prussia)
	First Treaty of Versailles (France and Austrian Habsburgs)
	Britain declares war against France; loss of Minorca
	Seven Years War begins
	Resignation of Newcastle; Devonshire–Pitt ministry (Dec.)
1757	Second Treaty of Versailles
	Battle of Plassey (Bengal)
	Newcastle–Pitt coalition ministry (June)
	First expedition against French coast
	Convention of Klosterseven – Hanoverian neutrality
	Frederick the Great's victory at Rossbach
1758	Second Convention of Westminster
	Second French coastal expedition
	British troops sent to Germany
	Fall of Louisburg
1759	*Annus mirabilis* of victories: Minden, Quebec, Guadeloupe, Lagos and Quiberon Bay
1760	Fall of Montreal completes conquest of Canada
	Accession of George III
1761	Bute appointed Secretary of State
	Unsuccessful peace negotiations
	Family Compact (France and Spain)
	Resignation of Pitt (Oct.)
1762	War with Spain
	Resignation of Newcastle; Bute ministry
1763	Peace of Paris
	Resignation of Bute; Grenville ministry
	First Wilkes episode: the *North Briton* affair
	Ministerial negotiations with Pitt fail
1764	Enactment of Grenville's American legislation begins
1765	Stamp Act passed
	Ministerial negotiations with Pitt fail
	Grenville dismissed; Rockingham ministry
	Stamp Act crisis
1766	Repeal of Stamp Act; Declaratory Act passed
	Rockingham dismissed; Pitt takes office as Earl of Chatham (July)
	Abortive negotiations with Prussia and Russia
1767	East India Company Enquiry
	Townshend American Duties Act
	Chatham disabled by illness (March)

1768	General election; Wilkes returned for Middlesex
	American protests over Townshend Duties
	Chatham resigns (Oct.); Grafton ministry
1769	Middlesex election affair: Wilkes's election disallowed
	Petitioning movement against this decision
	Chatham reappears at court (July)
	Radical movements in London
1770	'United' opposition of Rockinghamites and Chathamites
	Grafton resigns; North ministry
	Townshend Duties repealed except that on tea
	Dispute with Spain over Falklands Islands
1771	Printers' case pits City against Commons over publication of debates
	'United' opposition collapses
1772–74	Chatham in retirement
1773	Tea Act
	East India Regulating Act
	Boston Tea Party
1774	'Coercive' Acts to punish Massachusetts
	Chatham returns to opposition
	Quebec Act
	First Continental Congress of American colonies
1775	Proposals for American conciliation from Chatham (Provisional 'Act'), North, Burke
	British–American clashes at Lexington and Concord
	Second Continental Congress
	Proclamation of Rebellion
1775–77	Chatham in retirement
1776	American Declaration of Independence
1777	Chatham returns to opposition
	British defeat at Saratoga
1778	Franco-American Treaty
	Death of Chatham (May)
	War with France
1781	British surrender at Yorktown
1782	Resignation of North; Rockingham ministry
	Death of Rockingham; Shelburne ministry
1783	Peace of Versailles
	Resignation of Shelburne; Fox–North coalition
	Coalition dismissed; ministry of the Younger Pitt

MAJOR PERSONS MENTIONED
IN THE TEXT*

Anson	Admiral George (1697–1762), first Baron (1747), First Lord of the Admiralty 1751–56, 1757–62
Barré	Isaac (1726–1802), MP, follower of Shelburne
Bath	See Pulteney
Beckford	William (1709–70), MP, Alderman of London (1752) and Lord Mayor (1762–63, 1769–70), Pitt's leading supporter in the City
Bedford	John Russell, fourth Duke (1710–71), First Lord of the Admiralty 1744–48, Secretary of State 1748–51, Lord Lieutenant of Ireland 1757–61, Lord Privy Seal 1761–63, negotiator of the Peace of Paris 1762–63, independent Whig peer
Burke	Edmund (1729–97), MP, private secretary to Rockingham 1765, 'man of business' and publicist for the Rockingham party
Bute	John Stuart, third Earl (1713–92), tutor and Groom of the Stole (1756–60) to George, Prince of Wales, Secretary of State 1761–62, First Lord of the Treasury and prime minister 1762–63
Calcraft	John (1726–72), MP, holder of lesser offices in the Pay and War Offices c.1745–63, then follower of Shelburne and Pitt, 'man of business' to Chatham, especially 1769–72
Camden	See Pratt
Carteret	John (1690–1763), second Baron, second Earl Granville (1744), opposition Whig leader under Walpole, Secretary of State and prime

* Normally, offices held are given only for the period of Pitt's career; minor offices are indicated only in cases of particular interest.

263

	minister 1742–44, Lord President of the Council 1751–63
Chesterfield	Philip Dormer Stanhope, fourth Earl (1694–1773), dismissed from the royal household for opposition to the excise 1733, special Ambassador to the Dutch 1744, Lord Lieutenant of Ireland 1745–46, Secretary of State 1746–48
Clive	Robert (1725–74), first Baron (1762), won acclaim as a commander of East India Company forces 1740s and 1750s, victor at Plassey (1757), Governor and Commander-in-Chief, Bengal, 1764–67
Cobham	Richard Temple, first Viscount (1669?–1749), distinguished soldier, dismissed as Colonel of the King's Own Horse 1733 for opposition to the excise, restored 1742, patron of 'Cobham's Cubs' – Pitt, George Lyttelton and the Grenvilles
Conway	Henry Seymour (1719–95), MP, army officer, Secretary of State 1765–68, leader in the Commons, a Rockinghamite
Cumberland	William Augustus, Duke (1721–65), younger son of George II, Captain-General of the Army 1744–57, patron of Bedford and Fox in the 1750s, of the Newcastle–Rockingham group from 1763
Devonshire	William Cavendish, fourth Duke (1720–64), independent Whig peer, Lord Lieutenant of Ireland 1755–56, First Lord of the Treasury in coalition with Pitt 1756–57, Lord Chamberlain with cabinet seat 1757–62
Dunning	John (1731–83), lawyer, MP, Solicitor-General 1768–70, follower of Shelburne, made Baron Ashburton 1782
Ferdinand	Prince of Brunswick-Wolfenbüttel (1721–92), distinguished soldier, commander of the allied army in the Rhineland 1757–62
Fox	Henry (1705–74), first Baron Holland (1763), ex-Tory, Old Corps Whig and protégé of Cumberland 1746–57, Lord of the Treasury 1743–46, Secretary at War 1746–55, Secretary

	of State 1755–56, Paymaster-General 1757–65, leader in the Commons 1762–63
Glynn	John (1722–79), MP, Sergeant-at-Law 1763, Recorder of London 1772–79, Wilkite radical
Grafton	Augustus Henry Fitzroy, third Duke (1735–1811), Secretary of State 1765–66, First Lord of the Treasury 1766–70, prime minister 1768–70, Lord Privy Seal 1771–75, Chathamite in the 1760s and from 1775
Granby	John Manners, Marquess (1721–70), distinguished soldier, commander of British troops in Germany 1758–62, Commander-in-Chief 1766–70, Chathamite
Granville	See Carteret
Grenville	Richard, eldest of the Grenville brothers, see Temple
Grenville	George (1712–70), Lord of the Admiralty 1744–47, Lord of the Treasury 1747–54, Treasurer of the Navy 1754–55, 1756–57, 1757–62, Secretary of State 1762, First Lord of the Admiralty 1762–63, First Lord of the Treasury and prime minister, 1763–65, second of the Grenville brothers, a 'Cobham Cub', brother-in-law to Pitt, broke with him 1761
Grenville	James (1715–83), Lord of Trade and deputy Paymaster to the Forces 1746–55, Lord of the Treasury 1756–57, 1757–61, Joint Vice-Treasurer Ireland 1766–70, third of the Grenville brothers, loyal Chathamite
Hardwicke	Philip Yorke, first Baron (1733), first Earl (1754), Old Corps Whig and distinguished lawyer, Solicitor-General 1720–24, Attorney-General 1724–33, Chief Justice 1733–37, Lord Chancellor 1737–56, member of the cabinet without office 1757–62
Holderness	Robert D'Arcy, fourth Earl (1718–78), Secretary of State 1751–61
Holland	See Fox
Legge	Henry Bilson (1708–64), Old Corps Whig, minor offices 1735–45, Lord of the Admiralty 1745–46, Lord of the Treasury 1746–49,

Treasurer of the Navy 1749–54, Chancellor of the Exchequer 1754–55, 1756–57, 1757–61, associate of Pitt in the mid-1750s

Ligonier   Jean Louis, first Earl (1680–1770), distinguished military officer of Huguenot family, Commander-in-Chief 1757–59, Master-General of the Ordnance 1759–63

Lyttelton   George, first Baron (1709–73), Secretary to Frederick, Prince of Wales 1737–44, Lord of the Treasury 1744–54, Cofferer of the Household 1754–55, Chancellor of the Exchequer 1755–56, second-rank politician thereafter, man of letters, cousin to the Grenvilles, 'Cobham Cub', Pitt's oldest friend and political ally to 1755, reconciled 1769

Mansfield   William Murray, first Earl (1756), ex-Jacobite turned Old Corps Whig, distinguished lawyer, Solicitor-General 1742–54, Attorney-General 1754–56, Chief Justice 1756–88, Pitt's greatest debating rival in Commons and Lords

Murray   See Mansfield

Newcastle   Thomas Pelham-Hollis, first Duke (1693–1768), elder brother of Henry Pelham, Old Corps Whig leader, Secretary of State 1724–54, First Lord of the Treasury and prime minister 1754–56, 1757–62, in coalition with Pitt until 1761

North   Frederick, Lord North (1732–92), Lord of the Treasury 1759–65, joint Paymaster-General 1766–67, Chancellor of the Exchequer 1767–82, First Lord of the Treasury and prime minister, 1770–82, 'King's Friend'

Northington   Robert Henley (c.1708–72), Lord Henley (1760), first Earl (1764), Lord Keeper 1757–61, Lord Chancellor 1761–66, 'King's Friend'

Pelham   Henry (1695?–1754), Old Corps Whig leader, Lord of the Treasury 1721–24, Secretary at War, 1724–30, Paymaster-General 1730–43, First Lord of the Treasury and Chancellor of the Exchequer 1743–54, prime minister 1746–54

Potter   Thomas (1718?–59), MP, minor officeholder 1756–59, friend of Pitt and dissolute associate of Wilkes

Pratt   Charles (1714–94), first Baron Camden (1765), able lawyer, Attorney-General 1757–62, Chief Justice 1762–66, Lord Chancellor 1766–70, longstanding Chathamite

Pulteney   William (1684–1764), first Earl of Bath (1742), opposition Whig leader under Walpole, seat in the cabinet without office 1742–44

Richmond   Charles Lennox, third Duke (1735–1806), Ambassador to France 1765–66, Secretary of State 1766, Rockinghamite peer

Rockingham   Charles Watson-Wentworth, second Marquess (1730–82), Lord of the Bedchamber 1751–65, First Lord of the Treasury and prime minister 1765–66, 1782, successor to Newcastle as leader of those of the Old Corps who came to claim exclusively the name Whig

Sawbridge   John (1732?–95), MP, Alderman of London (1769), radical, friend of Shelburne

Shelburne   William Petty, second Earl (1737–1805), later first Marquess of Lansdowne (1784), President of the Board of Trade 1763, Secretary of State 1766–68, First Lord of the Treasury and prime minister 1782–83, Chathamite from 1763

Temple   Richard Grenville (1711–79), Lord Cobham (1749), Earl Temple (1752), First Lord of the Admiralty 1756–57, Lord Privy Seal 1757–61, eldest of the Grenville brothers, 'Cobham Cub', brother-in-law to Pitt, breaks with him 1766, reconciled 1769

Townsend   James (1737–87), MP, Alderman of London (1769), Lord Mayor (1772–73), radical, leader of Shelburne group in City

Townshend   Charles (1725–67), Lord of Trade 1749–54, Lord of the Admiralty 1754–55, Treasurer of the Chamber 1756–61, Secretary at War 1761–62, President of the Board of Trade 1763, Paymaster-General 1765–66, Chancellor of

	the Exchequer 1766–67, brilliant Whig politician of erratic personal loyalty
Townshend	George (1724–1807), elder brother of Charles, MP, distinguished soldier, independent Whig
Walpole	Horace (1717–97), MP, third son of Sir Robert, connoisseur of the arts and letters, memoirist and correspondent
Walpole	Horatio (1678–1757), brother of Sir Robert, able diplomat
Walpole	Sir Robert (1676–1745), first Earl of Orford (1742), First Lord of the Treasury and prime minister 1721–42
Wilkes	John (1727–97), MP, Alderman of London (1769), Lord Mayor (1774–75), famous radical and demagogue
Yorke	Charles (1722–70), second son of the first Earl of Hardwicke, Newcastle–Rockingham Whig, Solicitor-General 1756–61, Attorney-General 1762–63, 1765–66, Lord Chancellor for three days 1770
Yorke	Joseph (1724–92), younger brother of Charles, KB 1761, first Baron Dover 1788, soldier and diplomat, minister at The Hague 1751–61, Ambassador 1761–80

MAPS

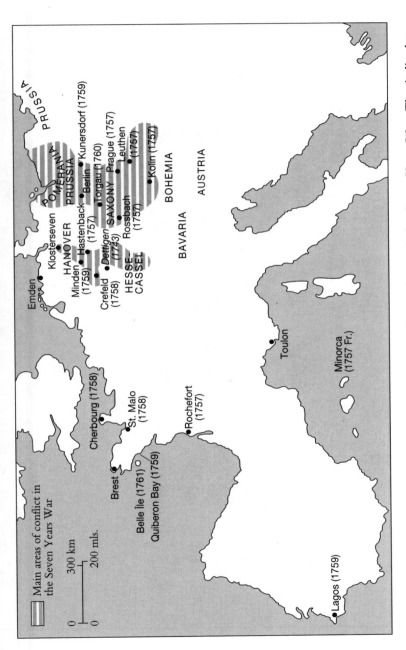

Map 1. European battles of the War of the Austrian Succession and the Seven Years War. The italic date refers to a battle of the War of the Austrian Succession; all other dates refer to battles of the Seven Years War.

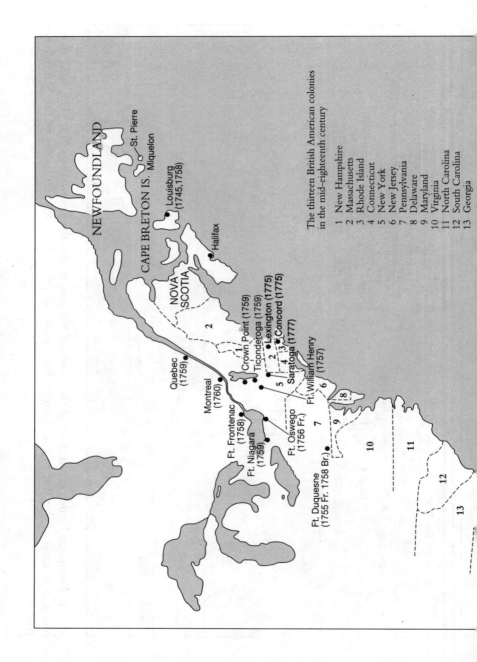

The thirteen British American colonies
in the mid-eighteenth century

1   New Hampshire
2   Massachusetts
3   Rhode Island
4   Connecticut
5   New York
6   New Jersey
7   Pennsylvania
8   Delaware
9   Maryland
10 Virginia
11 North Carolina
12 South Carolina
13 Georgia

NEWFOUNDLAND

CAPE BRETON IS.

St. Pierre
Miquelon

Louisburg
(1745, 1758)

Halifax

NOVA
SCOTIA

Quebec
(1759)

Montreal
(1760)

Crown Point (1759)
Ticonderoga (1759)
Lexington (1775)
Concord (1775)
Saratoga (1777)

Ft. William Henry
(1757)

Ft. Frontenac
(1758)

Ft. Niagara
(1759)

Ft. Oswego
(1756 Fr.)

Ft. Duquesne
(1755 Fr. 1758 Br.)

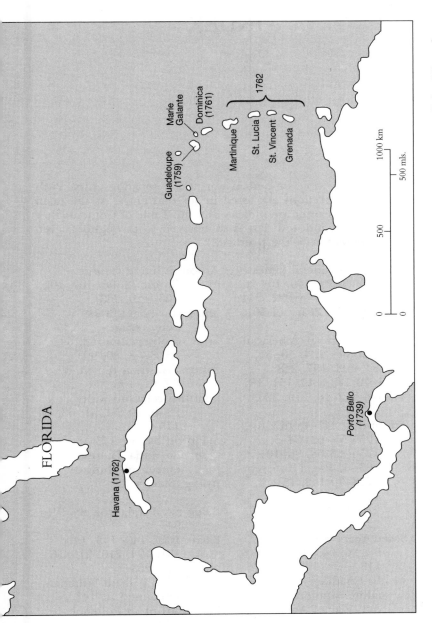

Map 2. North America and the West Indies. The italic date refers to an engagement of the War of the Austrian Succession; bold dates refer to engagements of the American War of Independence; all other dates refer to engagements in the Seven Years War.

INDEX